The Limits of Scripture

The Limits of Scripture

VIVEKANANDA'S REINTERPRETATION OF THE VEDAS

Anantanand Rambachan

University of Hawaii Press
HONOLULU

Printed in the United States of America

94 95 96 97 98 99 5 4 3 2 1

Library of Congress Cataloging-in-Publication Data
Rambachan, Anantanand, 1951–
The limits of scripture : Vivekananda's reinterpretation of the Vedas / Anantanand Rambachan.
p. cm.
Includes bibliographical references and index.
ISBN 0-8248-1542-4
1. Vivekananda, Swami, 1863–1902. 2. Advaita. 3. Vedas—Criticism, interpretation, etc. I. Title.
BL1280.292.V58R35 1994
294.5'921—dc20 93-44277
CIP

University of Hawaii Press books are printed on acid-free paper and meet the guidelines for permanence and durability of the Council on Library Resources

Designed by Ken Miyamoto

for Geeta, Ishanaa,
and Aksharananda

Contents

List of Abbreviations

A.U.	Aitareya Upaniṣad
BG	Bhagavadgītā
BS	Brahma-sūtra
B.U.	Bṛhadāraṇyaka Upaniṣad
C.U.	Chāndogya Upaniṣad
CW	*Complete Works of Swami Vivekananda*
K.U.	Kaṭha Upaniṣad
K.U.	Kena Upaniṣad
M.U.	Muṇḍaka Upaniṣad
NYSG	Nyāya Sūtras of Gotama
P.U.	Praśna Upaniṣad
T.U.	Taittirīya Upaniṣad

The letter *B* added to the abbreviation of any text as (e.g., BS = B) indicates the commentary *(bhāṣya)* of Śaṅkara on the said text. Unless otherwise indicated, the translations of these works used in the text are those included in the bibliography.

Acknowledgments

I AM GRATEFUL to Saint Olaf College for granting me a year's leave (1991–1992), which enabled me to complete this work. A grant from the college also helped defray some of the expenses incurred in the preparation of the manuscript for publication.

Our Religion Department secretary, Jody Greenslade, and my students Erik Skar and Karl Rosenquist assisted with the typing and formatting of this text. I am thankful for their assistance.

Sharon F. Yamamoto, my editor at the University of Hawaii Press, expressed an early interest in this manuscript, and her encouragement and guidance through the different stages of my work are deeply appreciated. I am also indebted to the readers of my manuscript for their many helpful criticisms. I believe that the incorporation of their suggestions has resulted in a better book.

I also wish to acknowledge the support of my wife, Geeta, whose encouragement of my research and writing has helped me, in so many ways, to complete this work. My children, Ishanaa and Aksharananda, have been speaking enthusiastically about the "making" of another book. The innocence of their joyful anticipation has been a source of delight and incentive to me.

Finally, I am thankful to the editors of *Religious Studies, Religion,* and *Philosophy East and West* for granting permission to use, in a revised form, some material that previously appeared in these journals.

INTRODUCTION

THE VARIOUS traditions of Hinduism are almost unanimous in the view that ignorance *(avidyā)* of absolute reality, however conceived, is the fundamental human predicament and the cause of suffering. The right knowledge of reality, therefore, becomes necessary for liberation from bondage and the attainment of happiness. Identifying the nature and source of this liberating knowledge and clarifying the means for its attainment are central concerns of these traditions.

In the particular case of the Advaita (nondual) tradition, with which this study is concerned, ignorance, as far as the individual is concerned, consists of an erroneous understanding of self *(ātman)*. The self is wrongly identified with the limited and changing qualities of the body and the mind and considered as being subject to birth, aging, and death. Its true nature as identical with the infinite reality of the universe (namely, *brahman*) and free from all limitations remains unknown. Liberation *(mokṣa)* is the correction of wrong notions about the self and an assimilated and doubtless knowledge of its true nature. It is the appreciation of oneself to be a full and complete being.

It will become obvious, however, that, while there is consensus within the Advaita tradition about the content of liberating knowledge, its interpreters cannot agree about the authoritative source of this knowledge or about the means by which it is attained. There are differences, for example, in the significance attributed to personal experience *(anubhava)* or to the scripture. It is with the clarification and assessment of these differences that this study is concerned. Since liberation is the highest goal of existence in Hinduism and right knowledge the means to its attainment, it is easy to appreciate the centrality of this issue.

My first encounter with Advaita Vedānta and the literature of neo-Hinduism was through the writings of Swami Vivekananda (1863–1902). My reading of Vivekananda convinced me that, as far as Advaita, and indeed Hinduism as a whole, was concerned, the authoritative source of knowledge was a very special experience *(anubhava)* that revealed beyond any doubts the basic truths about the meaning of human existence.[1]

This experience was presented as the very core of Hinduism, the only meaningful end to be sought after and the culmination of the Hindu spiritual journey. It was affirmed as offering the possibility of a direct insight into the nature of reality and, therefore, as the only ultimately credible source of spiritual knowledge. In relation to the knowledge of matters beyond the range of sense apprehension, Vivekananda asserted that this experience afforded a directness and conclusiveness that could be likened only to ordinary sense perception. *Anubhava* was presented by him as possessing a self-valid quality that obviated the need for faith or reliance on any source of spiritual knowledge that one could not personally verify. In fact, all authoritative sources were subordinate to *anubhava,* and all spiritual disciplines were intended only for its attainment.

Along with my understanding of the paramount epistemological status of this experience, I also gathered, from Vivekananda, what I considered, at that time, to be the established view of the Vedas or *śruti* in Advaita and Hinduism. *Śruti* was just a record, in words, of this experience as attained by others. At best, it informed us of what they had attained and the means that they employed. The aspirant, however, could not simply rely with faith on this testimony, which was only a secondhand report. As the testimony of another, the knowledge that one may gain by a study of the *śruti* lacks conclusiveness and freedom from doubt. This knowledge is presented by Vivekananda as "theoretical" information that cannot lead to liberation *(mokṣa).* To be definitive, this knowledge had to be verified, and this was possible only through a similar direct experience. As a source of knowledge, therefore, even the *śruti* was subordinate to *anubhava.*

My subsequent study of the commentaries of Śaṅkara (ca. 788–820), the principal systematizer and exponent of the Advaita system, convinced me of a radically different understanding of the nature and function of the *śruti* in relation to the gain of liberating knowledge. This understanding centered around Śaṅkara's treatment of *śruti* as *śabda-pramāṇa,* a source of valid knowledge *(pramāṇa)* composed of words *(śabda).* This view of the scripture, with all its implications, was in thorough and remarkable contrast to the status and functions assigned to *śruti* in Vivekananda's representation of Advaita. The *śabda-pramāṇa* approach offered a very different rationale for the necessity of the scripture.

Unlike Vivekananda, who presented the affirmations of *śruti* as having only a hypothetical or provisional validity and needing the verification that only *anubhava* could provide, Śaṅkara argued for *śruti* as the unique and self-valid source for our knowledge of absolute reality *(brahman).* In relation to the gain of this knowledge, all ways of knowing were subordinate to *śruti.* In important contrast to Vivekananda's argument that the declarations of *śruti* needed further verification to become conclusive was Śaṅkara's contention that liberation *(mokṣa)* is the immediate result of understanding the words of the *śruti.* For a qualified aspirant, nothing beyond a proper investigation of the meaning of those sentences in the *śruti* revealing *brahman* is required.

I also discovered that Vivekananda's interpretation of the significance of the *śruti* in connection with the acquisition of the knowledge of *brahman* (namely, *brahmajñāna*) was continuously identified by many modern commentators as being the original position adopted by Śaṅkara. According to these commentators, there is little or no deviation in Vivekananda's views from the Advaita Vedānta tradition as systematized and given expression by Śaṅkara. The late T. M. P. Mahadevan, a distinguished Hindu scholar, writes, "The *Advaita* which Swami Vivekananda teaches in his speeches and writings is, in essence, the same gospel whose consolidation and comprehensive exposition we owe to Śrī Śaṅkarācārya."[2] R. S. Srivastava comes to a similar conclusion: "The concept of salvation and *jñānayoga* as a path or discipline leading to it are ancient and traditional. The metaphysics and disciplines of Vivekananda do not deviate an inch from the standpoint of the *Advaita Vedānta* of Śaṅkarācārya."[3] Fundamental differences are uncritically overlooked, and Vivekananda is seen merely as a reviver of the Advaita of Śaṅkara.[4] These opinions suggest that, like Vivekananda, Śaṅkara also saw a special experience as the ultimately valid source of our knowledge of *brahman,* that Śaṅkara accorded only a provisional validity to the affirmations of the scripture and did not perceive these texts to be, in any way, a unique source of knowledge. Many felt that the only reason for Śaṅkara's recourse to *śruti* was the desire to gain the support of a traditional authority for his own views.

In an earlier published study, *Accomplishing the Accomplished,* I sought to establish that these interpreters misrepresent Śaṅkara's epistemology in failing to apprehend the meaning and significance that he ascribes to the *śruti* as the definitive source of the knowledge of *brahman.*[5] It is clear to me that, in relation to the gain of *brahma-jñāna,* Śaṅkara saw all other sources of knowledge as subordinate to the *śruti* and supported his views by well-reasoned arguments centered on the *śruti* as a logical, fruitful, and adequate source of knowledge.

It is obvious that many modern commentators on Śaṅkara are deeply influenced in their approach, directly or indirectly, by the interpretations of Vivekananda. In the light of this fact, my aim in this study is to clarify Vivekananda's understanding of the authority of the *śruti* and its relation to personal experience *(anubhava).* Because of the superior epistemological status that he accords to the latter, I will also examine the derivation and nature of this experience as presented by him. While I am concerned chiefly with his estimation of the relation between *śruti* and *anubhava,* this unavoidably leads me to consider other important aspects of his interpretation of Advaita, many of which are seen today as axiomatic features of Hinduism. Directly connected, for example, to Vivekananda's reinterpretation of the significance of the *śruti* is his elaboration of the methods of *karma* (work), *bhakti* (love), *jñāna* (knowledge), and *rājayoga* as direct and independent means to the attainment of *mokṣa.* This is a well-known argument in contemporary Hindu apologetics, and we are led to Vivekananda's treatment of this subject. There are other related issues concerning the nature and function of the teacher, the value of reason, etc.

In this study, however, I have not limited myself to the task of using historical-critical methods of analyzing textual sources to establish Vivekananda's views. I also seek to make evaluations, and it is important to clarify the criteria on which these are based. My assessments are in relation to the Advaita tradition to which Vivekananda professes his allegiance. I examine his innovations and contributions with reference to the fundamental premises of Advaita as formulated by Śaṅkara, retaining the attainment of *mokṣa* as the central concern. This method would be objectionable if it consisted of applying to Vivekananda a set of criteria and standards of judgment belonging to a system, Hindu or otherwise, with entirely different presuppositions. This is a definite problem, for example, when the norms and premises of one religious tradition are employed, consciously or unconsciously, in considering another tradition. In this case, however, my criteria are grounded in the presuppositions of the tradition with which Vivekananda identifies. Vivekananda's epistemology is rooted in the authority of a special experience, and, together with the methods derived from the Advaita tradition, I will also utilize forms of philosophical analysis developed in the recent study of mysticism and religious experience. My concern here, it must be clarified, is to question, not Vivekananda's right to reinterpret the source of authority in the Advaita tradition, but the consistency and persuasiveness of these interpretations.

Along with clarifying and assessing Vivekananda's interpretations, this study will also highlight significant areas of sharp difference with the views of Śaṅkara. The highlighting of these differences is also important since the Ramakrishna Mission and the Ramakrishna Order, founded by Vivekananda, see the teachings of Vivekananda as being in direct continuity with Śaṅkara. Swami Satprakashananda, a distinguished member of the Ramakrishna Order, minimizes the differences between Vivekananda and Śaṅkara: "It is Śaṅkara's Advaita philosophy that he [Vivekananda] accepted and expounded in modern terms and found its application in modern life. So far as the basic ideas of Advaita Vedānta are concerned he does not differ from Śaṅkara, but there are some differences in his way of presentation and the emphasis laid by him on its practical aspects." In particular, Satprakashananda argues for an identity of views between Vivekananda and Śaṅkara on the nature of the authority of the Upaniṣads, claiming that, "while Śaṅkara and Vivekananda accepted the *Upaniṣads* as the authoritative source of suprasensuous knowledge and acknowledged their allegiance to them, the Buddha did not."[6]

It is important, therefore, to show that the revival of Hinduism in the nineteenth and early twentieth centuries was not simply a reaffirmation of tradition but, in important ways, a new understanding of it. This study will also offer some comments on the legacy of Vivekananda and its continuing influence on the Hindu self-understanding.

In highlighting the differences between Śaṅkara and Vivekananda, the question of Vivekananda's knowledge of Śaṅkara's commentaries naturally arises. Vivekananda never studied the commentaries of Śaṅkara, at least not in the traditional manner, with a teacher affiliated with one of the religious orders *(saṁpradāya)* reputedly founded by Śaṅkara. His understanding of Śaṅkara came from his own study of the commentaries, and he clearly possessed a competence in Sanskrit to be able to read these works in the original. In a letter to Josephine MacLeod, for example, Vivekananda wrote of being "busy working on the great commentaries of Śaṅkara" with his friend E. T. Sturdy, a Sanskrit scholar. Vivekananda also gave class lectures on

Śaṅkara's commentary on the Brahma-sūtra and engaged in lengthy discussions with the scholar Pramadadas Mitra, of Varanasi, on various aspects of Śaṅkara's interpretations.[7]

Vivekananda appears to be most familiar with Śaṅkara's commentary on the Brahma-sūtra. In the *Complete Works of Swami Vivekananda,* references to this work significantly outnumber all other references to the commentaries of Śaṅkara. In addition to references to Śaṅkara's commentaries on other texts, including the Bhagavadgītā and various Upaniṣads, Vivekananda also cites the *Vivekacūḍāmaṇi* and other poems that he considered to be written by Śaṅkara. His knowledge of Advaita was also shaped by such works as the Yogavāsiṣṭha and Aṣṭāvakragītā.[8]

It is not within the scope of this study to sketch in full the system of Advaita as developed by either Śaṅkara or Vivekananda. At the same time, it is impossible to avoid wider doctrinal issues, and these are introduced at relevant points in the discussion. I have also not attempted to account for or to trace all the sources of Vivekananda's views. While specific influences are mentioned in the course of my discussion, a comprehensive consideration of the sources and development of his thought is beyond the scope of this work. Chapter 1, however, is entirely devoted to sketching the atmosphere in which his views developed and to outlining significant developments in the eighteenth and nineteenth centuries in India, particularly with reference to the authority of the Vedas, which would have influenced him. The diverse and complex influences shaping Hindu thought in this period still await detailed study. I have sought, wherever possible, to identify some of the sources of specific views.

The significance of the clarification that this study attempts has to be viewed in the light of Vivekananda's unquestionable impact on the contemporary understanding of Advaita and, more broadly, of Hinduism. As Ninian Smart points out, "Not only did he interpret Hinduism to the West so eloquently, but he also interpreted it to India itself." "A shrinking world," continues Smart, "will surely recognize how much it owes to him, the first man to bring home to the consciousness of the Western world at large the deeper significances of the *Sanātana Dharma.*"[9] A. L. Basham also assesses the legacy of Vivekananda in laudatory terms: "It is certainly far greater than any Western historian or most Indian historians would have suggested at the time of his death. The passing of the years and the many stupendous and unexpected events which have occurred since then suggest that in centuries to come he will be remembered as one of the main moulders of the modern world, especially as far as Asia is concerned, and as one of the most significant figures in the whole history of Indian religion, comparable in importance to such great teachers as Śaṅkara and Rāmānuja."[10] Agehananda Bharati was not exaggerating in asserting that "modern Hindus derive their knowledge of Hinduism from Vivekananda, directly or indirectly."[11]

In spite of the acknowledged influence of Vivekananda—perhaps because of it—the Hindu tradition has yet to assess the nature of this influence critically. More than ninety years after his death, the general attitude is still the adulation with which he was greeted on his return to India from the West. It seems as if the memory of the genuine pride and self-respect that Vivekananda instilled in Hindus still precludes critical evaluation of his contribution. As Wilhelm Halbfass correctly notes, "Critical assessments and attempts to 'demythologize' Vivekananda are much more rare, and rarer still are examples of thorough historical analysis and hermeneutical clarification of Vivekananda's work."[12] It is Vivekananda's widespread impact, however, that makes critical appraisal necessary, and it is hoped that this work will contribute to such studies and to the understanding of changes in religious and philosophical thought in modern India.

Vivekananda's influence is so pervasive that it is a difficult task to identify and extricate the individual elements that he contributed to the contemporary understanding of Hinduism. Not only did he largely formulate this interpretation, but he also gave it the language in which it is articulated. There is very little in modern Hindu, particularly Vedānta, apologetic writing that does not carry the clear imprint of Vivekananda's influence.

The fact that Vivekananda was a representative of the system of Advaita did not weaken the impression that he made on the whole of Hinduism. Because Advaita, through Vivekananda, was the first Hindu system to be so elaborately presented to the West, its comprehension has considerably shaped the approach to Hinduism in India and abroad. This was fostered by Vivekananda's vision and presentation of Advaita as the natural culmination of Hindu religious thought. From his basis in Advaita, he generalized in his lectures and writings about the nature and features of Hinduism as a whole. In his own time, he was perceived as the spokesperson and champion of Hinduism, not of any specific tradition within it.

The primary sources for this study of Vivekananda are his published writings, lectures, letters, and interviews. These, along with various miscellaneous sayings and newspaper reports, constitute the bulk of the material collected in the eight volumes of the *Complete Works*. Unlike Śaṅkara, Vivekananda did not use the medium of commentary *(bhāṣya)* to express his views, and his only written commentary, significantly on the Yoga-sūtras of Patañjali, is included in these volumes.

The *Complete Works* leaves much to be desired in terms of chronology, indexing, and the misleading titles of lectures, but it still remains the principal source for any study of Vivekananda's thought during his short public ministry—from his first major lecture on 11 September 1893 to his death on 4 July 1902. Vivekananda wrote very little, and, for the study of his views, we must rely mainly on his lectures as recorded by his faithful English secretary and disciple, J. J. Godwin. There is a considerable repetition of themes and ideas in these lectures that ensures their reliability. It is no exaggeration to say, however, that, because of poor ordering and indexing of the material, it is necessary to read the contents of every volume painstakingly to ascertain Vivekananda's views on any single issue.

Nevertheless, the *Complete Works* does indeed appear, as the volumes claim, to include all the available recorded writings, lectures, class notes, and conversations of Vivekananda. The contents are not limited to the English material but include translations of lectures, letters, conversations, poems, and articles from Bengali. The inclusiveness of the material in these volumes certainly contributes to their reliability as a guide to Vivekananda's views.[13]

This study is divided into six chapters. Chapter 1 traces developments in attitudes toward scriptural authority and revelation during the period from Rammohun Roy (1774–1833) to Ramakrishna (1836–1886) that appear to have influenced Vivekananda. Chapter 2 analyzes Vivekananda's understanding of the nature, authority, and functions of the Vedas. Following on this discussion, I seek in chapter 3 to describe, compare, and evaluate his arguments for different methods of attaining *mokṣa.* Chapter 4 tries to understand and evaluate the significance of the experience *(anubhava)* that Vivekananda posits as the ultimate source of valid spiritual knowledge. Chapter 5 identifies and discusses some of the principal areas of contrast between Vivekananda and Śaṅkara, while the final chapter assesses elements of his legacy to contemporary Hinduism.

Today, largely as a result of processes generated by Vivekananda himself, Hinduism no longer finds its adherents only among people of Indian descent. He initiated a worldwide interest in Hinduism and immeasurably influenced its contemporary understanding. In drawing the attention of the West to the richness of Hinduism, he also stimulated a renewed interest among Hindus themselves. Perhaps the latter would not have been possible without the former. The legacy of his influence continues in many parts of the world through the activities of the Ramakrishna Mission. This study hopes to contribute to the analysis and understanding of Indian religions and the wider study of religion by examining important aspects of the Vivekananda legacy. More important, I hope that it will lead to a more critical assessment of the character and value of this legacy.

The possibility of a human knowledge of God or reality is a problem with which every major religious tradition wrestles, and the issue of whether the authority of scripture takes precedence over that of individual experience transcends religious boundaries. Vivekananda universalized his claims for *anubhava* and argued for it as the ground and source of all religious traditions. A study of this debate within Hinduism will contribute to the wider community of discussion and stimulate fruitful dialogue among these traditions.

It will be apparent to the reader that I am personally engaged with the issues discussed here and that the subject matter is not only of scholarly interest to me. The divergences in understanding between Vivekananda and Śaṅkara about the nature and status of knowledge gained from inquiry into the words of the *śruti* determine the different methods employed to attain *mokṣa.*

If, as in the case of Vivekananda, the knowledge gained from inquiry into the meaning of the *śruti* lacks certitude and finality and must be confirmed by *anubhava* for *mokṣa* to be achieved, then the attainment of this experience becomes all important since liberation is impossible without it. In Vivekananda, as we will see, it is difficult to find an unconditional rationale for the *śruti.*

If, on the other hand, as in the case of Śaṅkara, the *śruti* is the valid source of knowledge *(pramāṇa)* for *brahman,* the implications are that such knowledge can be neither derived from any other source nor contradicted by another means of knowledge. This knowledge does not need to be validated or confirmed by another source of knowledge. As understood by Śaṅkara, *mokṣa* is identical with the nature of the self *(ātman),* which is free from all limitations. Through ignorance *(avidyā),* however, this self is erroneously identified with the finite characteristics of mind and body. A valid source of knowledge is needed, not to create or produce the ever-existent self, but to remove erroneous knowledge and unfold its true nature. Such a source, for Śaṅkara, can be found in the words of the *śruti.*

In this case, therefore, proper comprehension of the meaning of *śruti* sentences teaching about the self is all important since this is sufficient. Such knowledge reveals an existing and liberated self. The knowledge gained from the *śruti* does not have to be applied to produce an experience that validates *śruti.*

Since the *śruti* is the valid source of knowledge about *ātman-brahman,* it cannot be considered, like in Vivekananda, a nonessential aspect of religion. It is obvious, therefore, that the implications of the different views of *śruti* are significant. Where these differences concern the very means by which liberation is attained, the clarification of such differences, especially when they are widely overlooked, is much more than a matter of scholarly concern.

Chapter 1

ATTITUDES TOWARD SCRIPTURAL AUTHORITY AND REVELATION FROM RAMMOHUN ROY TO RAMAKRISHNA

MY AIM in this chapter is to identify and describe some of the salient developments in attitudes toward revelation and scriptural authority that constituted the immediate background for Swami Vivekananda and that influenced his interpretations.

The British Impact

In its long history, Hinduism has undergone innumerable changes and has responded and adapted itself to diverse influences. The most important challenge and stimulus has been its encounter with the West. The response to this meeting was change of the most radical kind, and the present form of Hinduism can be properly understood only in the light of this historic meeting. It is not, however, within the scope of this study to consider all the dimensions of this encounter; I can focus only on its effects in relation to the authority and status of the Vedas.

The uniqueness of the impact of the West on Hinduism is easily appreciated when one considers the different effects of Islam, in spite of a coexistence extending over seven hundred years. The reason lies, of course, in the nature of Islamic rule. Islamic dominance in many parts of India was primarily political and military, and the Islamic state did not set up an educational system. This is not to argue that both civilizations did not influence each other. As K. M. Panikkar points out, the general effect of Islam was a greater withdrawal into religious and social rigidity and orthodoxy:

> So far as Hindu society was considered, the impact of Islam seems on the whole to have made it more rigid. A study of the extensive *smṛti* literature of the Muslim period including the encyclopaedic *Todarananda,* composed under the orders of Akbar's famous Revenue Minister, Raja Toder Mal, would clearly demonstrate that Hinduism, far from liberalising itself under the impact of Islam, became stricter in its observations of rituals and caste rules, placing more emphasis on the *prayaścitta,* or the religious penances for social offences. Briefly, therefore, it may be said that the encounter between Islam and Hinduism became, after a short time, a problem of co-existence, with mutual toleration rather than the domination of one by another.[1]

The challenges to Hinduism have not come just from outside. The *bhakti* movements of medieval times disseminated ideas of religious and social reform, later echoed in the reformist movements of the eighteenth and nineteenth centuries. *Bhakti* teachers asserted that God was not embodied in a material object and that the human being had direct access to salvation without the mediation of priests. Most of the *bhakti* adherents were fervent monotheists, and the doctrine of direct access to salvation through *bhakti* offered dignity and equality to all who had been denied full participation in religious life under orthodox Hinduism. Some were anticaste, and women were considered spiritually equal by many of them and admitted to the inner ranks of disciples.

The *bhakti* movements, however, failed to effect widespread changes in the beliefs and institutions of orthodox Hinduism. Many reasons explain this failure.[2] Equality was an ideal of the religious and not the secular sphere. While criticizing certain social practices, the movements offered no alternative program of social and economic reorganization, never, in fact, building the organizations to carry out positive social programs. The saints of *bhakti* were of a pacific turn of mind, tolerant in outlook and eschewing controversy or conflict. Social reform was peripheral to the reconstitution of religious beliefs. Most of the sects fostered an otherworldly attitude toward life. Heimsath sees this as a result of their emphasis on mysticism:

> But it was not the primacy of spiritual concerns alone that caused the *bhakti* movements to fail in the transformation of social life; religious movements have been known to overturn social structures. Most *bhakti* sects, like other Hindu religious movements, leaned towards mysticism, as a method of spiritual revelation, and this often encouraged a drawing away from worldly concerns. Individual salvation, not the salvation of society or the group, was the reason for and the result of the religious quest through mysticism.[3]

In contrast to Hinduism's earlier encounters with other civilizations and cultures, the British challenge was total—economic, social, religious, and intellectual. The main thrust of the Western incursion was directed toward the religion of the Hindus. Missionaries questioned the validity of Hinduism, denouncing it as a mass of superstitions. Hinduism was condemned as idolatrous and polytheistic. Social customs for which religious legitimation was claimed invoked the severest disapproval. These included such practices as the burning of widows on the funeral pyres of their husbands, infant marriages, compulsory widowhood, and the institution of caste with the acceptance of untouchability. The structure of Hinduism was threatened by the concept of equality, which the British incorporated into the Indian legal system. Economically, India's handicraft industry was subjected to the pressures of industrialization; politically, the divisions and fragmentations within Indian society were confronted with the British sense of community and nationalistic pride. The British, in other words, offered an observable, functioning, and successful alternative to the Indian system.

The result was what is now commonly referred to as the Indian Renaissance, which was effected through English education, the preaching of Christian missionaries, and the research work of Orientalists. The first great impetus to English education was the establishment in Calcutta of the Hindu College in 1817. A large number of schools and colleges were founded during the next forty years in Bengal and in other parts of India, creating a small but influential English-educated class. The spread of English as a pan-Indian language, along with improved transportation, facilitated communication and the spread of ideas from one part of the country to another. Among the writers most influential in shaping Indian thinking around this time were J. S. Mill, Auguste Comte, and Herbert Spencer. Mill's political writings, in which he argued that social tyranny might be more oppressive than political subjugation, and his arguments in favor of women's equality were well known. Comte's influence came through his effort to discover "laws of progress." He argued that the key to progress was moral development leading to altruism; moral development depended on religion. Comte also insisted on the necessity of women's equality. Indians were also inspired by Spencer's application of the theory of evolution to human society, showing as it did that social change was a natural process that could be guided, that violent breaks with the past were unnecessary, and that ultimate progress was certain. Spencer's writings were translated into the major Indian languages, reaching a wide audience.[4] The significance of these philosophies was their emphasis on reason rather than tradition and authority as the factor determining the norms and values of society. The objective assessment of tradition was encouraged. Christian missionaries were among the leading vehicles of Western ideas and concepts. Their scathing criticisms of Hindu doctrine and practice were a major impetus to religious reform and revaluation. They were also influential in a positive manner through their example in education, welfare work, the uplifting of the backward classes, and women's emancipation.

The contribution of the Orientalists is well documented and accepted.[5] In the history of Indology, the names of W. Jones, H. H. Wilson, and H. T. Colebrooke are legendary. Jones related Hindu civilization to that of Europe by linking Sanskrit to the European language family and thereby reanimated the idea of a golden age in the past. The golden age concept was given further shape by the work of Colebrooke. Colebrooke argued that the West owed a debt of gratitude to the East for its contributions to the arts and sciences but that civilization, which had its origin in Asia, was now in a state of decline there, whereas the West was steadily progressing. He concentrated his research on the Vedic age of India, characterizing it as an age of gold and comparing it with the present decline. He demonstrated from textual sources that the practice of *satī* was a departure from the authentic tradition and discovered many other discrepancies between ancient texts and actual practices. Colebrooke romanticized the virtues of the Aryan inhabitants of North India, describing their worship as a non-idolatrous monotheistic faith, free from the fertility goddesses, rites, and rituals of contemporary Hinduism. Wilson, unlike Jones and Colebrooke, concentrated his efforts on translating, describing, and analyzing the Purāṇas. In contrast to Colebrooke, who was harsh in his judgment and evaluation of all post-Vedic developments in Hinduism, Wilson argued "that it was neither necessary nor desirable, and was perhaps even absurd, to eliminate traits that through the ages had become deeply ingrained in Hindu culture."[6] His work, as Kopf suggests, linked contemporary traditions with their "historically authenticated pristine forms." The conception of the golden age directly influenced the reformist arguments of men like Rammohun Roy and was perhaps the early Orientalists' greatest contribution: "Knowledge of this golden age would become the cohesive ideology underlying a new sense of community. It is doubtful that the rise of nationalism would have been possible without the sense of community, the sense of community without a collective feeling of self-respect, and self-respect without the stimulus of a rediscovered golden age."[7]

The Indian Renaissance had effects of the most far-reaching kind, touching almost every aspect of Indian life. It set up a high standard of rational thinking, leading to religious and social reform, and developed the political ideas and institutions that led eventually to the freedom of India. Its chief effect, relevant to the authority and status of the Vedas, was the growth of the spirit of criticism. Majumdar argues that this spirit of inquiry and criticism is the most important result of the Western incursion in India.[8] The claim of the Vedas to be an infallible revelation was questioned and their authoritativeness and role eventually redefined. This change, as will be shown later, had serious consequences for the understanding of the specific role of these texts and of Hinduism in general.[9] I will argue that, for various reasons, the reinterpretation that the texts underwent during this period eventually came to be accepted as having returned to their true and original role. One of the important consequences of this acceptance was a remarkable change in the understanding and interpretation of Śaṅkara's Advaita Vedānta.

A study centered on any aspect of this fecund period in the history of Hinduism must inevitably concern itself in large measure with the Brahmo Samaj. This study is no exception. From the days of Rammohun Roy until the death of Keshub Chandra Sen in 1884, the Brahmo Samaj, although numerically small, was the center of all progressive religious, social, and political movements and exerted considerable influence. The movement produced a series of charismatic leaders who determined its doctrine and direction.[10]

Rammohun Roy

Rammohun Roy (1774–1833) is the acknowledged pioneer of the Indian Renaissance. He was born into an orthodox Hindu *brahmin* family, and his early education in Persian and Arabic was intended to prepare him for a career in the Muslim administration. He also learned Sanskrit and possessed a working knowledge of Greek and Hebrew. During the years 1806–1814, when he worked with the East India Company, he acquired a considerable command of the English language. He settled in Calcutta in 1815 and involved himself in the campaign for religious and social reform, establishing the Brahmo Sabha in 1828.[11] Roy died on 27 September 1833 in Bristol, while on a visit to England.

The question of the significance of scriptural revelation is important with respect to Rammohun Roy, for the reason that his work on religion consists largely of attempting to interpret the scriptures to people who considered the texts to be of divine origin and therefore infallible. Opinions are divided among modern scholars on Roy's real attitude toward scriptural authority. S. K. Das is doubtful whether Roy really believed in the divine inspiration of the Vedas.[12] On the other hand, B. G. Ray sees Roy as a champion of Vedic infallibility.[13] Ray's opinion is shared by S. Mitra, who sees the Vedas as the authoritative basis of Hindu theism for Rammohun Roy. According to Mitra, the Vedas were for Roy "extremely luminous works, affirmed to be co-eval with the creation and containing the whole body of Hindu Theology, Law and Literature."[14]

The difficulty of ascertaining Roy's true position on the scripture arises from his tendency to use texts that he himself did not necessarily uphold but that his opponents did. He preferred to avoid questioning the authoritativeness of scripture in his controversies with Hindu opponents.[15] Like most other Brahmo Samaj leaders, Rammohun Roy was not a systematic theologian, and his purpose was not to provide a rounded, consistent theology. He had an abiding interest in social reform. It is difficult, however, to agree with Mitra and Ray that Roy upheld, without reservations, the traditional authority of the Vedas and their absolute infallibility. There is a strong case for modifying this view.[16]

Rammohun Roy saw the Vedas as directing our attention to the regular and orderly operation of the natural world, enabling us to form a concept of the creator: "The *Vedas* (or properly speaking the spiritual parts of them) . . . recommend mankind to direct all researches towards the surrounding objects, viewed either collectively or individually, bearing in mind their regular, wise and wonderful combinations and arrangements, since such researches cannot fail, they affirm, to lead an unbiased mind to the notion of a Supreme Existence, who so sublimely designs and disposes of them, as is everywhere traced through the universe."[17] It is very significant that, in this view, the Vedas do not themselves give certain knowledge of God but point to the means by which such knowledge may be gained. There is already a shift here in the nature of traditional scriptural authority. It is interesting to note that Roy expresses an idea that becomes very important in later Brahmo doctrine, the notion that nature provides the basis for a particular type of revelation. This idea figures prominently in the thought of Keshub Chandra Sen and will be explored more fully when he is treated.

For Rammohun Roy, the criterion by which the authoritativeness of any text may be evaluated is whether it teaches the "true" religion. This view enabled him to accept as authoritative texts of the Hindu tradition other than the Vedas. In this sense, the Vedas were not, for him, a unique and incomparable source of knowledge: "If the spiritual part of the *Vedas* can enable men to acquire salvation by teaching them the true and eternal existence of God, and the false and perishable being of the universe, and inducing them to hear and constantly reflect on these doctrines, it is consistent with reason to admit, that the *smṛti,* and *āgama,* and other works inculcating the same doctrines, afford means of attaining final beautitude."[18]

One may add that it is also consistent with reason and the logic of his thought that the texts of other traditions inculcating the "true" religion would also be accepted as authoritative. There is no reason to suppose that this view would have been disagreeable to him. His wide sympathies with Christian and Islamic thought are well known. This, of course, further erodes the uniqueness of the Vedas. The view that a text is authoritative only if it teaches the "true" religion implies that Roy has an extrascriptural concept of right doctrine that he brings to bear in his evaluation of any text. In his earliest known work, a Persian tract entitled *Tuhfatu'l al-Muwāhhidīn* (A gift to deists) from 1803–1804, Rammohun Roy outlines a minimal theology common to all religions.[19] The tenets of that theology include the existence of God, which is derived from the design of the universe and the human being's innate capacity to infer God from it, and a morally accountable soul existing after death, a belief necessary for the maintenance of social order. The minimal moral principle was a concern for the welfare of mankind. These basic beliefs were contrasted with the doctrinal diversity of historical religions, and they were seen as the converging points of all traditions. Here is the germ of the idea of the unity of all religions, which, in various forms, became a prominent feature of Hindu thought in the modern period.

A very important clue to Roy's attitude toward the Vedas emerges when his view is contrasted with Śaṅkara's on the question of *adhikāra* (entitlement). Roy differs from Śaṅkara in upholding the view that householders, not only *saṁnyāsins,* are entitled to the knowledge of *brahman.* The question of whether *śūdras* are able to know *brahman* is related to the question of the indispensability of the Vedas for a knowledge of *brahman.* Śaṅkara, who argues for the indispensability of the Vedas as a source of knowledge of *brahman,* sees the *śūdras,* who are debarred from Vedic study, as not being entitled to this knowledge. Rammohun Roy, however, in a dispute with one Subrahmanya Sastri, argues that knowledge of the Vedas is not necessary for a knowledge of God, wrongly citing Śaṅkara's support for this view.[20] As far as Roy was concerned, the entitlement of people to true or inferior forms of religion was determined not by formal qualifications of birth or ritual status but by inclination and ability.

It is clear, then, that, although Rammohun Roy did not unambiguously reject Vedic authority and infallibility, he had a considerably modified attitude to them. He never worked out a cohesive theology, but, if he had, it is difficult to see how he could have consistently maintained a position on the authority of the Vedas similar to that of Pūrva-Mīmāṁsā exegetes or Śaṅkara. His view of nature as revelation, his extrascriptural concept of a type of minimal theology, his idea that religious truth is not confined to the texts of the Vedas, and his argument that knowledge of the latter is not necessary for a knowledge of God all mollify the age-old attitudes toward the Vedas. It is also relevant to note that Roy adopted an extremely critical view of Biblical texts, expunging matters that he felt to be irrational. He sometimes argued, in fact, that the Vedic texts themselves, and not only the interpretations of them, must be subjected to rational analysis.[21] Rammohun Roy did not lay down a detailed set of doctrines for the Brahmo Samaj, but his general approach certainly influenced the theological evolution of the movement and its formulation of a definite stance toward the Vedas.

In this context, it is interesting to examine the conclusions of two subsequent leaders of the Brahmo Samaj on Roy's approach to the Vedas. Sivanath Sastri, who joined the movement in the early 1860s, along with Keshub Chandra Sen broke with Debendranath Tagore in 1866, and became the spiritual leader of the revolt against Keshub Chandra Sen in 1878, is critical of Roy's use of the Vedas. He sees Roy's reliance on the texts as vitiating his protest against idolatry. Over seventy-five years after Roy's death in England, Sastri writes:

> Proceeding on the strict lines of the *Śāstras,* he could not but concede to his adversaries that the old scriptures tolerated idolatrous practices as an inferior kind of culture necessary for the ignorant and innocuous in the case of the wise. The admission of this principle largely neutralized the effects of his earnest protest against the idolatry of his countrymen; and as a consequence the Brahmo Samaj long remained only as a meeting place of a number of educated and influential persons who intellectually sympathized with the doctrine of monotheism, but practically adhered to all the idolatrous rites in private life.[22]

Keshub Chandra Sen is very critical of the exclusion of all but *brahmins* from hearing the recitation of the Vedas during the services of the Samaj in Roy's time. It was an inconsistent anomaly in his eyes and militated against the universalistic ideals of the church. In spite of

Sen's suspicions about Roy's reverence for the Vedas and his censuring of the Hindu image that the Samaj projected under Roy's guidance, he warns against concluding that Roy maintained an orthodox view of the texts:

> We must not, however, rush to the extreme of supposing that Ram Mohun Roy was a thorough Vedāntist, and that he offered implicit obedience to the authority of the *Vedas* as the infallible scriptures of God. All that we could gather from his published writings tends to prove that his idea of revelation was catholic, that he measured the inspiration of the so-called scriptures by the truths which they inculcated. Hence he attached great value and importance to the Christian scriptures, and he published a compilation entitled, "The precepts of Jesus, the guide to Happiness," for the welfare of his countrymen. We are therefore, led to the inference that Ram Mohun Roy availed himself of the authority of the *Vedas* for emancipating his countrymen from the yoke of Purāṇic idolatry, not from an absolute belief of those ancient books having come from God himself, but on account of the sublime truths they set forth with all the weight of acknowledged authority on the unity of the Godhead and the spirituality of true worship.[23]

Debendranath Tagore

The watershed in the attitude of the Brahmo Samaj toward the Vedas came under the leadership of Debendranath Tagore (1817–1905). A definite stand was taken and the infallibility of the Vedas formally rejected. This was also the turning point in the general status of these texts in the ensuing history of modern Hinduism.[24] Debendranath Tagore was born in Calcutta in 1817. He received his early education in a school founded by Rammohun Roy. In 1834, he obtained admission to the Hindu College, where he spent about four years, before joining his father, Dwarkanath Tagore, a close associate of Rammohun Roy's, in the family business.[25] Debendranath Tagore was of a contemplative turn of mind, and the death of his grandmother, to whom he was deeply attached, aroused in him deep sorrow and an aversion to wealth and pleasure. A chance encounter with the Īśa Upaniṣad brought relief to his inner turmoil, and he took up the study of the Upaniṣads with great zeal. In 1839, Tagore founded the Tattvabodhini Sabha for propagating the ideas of the Upaniṣads. To carry out the objective of the Sabha, the Tattvabodhini Pathsala, a school for the training of the young, was established in 1840 and a monthly journal, the *Tattvabodhini Patrika,* started in 1843. Akshaykumar Datta (1820–1886), who proved to be an important influence on

Tagore and, indeed, on the whole movement, was a teacher at this school and editor of the journal. The relations between the vigorous Sabha and the Brahmo Samaj, which was in a state of decline after Roy's departure for England, were extremely close. The Tattvabodhini Sabha served as the organizational wing of the Brahmo Samaj, finally merging with the latter in 1859.[26] The assumption of leadership by Debendranath Tagore initiated a new phase in the growth of the Samaj. There was a rapid increase in the power and influence of the Brahmo movement. New rituals and ceremonies were added, the most important being a special form for initiation into membership.

Debendranath Tagore followed Rammohun Roy in his belief that original Hinduism was a spiritual theism and that the Upaniṣads were its source. The spark that led to a change in this view was ignited, strangely enough, by a controversy over missionary proselytization. In 1845, the Hindus of Calcutta were aroused and incensed by the conversion to Christianity of Umesh Chandra Sarkar and his young wife, and a movement in opposition to Dr. Alexander Duff's school, where Sarkar was a student, was launched. Duff's work *India and Indian Missions,* which appeared at that time, was assailed in the pages of the *Tattvabodhini Patrika.* Duff responded by denouncing the doctrines of the Samaj in the *Calcutta Review,* fixing his fury on the idea of the infallibility of the Vedas.[27] The initial response of the Samaj was to defend the concept: "We will not deny that the reviewer is correct in remarking that we consider the *Vedas* and the *Vedas* alone, as the authorized rule of Hindu theology. They are the sole foundation of all our beliefs and the truths of all other *Śāstras* must be judged of according to their agreement with them. What we consider as revelation is contained in the *Vedas* alone; and the last part of our holy Scriptures treating of the final dispensation of Hinduism forms what is called *Vedānta.*"[28] This categorical public declaration of adherence to Vedic infallibility soon provoked dissent and unease within the Samaj, which also found expression in print. Akshaykumar Datta was the leading dissident, and it is generally accepted that it was under his influence that Debendranath Tagore and the Samaj discarded the notion of infallibility.

It is important briefly to consider Datta's religious views because his linking of religion and science became a constantly reiterated theme throughout the period, one salient in Vivekananda's thought. Datta's notion of natural religion was also prominent.[29] Datta posited a deistic concept of God as the supreme maker, who created a purposeful universe. God's plan for the universe is apprehended through the discovery of natural laws that reveal the unity and interrelatedness of all phenomena. God was approached not through worship or monism but through the study of the natural sciences. A complete understanding of these natural laws, or "God's scripture," reveals the harmony of all things. The logic of this thinking led Datta to reject Vedānta as the revealed source of the Brahmo Samaj. Because of his belief in natural laws, he felt that the emphasis in the Brahmo Samaj should be less on national character and more on the religious impulses common to all men. In this way, the Samaj could offer itself to the world as a scientifically constructed natural religion. In his own way, Datta was developing the embryonic theme of Rammohun, which was further enlarged on by Keshub. Sastri is of the opinion that Datta's arguments against Vedic infallibility had wide support in the Samaj.[30]

As part of his effort to ascertain the truth of the issue, Debendranath Tagore sent four *brahmin* youths to Benares to study the Vedas. His own visit to that city in 1847 was partly in pursuit of the same inquiry.[31] In 1850, the doctrine of infallibility was finally abolished.[32] In order, however, to maintain the movement along the lines of Upaniṣadic monotheism, in 1850 Tagore published a compilation of carefully selected passages from the Upaniṣads entitled *Brahmo Dharma.* Perhaps the main cause that led Tagore to the final rejection of the authority of the Upaniṣads was his refusal to accept those passages proclaiming the identity of *ātman* and *brahman.* Earlier, Rammohun Roy had also refused to accept this identification. He preferred to treat *brahman* as the lord and regulator of the cosmos, related to the soul as its superintendent. Both the soul and the universe depend on God for existence.[33] In a revealing passage of his autobiography, worthy of being quoted in full, Tagore writes:

> How strange. Formerly I did not know of the existence of this thorny tangle of *Upaniṣads:* only eleven *Upaniṣads* were known to me, with the help of which I started the propagation of Brahma Dharma, making its foundation. But now I saw that even this foundation was shaky and built upon sand; even here I did not touch firm ground. First I went back to the *Vedas,* but could not lay the foundation of the Brahma Dharma there, then I came back to the eleven authentic *Upaniṣads,* but how unfortunate, even there I could not lay the foundation.[34] Our relation with god is that of worshipper and worshipped—this is the very essence of Brahmoism. When we found the opposite conclusion to this arrived at in Śaṅkarāchārya's *Śarīraka Mīmāṁsā* of the *Vedānta Darśana* we could no longer place any confidence in it; nor could we accept it as a support of our religion. I had thought that if I renounced the *Vedānta Darśana* and accepted the eleven *Upaniṣads* only, I would find support for

> Brahmanism, hence I had relied entirely upon these, leaving aside all else. But when in the *Upaniṣads* I came across, "I am He" and "Thou art That", then I became disappointed in them also.[35]

Here, one feels, is perhaps the real clue to his rejection of scriptural infallibility. The identity posited in the Upaniṣads between the self *(ātman)* and the ultimate reality of all existence *(brahman)* undermined, in Tagore's view, the necessary worshiper-worshiped relationship between the individual and God. This was, for him, unacceptable.

Henceforth, the nonauthoritative status of any text became enshrined in the creed of the Brahmo Samaj. This was a tenet adamantly and inflexibly upheld through all the fragmentations of the movement in later years.[36] In the absence of any authoritative standard of doctrine, nature and intuition became the twin sources of knowledge. Debendranath Tagore speaks of an innate knowledge of God hidden in the hearts of all human beings. This innate knowledge is kindled by the study of the universe, in which is revealed the wisdom, beneficence, glory, and majesty of God:

> Truth is revealed in an intuitive knowledge and our Self trusts in the truth. So this natural intuition is the only (ultimate) means of proving the existence of God. When the Infinite Person is revealed in our innate knowledge through intuition, our understanding finds proof of His wisdom in the creation of the universe and makes known to us His beneficent purpose. Though our infinite understanding cannot fully comprehend the Infinite Person, yet it greatly confirms our intuitive knowledge (of Him). Therefore the seeker of God desirous of salvation should never neglect the cultivation of understanding by the study of the mystery of the world, inner and outer. When understanding is cultivated we can clearly and thoroughly realise the meaning and scope of intuition.[37]

The few discussions in the *Brahmo Dharma* of the nature of intuition are not very lucid. At one point, the innate knowledge of God is presented as the presupposition of our sense of dependence and imperfection. There is no basis for considering ourselves to be dependent and imperfect, says Tagore, unless there is a perfect and independent being. This intuitive knowledge of God is described as being natural to every soul: "Doubt in intuition means cutting the root of all reasoning and leads to utter delusion. It will lead to doubt in our own existence as well as the existence of the outer world and of cause and effect resulting in complete nescience. He who does not believe in intuition can never believe unhesitatingly in the Almighty . . . who is revealed in knowledge and who is the support of all."[38] These views of Tagore's closely parallel the ideas of the Unitarians Channing and Parker discussed below and are suggestive of the influence of the Unitarians.

The basis of Brahmoism became "the pure heart filled with the light of intuitive knowledge."[39] Debendranath Tagore became increasingly reliant on personal intuition as his authority, and the concept of divine command *(ādeśa)* played an important part in his life. It was also to become an unquestionable source of authority with Keshub Chandra Sen. The idea of intuitive experience as an immediate source of spiritual knowledge, which rose to prominence at this time, became a leading idea of the period and has become a dominant motif in the rhetoric of modern Hinduism. In Vivekananda, it became associated with the idea of a scientific method of arriving at religious verification.

The rejection of the Vedas as revealed texts paved the way for an even more rigorous questioning of accepted articles of religious belief and intensified the clamor for social reform. Tagore's more conservative approach to social reform led to the first splinter in the Samaj. The decision to reject scriptural authority was not accepted without protest. Rajnarain Bose, for example, an early associate of Tagore's, was not pleased with the decision and left the employ of Tagore. The strongest voice of protest, however, came from Sitanath Tattvabhusan, who joined the movement under Keshub Chandra Sen in 1871 and later broke with him to become a member of the Sadharan Brahmo Samaj. Sitanath Tattvabhusan saw the weakness of the movement in its lack of any systematic theology. It is extremely interesting also that all efforts of the Brahmo Samaj to establish and maintain a regular theological school ended in failure. Tattvabhusan felt that the appeals to natural religion and intuition were tenuous, and he saw the difficulties of arriving at any philosophical consensus through these. The rejection of the Vedas by Debendranath Tagore, he felt, had led to a neglect of the scriptures and positively discouraged scholarship. He wanted a movement back to the Upaniṣad-based Vedānta. Unfortunately, voices like Tattvabhusan's, appealing for systematization, refinement, and clarity of doctrine, were solitary. Within the movement itself, Tattvabhusan was decried as an advocate of barren intellectualism and scholasticism. He was branded as a reactionary who wanted to abolish the spontaneity of the religious life and suspend the right to private judgment.[40] The opposition to any systematic and methodical approach to doctrine went hand in hand with the accentuation of the importance of the intuitive experience. It is another legacy to modern Hinduism, where the emphasis is very often on the lack of a necessity for any belief in doctrine or dogma. This was an outstanding argument in Vivekananda's presentation of Hinduism to the West.

As mentioned before, Debendranath Tagore adopted a very conservative attitude toward questions of social reform. In fact, he saw the mission of the Brahmo Samaj as a narrowly defined religious one and felt that, in matters of social reform, individual tastes and inclinations should prevail. This approach conflicted with the demands of the younger and radically minded members of the Samaj and led to the first split of the movement in 1866. The dissenting group wanted the Samaj actively to promote intercaste marriage and widow remarriage. These members were opposed to the wearing of the sacred thread. There was also a division of opinion over the quality and extent of women's education, many of the younger members advocating the ideal of complete social equality. In the vanguard of this progressive party was Keshub Chandra Sen (1838–1884).

Keshub Chandra Sen

Sen was born into a Vaiṣṇava family of Calcutta and educated at the Hindu College. Sen's Western education had eroded his childhood religious beliefs and created a void that left him restless and searching. He sought solace in Unitarian philosophy and the writings of Theodore Parker and established the Goodwill Fraternity in 1857. It was at a gathering of this society in that same year that he first met Debendranath Tagore. There was a mutual attraction, and Sen was soon active in the Brahmo Samaj. He was an enthusiastic worker and largely responsible for the reinvigoration of the movement and its attraction to the young. His tour in 1864 to the presidencies of Madras and Bombay facilitated the expansion of the Samaj as a pan-Indian movement. After the schism in 1866, he became the leader of the Brahmo Samaj of India. The section under Tagore called itself the Adi (Original) Brahmo Samaj.

In Sen's eyes, the rejection of the Vedas as inspired texts was a grand step in the evolution of the Samaj. Before this, it was simply revivalist in intention. In a sermon delivered during his visit to England at the Mill-Hill Chapel in Leeds on 28 August 1870, Sen contrasted the two stages of the Brahmo Samaj:

> For twenty years the movement was carried on in that spirit, based all the time upon the national Scriptures of the Hindoos. The same god that lifted this noble band of Hindoos out of the darkness of superstition and idolatry, the same God, led them further onward and heavenward, until they gave up completely and thoroughly the doctrine of the inspiration of the *Vedas*. They took a broader and more unexceptionable bases; they went into their own hearts in order to hear the voice of God, and they

> went forth throughout the amplitudes of nature in order to study in silence the direct revelation of God's spirit. Thus the Hindoo Pantheists became Hindoo Theists. They embraced pure monotheism, such as was not confined to Hindoo books, to the Scriptures of their own countrymen, but was to be found in human nature in all the races and tribes and nations in the world.[41]

Sen wanted to sever all links between the Brahmo Samaj of India and Hinduism. The Hindu image of the movement under Debendranath Tagore was a point of contention. When in 1872 the Brahmo Samaj of India proposed a Marriage Reform Bill, the Adi Samaj argued that the bill would lead to the separation of the Brahmos from the general body of Hindus. Interestingly, Sen countered this by rejoining that Brahmos were already not Hindus, using nonbelief in the Vedas as the dividing line.[42]

Of all the leaders of the Brahmo Samaj, Sen has left the largest legacy of speeches and writings, some of which contain very clear pronouncements on the nature of revelation and the sources of religious knowledge. The problem with Sen, as with other Brahmo leaders, is the unsystematic and often contradictory quality of his thought, a reflection perhaps of the paradoxical times in which he lived.[43]

In a lecture delivered at the Town Hall in Calcutta on 28 September 1866, Sen propounds what amounts to be a general theory of revelation. According to Sen, the primary and ordinary revelation of God, accessible and intelligible to all, is God's self-evident manifestation in nature: "The universe exhibits on all sides innumerable marks of design and beauty, of adaptation and method, which we cannot explain except by referring them to an Intelligent First Cause, the Creator of this vast universe. Each object in nature reminds us of its Maker, and draws the heart in spontaneous reverence to His infinite majesty." Nature, however, does not simply reveal God as creator, comparable to a maker who has invested his object with independent powers of functioning. It also reveals God's immanent function of sustaining and preserving and God's goodness in supplying daily needs: "Behold the Supreme Creator and Ruler of the universe—infinite in wisdom, power and goodness—immanent in matter, upholding it, and quickening all its movements, and mercifully dispensing joy and blessings to all His children. Such is the revelation of nature."[44]

In two lectures delivered the following year at the Calcutta Brahmo School, Sen repeats this argument. Here, however, he distinguishes between the importance of external and internal nature as sources of theological knowledge, undervaluing external nature as a type of revelation (an example of the inconsistency in his thinking): "There is nothing in matter itself, not even all the power and wisdom it manifests, which can lead us to the True God, whose spiritual nature, intelligence, personality, and holiness can only be deducted from the facts of our consciousness." As this quotation suggests, the mind is eulogized as the instrument of revelation. Theology, Sen claims, is essentially dependent on psychology, and the doctrines and arguments of religion are derived primarily from the constitution of the human mind: "The value and importance of the mind as an object of speculation through which we obtain a knowledge of the fundamental principles and main arguments of religion cannot be over-estimated. To what source are we to refer but to the human mind for our ideas of God, immortality and duty, and where do we seek for their proof but in the mind?"[45]

It is obvious that Sen was not consistent in the significance that he attributed to the different forms of revelation. After the revelation of God in nature, the next in Sen's typology is what he calls God in history. History, he contends, is not the mere chronicle of past events; if read properly, it is full of religious significance displaying the workings of Providence. The manner in which God reveals Godself in history is through "great men": "For what is history but the record of the achievements of those extraordinary personages who appear from time to time and lead mankind? and what is it that we read therein but the biography of such men? . . . It is through these great men, these leaders of mankind, that God reveals Himself to us in history: in short, they constitute what we mean by 'God in history.' "[46] Sen sees "great men" as the apostles and missionaries of God, owing their talents and success, not to personal exertions, but to an inherently superior constitution endowed by God. He is scrupulous, however, in distinguishing his "great men" theory from the Hindu notion of the *avatāra* and the Christian concept of incarnation.[47] With him, it is not a case of the perfection of divinity embodied in a mortal frame, the God of the universe in a human body. It is God manifest in man, "not God made man but God in man." These extraordinary men, who are representative of their country and age and also of specific ideas, are born as a result of a moral necessity in times of crisis and turmoil. They are characterized by originality of wisdom, sincerity, invincible power, and selflessness.[48] Christ commands a special regard from Sen, but he pleads for reverence for and honor of all dispensations: "And though Jesus Christ, the Prince of Prophets, effected greater wonders, and did infinitely more good to the world than the others, and deserves therefore our profoundest reverence, we must not neglect that chain, or any single link in that chain, of prophets that preceded him, and prepared the world for him; nor must we refuse honor to those who, coming after him, have carried on the blessed work of human regeneration for which he lived and died."[49]

In comparison with the final and highest category of revelation, the first two types, according to Sen, are merely external. Inspiration is the loftiest. It is direct communion with the spirit of God, vouchsafed only through God's mercy, and its effect on the human person is total. It is, in Sen's own words, "the direct breathing-in of God's spirit—which infuses an altogether new life into the soul, and exalts it above all that is earthly and impure. It is more powerful, being God's direct and immediate action on the human soul, while the revelation made through physical nature and biography is indirect and mediate.[50] It is very significant that, in this lecture, where we are provided with Sen's most detailed statements pertaining to revelation, no mention is made of any text or scripture as revelation, as these have no place in his scheme.

There are three tendencies in Sen's writings and lectures that have very important implications for our study of the changing status of scriptural authority and for our understanding of salient orientations in modern Hinduism. The first of these is his powerful invective against the importance of dogma and doctrine. These were seen to relate to intellectual cognition, reasoning, and logical thought, all of which were cold and lifeless, in contrast to the "fire of inspiration" and "direct communion with God." The former processes had nothing to do with the attainment of salvation. The following quotation will suffice to illustrate, as it is typical of his outbursts on this point: "Do not preach to me dogmas and traditions; talk not of saving my soul by mere theological arguments and inferences. These I do not want; I want the living God, that I may dwell in Him, away from the battle of the world."[51]It is interesting to compare Sen's aversion for doctrine with his criticism of Rammohun Roy, only three years earlier, in an article in which Sen is reviewing the growth of the Samaj and its structure under Roy's leadership: "The creed was of no consequence, unity in faith was not demanded except only in the idea of the Godhead; community of worship was all in all; such a baseless and incomplete system cannot last long: worship must be sustained by knowledge and faith and love, congregational worship must find its life in a community of dogmatic faith. This is an inevitable moral necessity."[52]

The second tendency, a direct consequence of the first, is his repudiation of all forms of authority, a type of spiritual anarchism. The claim was made that the Samaj was free from teachers, priests, books, ceremonies, and rites.[53] The third, and most important, tendency in his thought is his stress on direct perception as the means for gaining spiritual knowledge, foreshadowing an argument that rose to significance in Vivekananda. Sen sees the direct perception approach as a most familiar topic of the Upaniṣads: "No expression is more frequently used in the *Upaniṣads* than the 'perception' of God *(darśan)*. It appears that Hindu sages, not content with intellectual conceptions of the Almighty or abstract contemplation of certain Divine attributes, sought earnestly and indeed successfully, to behold the Supreme Spirit directly and to apprehend Him as a distinct and vivid Reality in their inner consciousness."[54] This certainty, Sen contends, which arises from the direct perception or realization of reality, is comparable to the assuredness arising from the sensual apprehension of objects around us. It is a self-evident truth, the only satisfactory kind of proof: "The Real God is seen as plainly as we see ourselves and the world. We must place our belief in God upon direct evidence or eyesight. I will apply the same demonstration in reference to God as we do to material objects. All arguments a priori or a posteriori are feeble."[55]

In 1878, the Brahmo Samaj underwent its second schism. This time the rebellion was against Sen, and the causes were many.[56] It is interesting that many of the issues that provoked the first rift were still very much alive, and on this occasion Sen was the accused. Sen's ideas on women's education and emancipation were seen as being retrograde. He was opposed to university education for women and their exposure to subjects like mathematics, philosophy, and science. He feared that they would lose their sexual identity. He refused the demand of some members that their wives be at their side during Samaj services. There was also opposition to Sen's authoritarian management of affairs and a demand for constitutional government and public control of Samaj property. There was a deep suspicion about Sen's perception of his own role in the movement and the attitude of hero worship that was growing around him. Sen was giving increasing prominence to the idea that he had received a special dispensation from God and that his decisions with regard to the movement were above question, being motivated by *ādeśa* (divine command).[57] From 1875 on, Sen emphasized the importance of asceticism in the religious life, giving prominence to meditation and withdrawal from the world. The social reform- and social welfare-oriented activities of the movement fell into neglect. The issue, however, that finally precipitated the split was Sen's consent to the marriage between his eldest daughter and the young maharaja of Cooch Behar, in violation of the principles of the Marriage Act of 1872, and in spite of considerable protest within the Samaj. Both had not attained the marriageable age stipulated by the act, and the rites were non-Brahmo. The schism led to the formation on 15 May 1878 of the Sadharan Brahmo Samaj. One year later, Sen inaugurated the Nava-Vidhan or New Dispensation.

The launching of the New Dispensation was motivated by Sen's conviction that he was inspired by a new revelation from God, the special feature of which was to harmonize and unify all conflicting creeds. It was not, he claimed, his intention to form a new sect. "It is the harmony of all scriptures, and prophets and dispensations. It is not an isolated creed, but the science which binds and explains and harmonizes all religions. It gives to history a meaning, to the action of Providence a consistency, to quarrelling churches a common bond and to successive dispensations a continuity. . . . It is the wonderful solvent, which fuses all dispensations into a new chemical compound. It is the mighty absorbent, which absorbs all that is good and true and beautiful in the objective world."[58]

The Nava-Vidhan did not alter Sen's attitude toward the scriptures even though his views on the necessity of authority in religious matters were dramatically reversed. He strongly refuted deism, for example, because of its disavowal of authority in religion.[59] In one of the most revealing pieces of writing belonging to this period, "Is the Bible Inspired?" Sen expounds what the New Dispensation understands by the concept of revelation.[60] His illustrations here, as in most of his speeches and writings, are drawn from the Christian tradition, but it is fair to assume that his views are applicable to the scriptures of other traditions as well. He draws a distinction between the New Dispensation and deism, claiming that the former, unlike the latter, does not deny revelation but reserves the right to interpret it in its own way. This interpretation is based on a contrast between the inspiration of words and the inspiration of events. The former is categorically denied:

> That a book has come down to us from heaven, cut and dry, containing lessons for our guidance and salvation, we do not believe. As a meteor falls from heavens, even so dropped a dazzling gospel-light! This story is too fantastic for our credence. Inspiration is not an ethereal rainbow delusion like that. It is real; it is solid. It is neither a written nor a printed book. Nor is it a voice behind the clouds speaking like thunder unto entire nations through their accredited prophet-leaders. We wholly disbelieve in the inspiration of words written or words spoken. Neither in the pen nor in the lips can there be inspiration.

Events alone, according to Sen, are inspired and revealed. In this sense, both the Old and New Testaments and the leading figures of the Bible's drama are inspired. By *revelation* he means

> the living history not the dead narrative; the fresh events as they occurred, not the lifeless traditions recorded on paper. The letter killeth. Convert a saint into a beautiful picture on canvas, convert living apostles into antiquated doctrines, transform living events into lifeless ceremonies, and burning enthusiasm into the cold dogmatism of books and creeds, and you kill inspiration. What you read in the Bible *was* inspired. It would be incorrect to say that the Bible *is* inspired. Inspiration dwells in the fact-Bible not in the book-Bible, in the living Gospel, not in the letter of the book.[61]

The effect of this kind of view was to reduce the significance of the scriptural text further. The unique claim of any scripture was dissolved in the unbounded eclecticism of Sen's thought. In fact, the scriptures of the Nava-Vidhan included "the whole of science, physical, metaphysical and moral and also the science of religion." Sen continued the trend noted earlier, especially with A. K. Datta in the time of Debendranath Tagore, of attempting to justify his religious experiments in the name of science. The special mission of the New Dispensation to unite all creeds was proclaimed as scientific, for "science and salvation" were identical, and its enemies were not atheists but "unscientific men." Its truths, Sen argued, were demonstrable, for they were based on observation and experiment, and the movement was ready to expunge any tenet falsified by scientific discoveries. Strange also, but perhaps not surprising, was his attempt to justify the Nava-Vidhan on the authority of Śaṅkara. The latter was seen as foreshadowing the Nava-Vidhan, which Sen described as a "New Śaṅkarāchārya, loftier and grander far than the Old Śaṅkara."[62]

Of all the leaders so far considered, Sen is significant as being the most influential of his times. He is important in any consideration of Vivekananda's thought, for the latter had also imbibed the legacy of Brahmoism. Early in his career, Vivekananda was active in the circles of the Brahmo Samaj. He was a member of Keshub's Band of Hope and acted on stage at Keshub's side.[63] Along with Ramakrishna, Sen was probably the strongest molding force in shaping Vivekananda's thought.[64] It is perhaps by no means inexplicable that Vivekananda first approached Ramakrishna with a strong skepticism of texts and doctrines, searching for someone who had personal experience of reality and who could lead him to such direct experience himself. This was the only kind of proof, which, as we have seen, Sen thought imperative and accepted as valid.

Ramakrishna

At the time of Keshub's death in January 1884, the center of religious attention in Calcutta had already shifted to Ramakrishna, who had taken up residence in the Kālī temple at Dakshineshwar. It was Sen, in fact, who brought Ramakrishna to public attention. Since their first meeting in 1875, a close relationship had developed between the two men. Primarily through Vivekananda and the Ramakrishna Mission founded in 1897, Ramakrishna, like the Brahmo Samaj, has exercised considerable influence on the character of modern Hinduism. My primary concern here being his attitude toward scriptural authority, only the briefest biographical details are necessary.[65]

Ramakrishna was born into a poor *brahmin* family of Kamarpukur, a village about seventy miles from Calcutta, on 18 February 1836. He seemed endowed with an extremely sensitive temperament and frequently experienced trancelike states of unconsciousness, once when struck by the spectacular contrast between a flock of white swans flying against the background of a dark band of clouds, and again while enacting the role of Śiva during a Śiva-*rātri* festival. Ramakrishna, then known by his childhood name Gadadhar, was averse to formal education, and his eldest brother, Ramkumar, who ran a Sanskrit school in Calcutta, took him to the city hoping to reform his attitudes. Ramkumar failed in this task, but Gadadhar became his assistant in performing the rituals of worship in several Calcutta homes where he served as family priest. When in 1855 Rani Rasmani, a wealthy Calcutta widow who built a temple dedicated to the goddess Kālī, had difficulties in securing the services of a *brahmin* priest because of her low caste status, Ramkumar accepted the offer, and, after an initial reluctance, Gadadhar also took up residence there. Here, also, he became his brother's acolyte, and, when the latter died suddenly in 1856, Gadadhar became the temple priest. He entered into the worship of Kālī with characteristic intensity and passion, yearning for a vision of the goddess. The agony and culminating ecstasy of his experience is best conveyed in his own words:

> There was then an intolerable anguish in my heart because I could not have Her vision. Just as a man wrings a towel forcibly to squeeze out all the water from it, I felt as if somebody caught hold of my heart and mind

> and was wringing them likewise. Greatly afflicted with the thought that I might never have Mother's vision, I was in great agony. I thought that there was no use in living such a life. My eyes suddenly fell upon the sword that was there in the Mother's temple. I made up my mind to put an end to my life with it that very moment. Like one mad, I ran and caught hold of it, when suddenly I had the wonderful vision of Mother and fell down unconscious. I did not know what happened then in the external world—how that day and the next slipped away. But, in my heart of hearts, there was flowing a current of intense bliss, never experienced before, and I had the immediate knowledge of the Light that is Mother.[66]

Ramakrishna's intense spiritual life aroused fears concerning his sanity, and his mother implored him to return to his village, hoping that marriage might lead to a more settled and normal course of life. Accordingly, in May 1859, he was married to Saradamani, who eventually became known as the Holy Mother, and assumed an important role in the Mission's activities after his death. In 1860, Ramakrishna returned to Dakshineshwar temple, practicing over the next few years various forms of *sādhana.* Under the guidance of Bhairavi Brahmani, a female ascetic, he went through the disciplines of *Tantra.* Incidentally, it was Bhairavi who proclaimed him an *avatāra* and made efforts to have him accepted as such. Ramakrishna was also initiated into the study and practice of Advaita Vedānta by a wandering monk, Tota Puri, a phase claimed to be the climax of his *sādhana.* He is also said to have been exposed to the Christian and Islamic paths.[67] Ramakrishna soon settled into the role of spiritual mentor to the large body of disciples who gathered around him, venturing only occasionally from his abode in the Dakshineshwar temple. He died of throat cancer on 16 August 1886.

Ramakrishna's instructions as a spiritual teacher cover a wide variety of subjects, and I have selected for analysis only those that are relevant to an understanding of his attitude toward scripture.[68] Ramakrishna's antipathy to formal education has already been noted. He felt that it was useful only for prosperity in the world, and this theme often recurred in his talks. Two of his favorite parables centered on this idea. Learned men were compared by him to kites and vultures, which soar to great heights in the sky but whose eyes are forever focused on the decaying carcasses below. They were also likened to foolish men in a mango orchard, who count the leaves and fruit and argue to estimate their value instead of plucking and relishing the juicy fruit. Along with this strong censure of the pedantic mind, he attributed little importance to reason and the intellect in the religious life.[69]

He often qualified this denunciation, however, by praising knowledge that led to mental purification.

In terms of the actual role of the scriptures, he drew a parallel with a map. Sacred books, he contended, only point the way to God. The most that one can derive from a study of the scriptures is a feeling that God exists.[70] At times he was even more pessimistic about what could be accomplished by textual studies. The scriptures are diluted, containing, as he puts it, a "mixture of sand and sugar," difficult to distinguish and separate. Their essence is much better learned from a spiritual teacher. They are of no use in conveying the feeling of God: "This feeling is something very different from book-learning. Books, scriptures and science appear as mere dirt and straw after the realization of God."There is also the implication in Ramakrishna that the Vedas are by no means unique, for there are many other such texts. Direct vision of God was the central idea of his entire instruction. It was the only form of verification: "But seeing is far better than hearing. Then all doubts disappear. It is true that many things are recorded in the scriptures; but all these are useless without the direct realization of God, without devotion to His Lotus Feet, without purity of heart. The almanac forecasts the rainfall of the year. But not a drop of water will you get by squeezing the almanac. No, not even one drop."[71] The awakening of the *kuṇḍalinī* in the state of *samādhi* alone led to *jñāna* (knowledge) and the realization of *brahman.*[72]

It is interesting to look at the references to Śaṅkara in the conversations of Ramakrishna. One expects to find significant mention of Śaṅkara, in the light of his tuition under Tota Puri, a member of one of the ten monastic orders reputedly founded by Śaṅkara.[73] There are, however, only six references to Śaṅkara recorded by Gupta. Five of these relate, with minor variations, an unflattering incident in Śaṅkara's life. One day, after emerging from a bath in the Ganges, Śaṅkara was accidentally brushed by an untouchable. Śaṅkara reproached the man, who then surprisingly questioned him on the nature of his identification with the body. The pure self, argued the untouchable, neither touches nor is touched. In the sixth reference, Ramakrishna uses Śaṅkara to illustrate the example of a *jñānī* who retains his sense of ego for the purposes of instructing others.

The very few references to Śaṅkara in Ramakrishna's conversations raises the important question of the sources of Ramakrishna's ideas. It is a matter well worth examination in view of Ramakrishna's cardinal place in the modern revival of Hinduism. Unfortunately, critical studies of Ramakrishna's thought are few, and the work of W. G. Neevel is perhaps the only attempt to explore this question. Neevel does not specifically investigate Ramakrishna's attitude toward the Vedas, but he raises questions and suggests answers that shed light on this problem. He goes into great detail in examining textual sources, but the principal lines of his argument are well worth outlining here. Neevel reiterates the point already noted about Ramakrishna's disregard for philosophical and theological deliberations and his devaluation of the role of reason. He contrasts this with the systematic presentation of Ramakrishna's ideas by Vivekananda as a reinterpretation of Śaṅkara. Neevel suggests that this methodic arrangement was a response to the foreign audience that Vivekananda sought to reach:

> Swami Vivekananda and the succeeding Rāmakrishna missionaries were concerned to present the Hindu tradition and Śri Rāmakrishna's message in a manner most comprehensible and appealing to Americans and Europeans. The *Upaniṣads* and the *Vedānta* school of religious thought *(darśana)* based upon them had already found ready acceptance and praise, especially within certain non-traditional and non-Christian circles. Moreover, the currency of transcendental idealism and vitalistic monism within Western philosophy provided a ready basis for an acceptance of the profundity of Śaṅkarācārya's idealistic non-dualism *(advaita).* Since Śrī Rāmakrishna held such a widely inclusive Hindu position, it was not at all difficult to emphasize or highlight the more appealing and acceptable Vedantic and *advaitic* aspects of his teachings.

By contrasting the standard biographies of Ramakrishna with earlier historical evidence, Neevel calls into question the systematic arrangement of Ramakrishna's *sādhana.* This is usually presented in an orderly sequence from certain preliminary forms of discipline to the pivot of his nondual experience. Neevel's view is that this is a reconstruction, "derived more from the views of Swami Vivekananda and the later Ramakrishna Mission than from the teachings of Śrī Ramakrishna himself. I propose that Saradananda and other official biographers were moved to establish this particular order by their conviction that *Advaita Vedānta* is the ultimate expression of religious truth and therefore the ultimate and finally satisfying phase of Ramakrishna's *sādhana.*"[74]

Neevel's thesis is that the primary influence on Ramakrishna's thought, forming the basic framework through which all his later experiences were interpreted, was his Tantra *sādhana* and that his views are more adequately understood in the terms of Tantra than in those of Śaṅkara's Advaita. Neevel proceeds to emphasize several significant differences in method and content between Śaṅkara and Ramakrishna, illustrating the derivation of the latter from Tantra sources.[75] To the many points of difference for which Neevel argues, I would also add the important area of attitudes toward the authority and role of the Vedas. As we have seen, Ramakrishna did not reject outright the authority of the scriptures as much as redefine it, and this accords with Tantra perceptions of the texts.[76] The sources of Ramakrishna's attitude toward the scriptures provide, of course, another important clue to the comprehension of Vivekananda's position.

The Influence of the Unitarians

Throughout this period, Unitarian influences were most significant in prompting the questioning of scriptural authority and also in formulating the new attitudes that eventually emerged. The Unitarian association with the Brahmo Samaj began in the time of Rammohun Roy, continued through all the movement's vicissitudes, and was strong under the Sadharan Brahmo Samaj at the close of the nineteenth century. Incidentally, Roy died at the Bristol estate of the Reverend Lant Carpenter, the well-known English Unitarian. He also corresponded with such famous American Unitarians as William Ellery Channing and Joseph Tuckerman and had planned to visit America in the hope of meeting Channing.[77] He often referred to himself as a Hindu Unitarian.[78] In the time of Keshub Chandra Sen, the American missionary C. H. A. Dall was active in the circles of the Samaj, even though both men later parted ways as Sen became less interested in social reform.[79] As late as 1896, the Sadharan Brahmo Samaj was visited by R. J. T. Sunderland, a representative of the British and Foreign Unitarian Association. The Brahmo Samaj Committee was organized by Sunderland for the annual selection of a suitable candidate, one interested in the propagation of Brahmoism, for theological training at the Manchester New College of Oxford. Funds for the scholarship were provided by an English Unitarian gentleman, and many were trained under the scheme.[80] There were further visits by representatives of the same organization in 1897 and 1899.

The attraction of Unitarianism for Rammohun Roy was perhaps the critique of Trinitarian Christianity that it provided, which he used in his disputation with the missionaries. The entire critique was adopted by the Brahmo Samaj. Following the Unitarians, the Samaj objected to the doctrine of the Trinity, arguing that it subverted the unity of God. They felt that Christ ought to be regarded as distinct from and inferior to God and discussed the problems of representing him as both human and divine. He was an emissary of God to effect a spiritual regeneration of mankind, and his agony and suffering were real. Unitarians rejected the idea that Christ's death made God more placable and merciful. They also opposed the doctrines about the natural depravity of man and the predestination of a select few for salvation.[81]

The Unitarian thinkers who exercised the greatest influence on the formation of Brahmo theology were Channing and Theodore Parker. The works of both men were widely circulated among Brahmos, and the latter's writings were translated into Bengali. The strength and extent of the influence become very clear when the writings of both men are compared particularly with those of the prolific Keshub Chandra Sen. Channing, for example, does not appear to question the existence of a valid scriptural revelation but argues for a wider concept of revelation: "But we shall err greatly, if we imagine that his Gospel is the only light, that every ray comes to us from a single Book, that no splendours issue from God's Works and Providence, that we have no teacher in religion but the few pages bound up in our Bibles. Jesus Christ came, not only to give us his peculiar teaching, but to introduce us to the imperishable lesson which God for ever furnishes in our own and all Human Experience, and in the laws and movements of the Universe." He does not appear to question the significance and status of the Bible as revelation but argues for the thorough exercise of reason in its interpretation, for it is a book "written for men, in the language of men, and its meaning is to be sought in the same manner as that of other books."[82] His concern is with enunciating the principles of the Bible's right interpretation. Rammohun Roy appears more akin to Channing in his attitude toward the scriptures, whereas Sen seems to have imbibed his views mainly from Parker, who rejected any idea of scriptural infallibility and argued for the human origin and character of all scriptures:

> Laying aside all prejudices, if we look into the Bible in a general way, as into any other books, we find facts which force the conclusion upon us, that the Bible is a human work, as much as the Principia of Newton or Descartes, or the Vedas and Koran. Some things are beautiful and true, but others no man, in his reason, can accept. Here are the works of various writers, from the eleventh century before, to the second century after Christ, thrown capriciously together, and united by no common tie but the lids of the bookbinder."[83]

The alternative forms of revelation suggested by Sen are culled from the writings of Channing and Parker. Sen's views on internal and external nature as revelation were earlier affirmed by Channing, and his ideas on inspiration are a close restatement of Parker's own. The "infinite," according the Channing, is revealed in all things, and, until we have learned to see the infinite in nature, we have missed a lesson that is continuously taught to us. He describes the universe as a symbol of "Infinite Power, Intelligence, Purity, Bliss and Love": "Nature everywhere testifies to the Infinity of its Author. It bears throughout the impress of the Infinite. It proclaims a Perfection illimitable, unsearchable, transcending all thought and utterance. It is modelled and moulded, as a whole and in its least molecule, with grandeur, unfathomable intelligence, and inexhaustible bounty. This is the glory of the universe. And to behold this is to understand the universe." Channing understood internal human nature to be a revelation in the sense that our primary emotions urge a relationship with a perfect being. In human nature is wrapped up the idea of God, and God's image is carried in our moral and intellectual powers:

> Thus we see that human nature is impelled by affections of gratitude, esteem, veneration, joy, not to mention various others, which prepare us to be touched and penetrated by the infinite goodness of God, and which when directed to Him, constitute piety. That these emotions are designed to be devoted particularly to the Creator, we learn from the fact that they are boundless in their range and demand an Unbounded Object. They cannot satisfy themselves with the degrees of love, intelligence, and power which are found in human beings. . . . They delight in the infinite, and never can find repose but in an Infinite Being, who combines all good.[84]

Parker argues that inspiration is superior to the revelation of God in nature and is a regular mode of God's operation on the human spirit. It is universal, varying in degree, not in kind, and its revelation is modified by the peculiar circumstances of the individual who receives it: "It is the direct and intuitive perception of some truth, either of thought or of sentiment. There can be but one mode of Inspiration: it is the action of the Highest within the soul, the divine presence imparting light." Inspiration, according to Parker, is the only means by which we gain knowledge of what is not seen and felt, and it is not confined to any single religious tradition, nation, or age. The variation in the degree of inspiration, however, depends on the natural intellectual, moral, and religious endowment of the individual as well as on the use that each individual makes of this inheritance. It results from the faithful use of our faculties; the purer the moral character, the loftier and more complete is the inspiration. Inspiration, says Parker, can assume a variety of forms, modified by the country, character, and education of the one who receives it. It can motivate action as well as words. Parker laments the fact that, in modern times, men have ceased to believe in the possibility of inspiration. It is accepted as an experience of the past, and guidance is sought instead in tradition, "the poor and flickering light which we get of the priest."[85]

The study of Parker's writings throws great light on many of Sen's arguments, particularly on what he means by the intuitive knowledge of God. It is Parker's contention that the institution of religion is founded in the very constitution of the human being. The principle that gives rise to religion is our inborn sense of dependence. He argues further that this religious element presupposes the existence of its object of satisfaction: "A natural want in Man's constitution implies satisfaction in some quarter, just as the faculty of seeing implies something to correspond to this faculty, namely, objects to be seen and, a medium of light to see by. As the tendency to love implies something lovely for its object, so the religious consciousness implies its object. If it is regarded as a sense of absolute dependence, it implies the absolute on which this dependence rests, independent of ourselves."[86] The knowledge of God, then, in Parker's view, is a "spontaneous intuition of reason." He argues, as Sen later does, that belief does not depend on any a posteriori or a priori argument but preceded proof and is gained through "natural revelation." It is the result of the interaction of the intellectual and religious faculties of man. The identical argument has been suggested by Keshub. After alluding to the sense of dependence, Sen concludes, "When a man feels this dependence then he has proclaimed himself a theist. Atheism is impossible. The very consciousness of self repudiates atheism."[87] It is obvious then, that the rejection of Vedic infallibility created a gap that the alternative forms of revelation suggested by Unitarianism quickly filled.

Throughout the period under survey, Swami Dayananda Saraswati (1824–1883), founder of the Arya Samaj, was the solitary champion of Vedic authority and infallibility. Born at Kathiawar in the state of Gujarat, Dayananda left home at an early age after a dispute with his father over the worship of idols and wandered across India for many years before finally becoming the disciple of Virajananda, a blind *saṅnyāsin* of Mathura.[88] He founded the Arya Samaj in 1875 at Bombay. Belief in the infallibility of the Vedas was the cornerstone of all the doctrines of the movement. The four Vedas were held by him to be the eternal utterances of God, containing all religious truth. This was his major difference with the leaders of the Brahmo Samaj, and their attempts to convince him to reject this view were unsuccessful.[89] All post-Vedic developments in Hinduism contradicted in the Vedas or not expressly approved by them were denounced by Dayananda. This view was also extended to other texts of the Hindu tradition, and the

Purāṇas, for example, were repudiated by him as being false. Dayananda, however, did not accord equal authoritativeness to all portions of the Vedas. He accorded primacy to the *saṁhitās* (hymns) alone. He was positively antibrahminic, attacked the doctrine of caste, and, like the Brahmo Samaj, dismissed the idea of the *avatāra.*

The Arya Samaj, however, had a limited impact. At the time of Dayananda's death in 1883, the total membership was around twenty thousand, and the movement never really had an appeal outside the Punjab.[90] Panikkar suggests several reasons for this.[91] Dayananda's call for a return to the Vedas involved a denial of all the developments of medieval Hinduism, which he bitterly opposed. The Vedic religion was no longer related to the religious experiences of the masses, and Panikkar feels that Dayananda's intolerant attitude toward other religions, especially Islam and Christianity, even though explicable in the context of his times, was inconsistent with Hindu tradition.

We have traversed a period of over one hundred years in this survey of attitudes toward scriptural authority from Rammohun Roy to Ramakrishna. I have argued that, in order to be consistent, Roy's position compelled him to adopt a considerably modified view of Vedic authority, even though he did not unambiguously reject the doctrine of Vedic infallibility. I sought to demonstrate how many of the ideas that influenced his view of the scriptures were made more explicit and their implications drawn out in greater detail by subsequent leaders of the movement. Of all the thinkers reviewed, however, Rammohun Roy strove most assiduously to justify his views by resorting to scriptural authority. With the formal rejection of the authoritativeness of the Vedas in the time of Debendranath Tagore, appeals to Vedic authority were no longer indispensable, for then intuition emerged as the alternative source of religious knowledge. The hermeneutical approach was almost totally disregarded, a legacy most manifest in the history of modern Hinduism in its lack of development in this method. This turning point came about in Tagore's time when, in controversy with Christian missionaries, the doctrine of infallibility became a positive embarrassment and dissidents under A. K. Datta clamored for its expurgation. We have seen how Keshub Chandra Sen welcomed the decision as the most important stride in the doctrinal growth of the Samaj. This direction of development continued under Sen, and the triumph of individual intuitive experience over all forms of religious authority may be said to have attained its climax in his time. With Sen, the Brahmo Samaj completed a full, paradoxical circle. Founded in the name of rationalism, it ended with a denial of the role of reason and the intellect in the religious quest, upholding personal experience as unquestionable and sacrosant. Also noted has been Sen's argument against dogma. This most probably had its origin when, under the barrage of missionary criticism, Roy attempted to prune the unwieldy mass of Hindu beliefs, seeking to introduce a definiteness of shape and a facility of comprehension, rivaling what he saw as positive features of Christianity. With the rejection of Vedic infallibility and the introduction of the authority of intuitive experience, the argument against doctrine took on new meaning. Doctrines became antithetical to direct intuitive realization, and the importance of the latter was argued in contradistinction to the former.

Ramakrishna's background was different from that of the Brahmo Samaj leaders in that he was virtually unexposed to Western influences. He was rooted, as we have seen, in the traditions of Hinduism, but in the strands that emphasized the authority of mystic experience. His claim to have had direct personal experience of the truths of religion was undoubtedly the most important factor in explaining Sen's attraction to him. In one of those strange and consequential coincidences of history, two different but very important and influential figures of modern Hinduism concurred on the supremacy of personal spiritual experience and a relative scorn of scripture.[92]

Chapter 2

VIVEKANANDA'S CONCEPT OF THE NATURE, ROLE, AND AUTHORITY OF THE VEDAS

IN CHAPTER 1, my aim was to trace the development of attitudes toward scriptural authority and revelation during the period from Rammohun Roy to Ramakrishna. We discovered, in this interval, an increasing rejection of orthodox interpretations of the authority of the scriptures. We saw Debendranath Tagore formally renouncing the authoritative supremacy of the Vedas and Keshub Chandra Sen seeking to establish the sacrosanctity of individual intuitive experience over all forms of religious authority. Ramakrishna was derogatory and cynical about the value of scriptural study and negative in his views about the overall importance of scripture. He maintained the primacy of direct personal experience. Vivekananda, of course, as a direct disciple of Ramakrishna, was the heir of this legacy. Many of the attitudes of the time were given renewed emphasis by him, and some of its mere suggestions and outlines were elaborately detailed and expanded.

In the present chapter, I seek to examine the direction and development given to this legacy by Vivekananda. In general, my concern is to unfold his understanding of the origin of the Vedas, the nature and scope of their authority, his principles of interpretation, and significant differences of emphasis between the views he expressed abroad and those he expressed in his homeland.

The Genesis of the Vedas and the Personal Foundations of Their Authority

Perhaps the clearest statements in all the writings and lectures of Vivekananda on the origin of the Vedas and the personal basis of their authority occur in his commentary on the Yoga-sūtras of Patañjali.[1]

Vivekananda comments on the *sūtra* "pratyakṣānumānāgamāḥ pramāṇāni," which enumerates the valid sources of knowledge acceptable to the Yoga school of Indian philosophy. Vivekananda renders *pramāṇāni* as "proofs" and translates the *sūtra,* "Direct perception, inference, and competent evidence are proofs." *Pratyakṣa,* for him, is knowledge directly derived from the senses, and this is valid as long as the sense instruments are accurate and free from error. *Anumāna* is the inference of a signified object through an appropriate sign. Very significantly, the term *āgama,* which he first translated as "competent evidence," is now given as *āptavākya.*[2] The latter he defines as "the direct evidence of the *yogis,* of those who have seen the truth." The difference between such a person and the ordinary individual in the matter of acquiring knowledge is the freedom of the former from the effort of intellectualizing: "Before his mind, the past, the present, and the future are alike, one book for him to read; he does not require to go through the tedious processes for knowledge we have to; his words are proof, because he sees knowledge in himself" (*CW,* 1:204). Vivekananda distinguishes between two kinds of knowledge or truths. Science, according to him, is knowledge derived from the application of reason to data acquired through the senses. The Vedas, on the other hand, represent knowledge acquired by the "subtle, supersensuous power of *Yoga*" (*CW,* 6:181). He considers the latter to be valid because that knowledge is derived from direct perception.

In his commentary on this *sūtra,* Vivekananda shows a certain awareness of the immediate problem of determining whether a particular *āptavākya* is valid knowledge. He proposes, therefore, a set of criteria for evaluating the authenticity of the *āpta* and his or her perceptions. First, Vivekananda emphasizes the character of the *āpta.* Unlike other fields of endeavor, where the discovery of truth is independent of and not conditional on the moral character of the inquirer, here the reverse is true: "No impure man will ever have the power to reach the truths of religion" (*CW,* 1:205). We must first ascertain, therefore, that the *āpta* is perfectly unselfish and holy. In imparting knowledge, Vivekananda advances, we must be clear that the *āpta* has no motive for material gain or acclaim. Second, we must be certain that the *āpta* has reached beyond the senses. The content of his knowledge should be information unobtainable through the application of our senses.[3] Third, the perceptions of the *āpta* should not contradict truths derived from other valid sources of knowledge. A perception should be immediately rejected, for example, if it contradicts scientific knowledge: "Because whatever I see is proof, and whatever you see is proof, if it does not contradict any past knowledge. There is knowledge beyond the senses, and whenever it does not contradict reason and past human experience, that knowledge is proof" (*CW,* 1:205).[4] Finally, according to Vivekananda, the assertions of the *āpta* must have a possibility of verification. The *āpta* should never claim any singular or unique faculty of perception and must represent only the possibilities of all persons. The perceptions of the *āpta* must be directly accessible to everyone.

It is these *āptas,* adds Vivekananda, who are the authors of the sacred scriptures, and the latter are proof only because of this fact. The authority of the scripture is, therefore, one derived from the personal authority of the *āpta:* "Who is a true witness? He is a true witness to whom the thing said is a direct perception. Therefore the *Vedas* are true, because they consist of the evidence of competent persons" (*CW,* 8:270; also 4:340, 1:232).[5] Vivekananda uses the word ṛṣi synonymously with *āpta* and often describes the Vedas as the documentation of their perceptions: "The *Vedas* are said to be written by the ṛṣis. The ṛṣis were sages who realized certain facts. The exact definition of the Sanskrit word ṛṣi is a Seer of *mantras*—of the thoughts conveyed in the Vedic hymns. These men declared that they had realized—sensed, if that word can be used with regard to the superconscious—certain facts, and these they proceeded to put on record" (*CW,* 2:60). This, of course, accords with his view of revelation as "later reports of spiritual discoveries" (*CW,* 3:494). It is important to note, however, that Vivekananda does not see the ṛṣis as the creators of the truths that they advocate. Like scientists in relation to the natural world, they are only discoverers. He characterizes the Vedas as a collection of spiritual laws discovered at different times by different persons: "Just as the law of gravitation existed before its discovery, and would exist if all humanity forgot it, so is it with the laws that govern the spiritual world. The moral, ethical, and spiritual relations between soul and soul and between spirits and the Father of all spirits, were there before discovery, and would remain even if we forgot them" (*CW,* 1:7).[6] We may briefly note here that these spiritual laws are not conceived to be existing anywhere outside but are described by him as "the eternal laws living in every soul" (*CW,* 3:409).[7] It is to substantiate this claim that he describes the Vedas as being "expired" rather than "inspired."

The Provisional and Limited Character of the Authority of the Vedas

The nature of the authoritative claim of the Vedas, as perceived by Vivekananda, is best illustrated by beginning with two analogies that he repeatedly employs. The adequacy of the scriptures is compared to the value and utility of a map to a traveler, before visiting a country (see *CW,* 1:185–186, 6:14). The map, according to Vivekananda, can create only curiosity for firsthand knowledge of the place and can communicate only a vague conception of its reality. Maps are in no way equivalent to the direct knowledge of the country, gathered by actually being there. The second analogy to which Vivekananda resorts is that to the almanac or calendar (see *CW,* 1:326, 7:210). The difference between the knowledge derived from a study of the scriptures and true spiritual knowledge is compared by him to predictions of rainfall in an almanac and actual rainfall. The rain is not to be found in the calendar. The significant point of both analogies is the same. The knowledge that we may gain from scripture is not self-sufficient. Something over and beyond this is required. Like maps, scriptures can only arouse our curiosity and stimulate us to make the discoveries for ourselves.

In the view of Vivekananda, the Vedānta does not accept the authority of any text, denies the validity of any one text over another, and refuses to concede that any one text can exhaust all truths about ultimate reality (see *CW,* 8:124). It is clear that, for him, the Vedas do not possess any intrinsic validity. Consistent with his views on their origin and the personal foundations of their authority, he envisages them as simply recording the spiritual discoveries of others and the methods by which such discoveries have been made. These findings, however, must be personally rediscovered by every individual before they are valid for him or her:

> There are certain religious facts which, as in external science, have to be perceived, and upon them religion will be built. Of course, the extreme claims that you must believe every dogma of a religion is degrading to the human mind. The man who asks you to believe everything, degrades himself, and, if you believe, degrades you too. The sages of the world have only the right to tell us that they have analyzed their minds and have found these facts, and if we do the same we shall also believe, and not before. That is all there is in religion. (*CW,* 2:163)

The text, therefore, is only an indication of the way to the discovery of certain facts (see *CW,* 4:191, 7:89). The proof of truth is the direct knowledge of the individual, not the fact of its embodiment in any text. The individual verifies and must verify the text.[8] This verification is likened to ordinary direct perception and constitutes the ultimately valid knowledge:

> The proof, therefore, of the *Vedas* is just the same as the proof of this table before me, *pratyakṣa,* direct perception. This I see with the senses, and the truths of spirituality we also see in a superconscious state of the human soul.
>
> Books are not an end-all. Verification is the only proof of religious truth. Each must verify for himself; and no teacher who says, "I have seen but you cannot," is to be trusted, only that one who says, "You can see too." All scriptures, all truths are *Vedas* in all times, in all countries; because these truths are to be *seen,* and any one may discover them. (*CW,* 3:253, 7:9)

For Vivekananda, the fact of one individual gaining knowledge is proof of the ability and necessity of every other individual to do the same (*CW,* 1:185). A scriptural text is represented by him as second-hand religion. As a record of the experiences of others, it may stimulate our own desires, but, even as one person's eating is of little value to another, so too is the record of another person's experiences until we attain the same end (see *CW,* 2:473, 5:410).

The imperative, therefore, for Vivekananda, is that everyone should become a ṛṣi. Until that time, the religious life remains empty; indeed, it has not even commenced. The chief characteristic of ṛṣi status is the possibility of a direct apprehension of religious truth: "He is a man who sees religion, to whom religion is not merely book-learning, not argumentation, nor speculation, nor much talking, but actual realization, a coming face to face with truths that transcend the senses" (*CW,* 3:175).[9] This possibility and requirement of every individual to become a ṛṣi is one of the important points of contrast that Vivekananda emphasized between Hinduism and other religious traditions. In the latter, he claims, insight is limited to a few select individuals, through whom truth is made available to the many: "Truth came to Jesus of Nazareth, and we must all obey him. But the truth came to the ṛṣis of India—the *mantra-draṣṭās,* the seers of thought—and will come to all ṛṣis in the future, not to talkers, not to book-swallowers, not to scholars, not to philologists, but to seers of thought" (*CW,* 3:283).[10]

Not only did Vivekananda advocate the necessity of each one becoming a ṛṣi and verifying firsthand the experiences of others recorded in the Vedas, but he also often asserted that only in becoming a ṛṣi does one understand the scriptures properly (*CW,* 3:284). His justification for this view seems to be that, as products and records of direct perception, these texts were not written for the intellect or for understanding through a process of rational inquiry and analysis.

They become meaningful only when one has lifted oneself to the same heights of perception. At that point, however, they are useful only to the extent that they confirm what one has known directly (see *CW,* 4:165, 7:85, 89). One peculiarity of the Vedas, Vivekananda says, in contrast to the scriptures of other religious traditions, is that they are the only ones asserting the need for going beyond them. They are written only for the adult who is in the childhood state of religious growth. One must, therefore, outgrow reliance on them. He likens the texts to tubs or hedges around a tiny plant, the confines of which it must eventually transcend (see *CW,* 3:283; 5:311, 411; 7:6; 8:27).

The Distinction between Scriptural Revelation and Realization

It is possible to make a clear and significant distinction, in Vivekananda, between the knowledge that is gathered from inquiry into scriptural revelation and what he understands as realization.[11] The former is not perceived as a self-sufficient end, capable of taking one directly to liberation. This is, of course, consistent with his call for verification of scriptural declarations: "We can read all the *Vedas,* and yet will not realize anything, but when we practice their teachings, then we attain to that state which realizes what the scriptures say, which penetrates where neither reason nor perception nor inference can go, and where the testimony of others cannot avail" (*CW,* 1:232). The real study, according to Vivekananda, is that by which the unchangeable is realized, and he distinguishes this from reading, reasoning, and believing. He identifies it with superconscious perception (see *CW,* 8:255). In fact, distinguishing Vedānta from scriptural texts, Vivekananda says that the former is necessary because neither books nor reasoning can lead us to God. He identifies Vedānta here as a method for attaining superconscious perception (*CW,* 7:41). He accepts the legitimacy of one of his disciples' complaint that he had read of everything in the scriptures but had realized nothing (*CW,* 7:253). He saw the ultimate end of the religious quest, the realization of God within oneself, as being beyond all books: "Talking, arguing, and reading books, the highest flights of the intellect, the *Vedas* themselves, all these cannot give knowledge of the self" (*CW,* 7:70).[12] Vivekananda sometimes adopted the extreme position of asserting that no scriptural text can make us religious and that the latter can be attained only by dispensing with such texts (see *CW,* 1:412, 4:34, 190).

The process of inquiring into scriptural texts is identified by Vivekananda with activity at the intellectual level and is seen as benefiting only that level of our personalities. He points out, however, that there is no equation between a high order of intellectual development and spiritual growth. Scriptural analysis can easily delude us into believing that we are growing spiritually. He describes it as intellectual opium eating (see *CW,* 1:45, 4:168). Scriptures are specified by him as theoretical religion, which is ultimately unsatisfactory: "Knowledge of the absolute depends upon no book, nor upon anything; it is absolute in itself. No amount of study will give this knowledge; it is not theory, it is realization" (*CW,* 7:34; see also 4:166, 238; 6:101). Vivekananda distinguishes between the essentials and the nonessentials of every religion, between what he terms the *essential truth* and the *nonessential receptacle* in which this truth is held. Scriptures and belief in their validity are classified by him along with the nonessentials of religion (*CW,* 8:218, 2:483). Among other nonessentials, he listed doctrines, dogmas, rituals, temples, images, and forms. He describes these as only preparations for removing internal impurities (*CW,* 1:257, 2:38–39, 46).

With his clear definition of scripture as theoretical religion and his association of inquiry into them with limited intellectual activity and achievement, it is not surprising to find Vivekananda distinguishing the aims of *śravaṇa, manana,* and *nididhyāsana.* These distinctions are, of course, closely related to the view that the claims of any scripture are to be verified and that the knowledge that one can derive from investigating the words and sentences of the same is not definitive. We must remark, however, that there is little discussion, elaboration, or definition of these processes in his lectures and writings. He rarely refers to the original Sanskrit terms. There is still enough evidence, however, to show that he differentiates their natures and aims.

In one of his revealing analogies about the usefulness of scripture, he refers to the relation between surgical texts and the making of a surgeon (*CW,* 1:185). His purport is that textual knowledge is not adequate but must, in some way or other, be further applied to produce the desirable end. This seems to be the leading idea in his distinction among *śravaṇa, manana,* and *nididhyāsana.* From the brief references that are available to us, *śravaṇa* is identified by him with hearing or listening. This hearing is from the teacher, and its essential content is the reality of the *ātman* and the *māyā* nature of everything else.[13] *Manana* seems generally to be the process of understanding. It is thinking or reasoning from different standpoints on what has been heard. Its purpose is to establish knowledge in oneself by reason so that belief is not founded on ignorance. This is only preliminary: "You may reason it out and understand it intellectually, but there is a long way between intellectual understanding and the practical realization of it. Between the plan of the building and the building itself there is quite a long distance" (*CW,* 1:504). The processes of hearing and reasoning are followed by *nididhyāsana,* described by Vivekananda as meditation. It is the stage when all arguments are put behind and one is concerned with developing the truth within oneself. He continuously affirms that the aim of meditation is realization, ensuring that knowledge is not merely intellectual assent or theory. While many may grasp the truth intellectually, only very few will attain realization. In his few and brief discussions of the threefold processes, the nature of this meditation is not outlined. At one point, he describes it as the constant assertion of the truth of one's identity with *brahman:* "It must be heard, apprehended intellectually, and lastly realized. Cogitating is applying reason and establishing this knowledge in ourselves by reason. Realizing is making it a part of our lives by constant thinking of it . . . realization will come as a result of this continuous cogitation" (*CW,* 7:37–38; see also 3:25).

One of the important results of Vivekananda's characterization of scriptural texts as the records of other people's experiences, as mere theoretical religion incapable of giving rise to liberating knowledge, was a strong denunciation of the value of learning and scholarship in the quest for satisfactory spiritual knowledge. He affirmed that learning was not necessary for salvation and that its only value lay in the strengthening and disciplining of the mind:

> We attend lectures and read books, argue and reason about God and soul, religion and salvation. These are not spirituality, because spirituality does not exist in books or in theories or in philosophies. It is not in learning or in reasoning, but in actual inner growth. Even parrots can learn things by heart and repeat them. If you become learned what of it? Asses can carry whole libraries. So when real light will come, there will be no more of this learning from books—no book-learning. The man who cannot write even his own name can be perfectly religious, and the man with all the libraries of the world in his head may fail to be. Learning is not a condition of spiritual growth; scholarship is not a condition. (*CW,* 8:114; see also 4:148, 6:64)

The great teachers of the world, according to Vivekananda, were not the ones who went into detailed analysis and explanations of texts. The ideal spiritual teacher, in his view, is not one who commands a mastery of the texts but one who knows their spirit (*CW,* 4:24). His own teacher, Ramakrishna, was presented by him as an example of one who spurned scholarship, apprehending religious truths directly. Perhaps the strength of Vivekananda's views on this matter is best demonstrated by the fact that he understood the central purpose of Ramakrishna's life as an illustration of this principle:

> In order to show how Vedic truths—eternally existent as the instrument with the Creator in His work of creation, preservation, and dissolution—reveal themselves spontaneously in the minds of the ṛṣis purified from all impressions of worldly attachment, and because such verification and confirmation of the scriptural truths will help the revival, reinstatement, and spread of religion—the Lord, though the very embodiment of the *Vedas,* in this new incarnation has discarded all external forms of learning. (*CW,* 6:184)[14]

The obvious conclusion of this study, at this point, is that, as far as Vivekananda was concerned, the value and functions of scriptural texts were minimal in the search for genuine religious understanding. Vivekananda never seemed to miss an opportunity for deprecating their importance and calling into question their usefulness. Almost every one of his addresses contains such denunciations. These were directed toward both scriptures in general and the Vedas in particular.

Vivekananda confesses a general skepticism of the accuracy of scriptural testimony (see *CW,* 1:328).[15] He sees the view that all God's knowledge could be confined to any particular text as horribly blasphemous (*CW,* 1:186). Scriptural infallibility was understood by him to be a denial of the freedom to question and inquire and book worship as the worst form of idolatry (*CW,* 1:453, 8:34).[16] He reviled the view that even incarnations must conform to the text:

> There are sects in my country who believe that God incarnates and becomes man, but even God incarnate as man must conform to the *Vedas,* and if His teachings do not so conform, they will not take Him. Buddha is worshipped by the Hindus, but if you say to them, "If you worship Buddha, why don't you take His teachings?" they will say, because they, the Buddhist, deny the *Vedas.* Such is the meaning of book-worship. Any number of lies in the name of a religious book are all right. In India, if I want to teach anything new, and simply state it on my own authority, as what I think, nobody will come to listen to me; but if I take some passage from the *Vedas,* and juggle with it, and give it the most impossible meaning, murder everything that is reasonable in it, and bring out my own ideas as the ideas that were meant by the *Vedas,* all the fools would follow me in a crowd. (*CW,* 4:42)[17]

Vivekananda criticizes and rejects the view that the Vedas are the only authentic revelation of God or that they alone contain all the truths of religion (*CW,* 1:329, 6:47). He seems to see religious revelation as an eternal process: "The Bible, the *Vedas,* the *Koran,* and all other sacred books are but so many pages, and an infinite number of pages remain yet to be unfolded" (*CW,* 2:374). Revelation is also continuing in the sense that any individual who is suitably prepared may discover the fundamental truths (*CW,* 8:34). Vivekananda alleged that parts of the Vedas are apparently contradictory, that they contain many crude ideas, and that the Upaniṣads offered varying advice on the methods of gaining knowledge of the *ātman* (*CW,* 2:195, 3:521, 8:255). He felt that only those parts of the Vedas that are in harmony with reason should be accepted as being authoritative (*CW,* 5:315, 411). In this connection, he expressed the view that many of the rituals and sacrifices of the Vedas are held in reverence only because of their antiquity and because their perpetuation became the business of the priestly class (*CW,* 2:159–160). Vivekananda ridiculed the Mīmāṁsā view, which he interpreted as implying that the existence of anything is dependent on its mention in the Vedas: "The Hindus believe that creation has come out of the *Vedas.* How do you know that there is a cow? Because the word 'cow' is in the *Vedas.* How do you know there is a man outside? Because the word 'man' is there. If it had not been, there would have been no man outside. That is what they say. Authority with a vengeance!" (*CW,* 2:336; see also 6:47).[18]

The Connection between Sādhana-catuṣṭaya *and the Acquisition of Liberating Knowledge*

An important area of study, one that sheds further light on Vivekananda's understanding of the significance of the Vedas, is his treatment of *sādhana-catuṣṭaya* (the fourfold means). *Sādhana-catuṣṭaya* refers in Advaita Vedānta to the fourfold qualifications (namely, *viveka, vairāgya, śamādisādhanasampatti,* and *mumukṣutvam*) that are seen by Śaṅkara as indispensable qualities of intellect, volition, and emotion for inquiry into and assimilation of knowledge from the Upaniṣads. The cultivation of these qualities, for Śaṅkara, is only preparatory to inquiry into the Upaniṣads, not an alternative to this inquiry. They do not replace the Upaniṣads as a valid source of knowledge but ensure the gain and integration of knowledge.[19]

Vivekananda defines *viveka* as the discrimination of the true or real from that which is untrue or unreal, the eternal from the transitory. It is the recognition of the reality of God and the changeful and illusory character of everything else.[20] *Vairāgya* is a renunciation of the desire for gain in this life or in the life to come. Vivekananda emphasizes the abnegation of the desire for heaven. The gain of heaven is not the attainment of truth or freedom from original false notions about oneself: "What is heaven? Only the continuation of this earth. We would be better and the little foolish dreams we are dreaming would break sooner if there were no heaven, no continuation of this silly life on earth. By going to heaven we only prolong the miserable illusions" (*CW,* 8:107).

Vivekananda defines *śama* and *dama* as "the keeping of the organs in their own centers without allowing them to stray out" (*CW,* 1:405). In this connection, he distinguishes between the "organs" and the "instruments." The organs are the nerve centers in the brain and are the true instruments of perception, while the "instruments" are the external perceptible sense vehicles. Any act of external perception, according to Vivekananda, requires the conjunction of the mind, the organs, and the instruments. The mind and the organs can be internally active even when there is no external perception. By *śama* and *dama,* therefore, he means the checking of the internal and external activities of the mind, the restraint of the organs in their centers, and the control of the external instruments. He defines *uparati* as "not thinking of things of the senses." This includes not recalling pleasurable experiences of the past and not anticipating future ones (*CW,* 1:406).

Titikṣa is forbearance. In amplifying this quality, Vivekananda focuses on the internal dimensions of restraint. *Titikṣa* is not merely desisting from an external response but not reacting with feelings of anger or hatred. It is the ability, he says, to tolerate the inevitable miseries of life, and he sees Christ as the exemplar of this capacity. He presents *śraddhā* as faith in religion and God and a fervent eagerness to reach God. He also points to the necessity of faith in the teacher (*CW,* 8:112–113). *Samādhāna* is the constant practice of fixing the mind on God, while *mumukṣutvam* is the intense desire to be free, born out of an appreciation of the vanity and limitations of sense enjoyments (*CW,* 1:407–411).

Whereas Śaṅkara argues for *sādhana-catuṣṭaya* as a preparation for inquiry into the Upaniṣads with the aid of a teacher, Vivekananda adopts the reverse position, using the *sādhana-catuṣṭaya* to argue against scriptural necessity, to denounce the need for study and learning, and to emphasize the secondary role of the intellect in the quest for spiritual knowledge. Nothing more than the cultivation of these disciplines is required, he adds, because the knowledge sought is all within (*CW,* 1:412). He sees *sādhana-catuṣṭaya* as preparation for the purification of the heart rather than as training of the intellect or reason. This purification is all that is necessary:

> The pure heart is the best mirror for the reflection of truth, so all these disciplines are for the purification of the heart. And as soon as it is pure, all truths flash upon it in a minute; all the truth in the universe will manifest in your heart, if you are sufficiently pure.
>
> The great truths about atoms, and the finer elements, and the fine perceptions of men, were discovered ages ago by men who never saw a telescope, or a microscope, or a laboratory. How did they know all these things? It was through the heart; they purified the heart. (*CW,* 1:414)

This training, he contends, takes us beyond the senses, and he seems to suggest that all bondages will naturally fall off when one has cultivated these qualities (*CW,* 1:416).

As far as other general qualifications are concerned, Vivekananda adopted a much more liberal attitude, in some respects, than Śaṅkara. Śaṅkara did not challenge the orthodox position of the right of only the three upper castes to study the Vedas. The *sūdras* were debarred.[21] Vivekananda adopted the position that there was no bar of sex, race, or caste to realization. He severely chastises Śaṅkara for his lack of liberality in this respect and accuses him of fanatical *brahmin* pride (*CW,* 7:117–118). He seems, on the other hand, to support Śaṅkara's position that only the *saṁnyāsin* can attain to the fullness of *brahmajñāna:*

> Nobody attains freedom without shaking off the coils of worldly worries. The very fact that somebody lives the worldly life proves that he is tied down to it as the bond-slave of some craving or other. Why otherwise would he cling to that life at all? He is the slave either of lust or gold, of position or of fame, of learning or of scholarship. It is only after freeing oneself from all this thraldom that one can get along on the way of freedom. Let people argue as loud as they please; I have got this conviction that unless the monastic life is embraced, none is going to be saved, no attainment of *brahmajñāna* is possible. (*CW,* 6:505; see also 1:184, 410; 5:261; 7:193)[22]

His attacks on householders were often quite scathing. He suggested that the gulf between the householder and the *saṁnyāsin* was wide and unbridgeable and that the former are incapable of sincerity but of necessity must possess some selfish motive. He would not believe God to be sincere if he incarnated as a householder. He even spoke of the repulsive odor of householders. In this context, one must admit that Vivekananda appears as partisan as Śaṅkara was with respect to caste. Views like these seem to contradict his declared aim of making Vedānta a practical religion, accessible to all.

The Claim to a New Formula for Vedic Exegesis

According to Śaṅkara, the single purport of the Upaniṣads is to reveal the identity between *ātman* and *brahman:*[23] "And it is not proper to explain these texts otherwise than literally, for they are meant to show that the individual Self is no other than the Supreme *Brahman*" (Br. U = B 2.3.6, p. 236). Moreover, the ultimate aim of all the Upaniṣads is to teach Self-knowledge (Br.U = B 3.5.1, p. 336). This conviction about the cardinal intention of all sentences of the Upaniṣads is the governing principle of Śaṅkara's exegetical method. In his commentaries, he sets himself the task of resolving apparent contradictions and establishing that all the sentences of the Upaniṣads could be reconciled in the light of this central aim.

Vivekananda, on the other hand, claims this assumption to be an unsatisfactory criterion for Vedic exegesis. He suggests that both Advaita and Dvaita commentators are constrained to resort to text torturing in their attempt to prove that either view is the exclusive theme of the Upaniṣads. The Advaita commentator retains Advaita texts and juggles with the Dvaita ones, while his rival adopts the reverse procedure. Vivekananda feels that this is facilitated by the intricacy and complexity of the Sanskrit language (*CW,* 3:233). Vivekananda clearly seems to accept that there are texts in the Vedas that are entirely dualistic and others that are truly monistic. He suggests that it is absurd to set out to demonstrate that all texts are either monistic or dualistic and accuses Śaṅkara of occasionally resorting to sophistry to sustain his conclusions (*CW,* 7:40).[24] Vivekananda felt that the time had come for a better and more faithful interpretation of the purport of the Vedas and reconciliation of their apparent contradictions. It was just such an interpretation, he claims, that was suggested to him by his acquaintance with Ramakrishna: "It was given to me to live with a man who was as ardent a dualist, as ardent an *advaitist,* as ardent a *bhakta,* as a *jñāni.* And living with this man first put it into my head to understand the *Upaniṣads* and the texts of the scriptures from an independent and better basis than by blindly following the commentators; and in my opinion and in my researches, I came to the conclusion that these texts are not at all contradictory" (*CW,* 3:233).[25]

Vivekananda's new formula for Vedic exegesis is derived from his conclusion that it is possible to trace three distinct phases in the evolution of Vedic thought about the nature of God. First, there was a very personal concept of God as an extracosmic deity. This soon gave way to an emphasis on the immanence of God in the universe and culminated in identifying the human soul with God. This development is one from dualism to qualified monism, ending in monism (see, e.g., *CW,* 2:240–253). He denies that Advaita is the only phase of thought represented in the Vedas. The significant exegetical point about this claim, however, is his denial that these three phases of thought are in any way contradictory: "One cannot exist without the other; one is the fulfillment of the other; one is the building, the other is the top; the one the root, and other the fruit, and so on" (*CW,* 3:234). Vivekananda sees it as a deliberate method of the Vedas to reveal a progressive development to the ultimate goal (*CW,* 3:281–282). In these texts, he contends, it is possible to trace the evolution of religious ideas because old ideas were not discarded when higher truths were discovered. The authors realized that there would always be aspirants for whom the earlier steps were still necessary (*CW,* 8:24–25).[26] Vivekananda is alluding to the doctrine of *adhikārībheda,* the idea of different grades of aspirants. He also refers to the method of *arundhatī darśana nyāya,* which Śaṅkara uses to demonstrate a particular method of unfolding *brahman* in the Upaniṣads (see Ch.U = B 8.12.1, p. 472). Vivekananda, however, sees it as the wider method of progressive development from dualism to nondualism (*CW,* 3:397–398).

In spite of Vivekananda's powerful advocacy of this formula for reconciling conflicting texts in the Vedas, there were occasions when he expressed equally strong reservations about this view and method. In fact, he seems to repudiate it entirely, challenging what he sees as the expression of this doctrine in the Bhagavadgītā (3.26): "Let no wise man unsettle the mind of the ignorant people attached to action; but acting in harmony with Me let him render all action attractive." It is contradictory, he claims, to argue that knowledge and enlightenment can lead to error and confusion. It is a doctrine of compromise, he avers, born out of a fear of challenging local and regional customs and prejudices. He accuses the ṛṣis of having a selfish motive:

> They knew that by this enlightenment on their special subject they would lose their superior position of instructors to the people. Hence their endeavor to support this theory. If you consider a man too weak to receive these lessons, you should give him the advantage of more teaching, instead of less, to train up his intellect, so as to enable him to comprehend the more subtle problems. These advocates of *adhikārīvāda* ignored the tremendous fact of the infinite possibilities of the human soul. Every man is capable of receiving knowledge if it is imparted in his own language. (*CW,* 5:263; see also 8:139–140)

Although it is not within the scope of this study to treat in full the wider implications of Vivekananda's theory of the progressive development of religious thought in the Vedas, we may note briefly that he applied this view to the understanding of the growth of ideas in other religious traditions as well and employed it as a central concept for interreligious harmony. The fundamental premise, however, is that nonduality is the unavoidable goal of the human religious quest. Movement in religious thought is, therefore, a growth, not from error to truth, but from a lower to a higher truth. All religions, he claims, from the lowest fetishism to the highest absolutism, reflect attempts to grasp the infinite. The religions of the world are, as he puts it, "only a travelling, a coming up, of different men and women, through various conditions and circumstances, to the same goal" (*CW,* 1:18). The end here is the infinity of the self, and this is attained by different paths. Vivekananda distinguishes between the paths and the goals. Each one is entitled to choose his own path, but the path is not the goal. This is the clue to his often-voiced concept of unity in diversity. The unifying factor is the common goal, and diversity can be found in the means adopted for its attainment. Each religion, therefore, can be positioned at some point along the approach to the final, nondual truth: "All religions are so many stages. Each one of them represents the stages through which the human soul passes to realize God. Therefore, not one of them should be neglected. None of the stages are dangerous or bad. They are good. Just as a child becomes a young man, and a young man becomes an old man, so they are travelling from truth to truth; they become dangerous only when they become rigid, and will not move further—when he ceases to grow" (*CW,* 2:500). In this broad view, he sees the possibility of accepting all religious doctrines, not as an act of patronizing, but with the full conviction that "they are true manifestations of the same truth, and that they all lead to the same conclusions as the *Advaita* has reached" (*CW,* 2:347). He also traces, for all religious traditions, the three major phases of development that he claimed to have discovered in the Vedas (see, e.g., *CW,* 1:322–323).

Although Vivekananda's supposedly novel and more satisfactory way of interpreting and reconciling apparently conflicting texts of the Upaniṣads appears at first sight to differ from Śaṅkara's method, the divergence does not seem to be an absolutely radical one. Śaṅkara does not deny the presence of dualistic texts in the whole of the Vedas. He accepts, for example, that the ritualistic prescriptions of the *karmakāṇḍa* are based on an outlook of duality and that these are intended for aspirants of a different order as compared to the *jñāna-*

kāṇḍa. Śaṅkara, therefore, clearly accepts the fact of differing needs and capabilities in individuals and sees the *śruti* as recognizing this diversity as well. What he strongly denies, however, is the ultimate truth or reality of this duality. It appears to me that, from an exegetical viewpoint, the really important argument is that nonduality is the final and ultimately valid doctrine of the Vedas. On this question, there is no difference between Vivekananda and Śaṅkara.

Contrasts between the Statements of Vivekananda on the Vedas in the West and in India

In trying to form a composite picture of Vivekananda's understanding of the nature, role, and authority of the Vedas, one is struck by significant divergences of content and tone between views expressed in America and Europe and those expressed in India. The differences are particularly apparent on a close analysis of the series of talks that he delivered in India after returning from his first visit to the West (15 January 1897) and before his departure for his second lecture tour (20 June 1899). In the *Complete Works,* the talks are famously titled "Lectures from Colombo to Almora" (*CW,* 3:103–461). It is to a consideration of the significance of these differences that I now turn.

In India, there was a greater overall emphasis on the authority of the Vedas, and this took different forms of expression. One of the common methods was a reiteration of the orthodox distinction between *śruti* and *smṛti.*[27] The latter, according to him, are written by the sages, but they are not the final authority. In instances of contradiction between both groups of texts, *smṛti* has to be rejected. He saw the declarations of the *smṛtis* as being binding under particular circumstances, times, and places. *Smṛtis,* in other words, treat the variable dimensions of religion, while *śruti* is concerned with its eternal aspects:

> As essential conditions changed, as various circumstances came to have their influence on the race, manners and customs had to be changed, and these *smṛtis,* as mainly regulating the manners and customs of the nation, had also to be changed from time to time. . . . The principles of religion that are in the *Vedānta* are unchangeable. Why? Because they are all built upon the eternal principles that are in man and nature; they can never change. Ideas about the soul, going to heaven, and so on can never change; they were the same thousands of years ago, they are the same today, they will be the same millions of years hence. But those religious practices which are based entirely upon our social position and correlation must change with the changes in society. Such an order, there-

> fore, would be good and true at a certain period and not at another. (*CW,* 3:121)

One of the clear reasons for Vivekananda's reassertion of the traditional distinction between *śruti* and *smṛti* was his attempt to employ it as a suitable basis for the introduction of order and the standardization of religious belief and practice in India. He was disturbed by the prevalence, at the local level, of practices that he saw as being superstitious and the tendency to assign an authoritative sanction to these. He was particularly incensed by the wide prevalence of certain Tantra practices in his native Bengal and saw the primacy of the *śruti* as a way of challenging the authority of texts that approved such customs.[28]

In India, Vivekananda identified orthodoxy with the acceptance of the authority of the Vedas: "All the philosophers of India who are orthodox have to acknowledge the authority of the *Vedānta*" (*CW,* 3:120). He saw clearly that the acceptance of the authority of the Vedas was one of the few common points around which different religious allegiances in India could be united: "The only point where, perhaps, all our sects agree is that we all believe in the scriptures—the *Vedas.* This perhaps is certain that no man can have a right to be called a Hindu who does not admit the supreme authority of the *Vedas*" (*CW,* 3:228).[29] Like his employment of the distinction between *śruti* and *smṛti,* Vivekananda's stress on the common authority of the Vedas and his equation of it with orthodoxy must be placed in the wider context of his anxiety for and commitment to national and religious unity. One of the most common of Vivekananda's themes throughout this triumphal lecture tour was the view that religion constituted the central, indispensable characteristic of national life in India. Almost every one of his major addresses opened on it:

> I see that each nation, like each individual, has one theme in this life which is its center, the principal note round which every other note comes to form the harmony. In one nation political power is its validity, as in England, artistic life in another, and so on. In India, religious life forms the center, the keynote of the whole music of national life; and if any nation attempts to throw off its national vitality—the direction which has become its own through the transmission of centuries—that nation dies if it succeeds in the attempt. (*CW,* 3:220)

In the light of this view on the place of religion in Indian life, Vivekananda thought that all kinds of reform, social and political, should be preceded by and founded on religious unity and reform. He felt that no other approach would have a sufficient impact. Vivekananda saw quite clearly the difficulties of trying to found a nation on the basis of common ethnicity, language, or customs. As far as these factors were concerned, India exhibited a bewildering variety. He felt that religion could be used as the nucleus of an emerging Indian nation: "The one common ground that we have is our sacred tradition, our religion. That is the only common ground, and upon that we shall have to build. In Europe, political ideas form the national unity. In Asia, religious ideals form the national unity. The unity in religion, therefore, is absolutely necessary as the first condition of the future of India" (*CW,* 3:286–287).[30] Even religion, however, was not an obvious common factor. Hinduism presented a challenging medley. This is the explanation behind Vivekananda's exertion throughout this lecture tour, perhaps for the first time in the history of modern Hinduism, to identify and extol what he saw as the common bases of Hinduism. Acceptance of the authority of the Vedas was the paramount tenet of the common features he presented. Among the other common features that he mentioned are the concepts of *karma* and *saṁsāra,* the cyclic view of creation and dissolution, and the acceptance of the soul to be free from birth and death. He also points to the notion of religion as realization or direct perception.

Along with a new emphasis on orthodoxy and the Vedas as the fountainhead of Hinduism, another revealing contrast is also apparent from his Western statements. In the West, whenever he made a critical statement about the insignificance of scriptural texts, the Vedas were always treated on the same footing with the scriptures of other religions. In India, however, this equality was replaced by an equation of non-Hindu scriptures with the *smṛtis.* Like the *smṛti* texts of Hinduism, their validity is now seen as a secondary one, to be evaluated only with reference to the *śruti:* "Therein lies the difference between the scriptures of the Christians or the Buddhists and ours; theirs are all *Purāṇas,* and not scriptures, because they describe the history of the deluge, and the history of kings and reigning families, and record the lives of great men, and so on. This is the work of the *Purāṇas,* and so far as they agree with the *Vedas,* they are perfectly good, but when they do not agree, they are no more to be accepted" (*CW,* 3:333).

Vivekananda describes the Vedas as the best-preserved scriptures of all religious traditions (*CW,* 3:280). Like the *smṛtis,* non-Hindu scriptures have been written by particular sages (*CW,* 3:120). Although Vivekananda does not deny the efficacy of other texts, he asserts the primacy of the Vedas: "Although the supersensuous vision of truth is to be met with in some measure in our *Purāṇas* and *Itihāsas* and in the religious scriptures of other races, still the fourfold scripture known among the Aryan race as the *Vedas* being the first, the most complete, and the most undistorted collection of spiritual truths, deserve to occupy the highest place among all scriptures, command the respect of all nations of the earth, and furnish the rationale of all their respective scriptures" (*CW,* 6:182). In India, he asserted that everything necessary for the perfection and freedom of the human being could be found in the Vedas. *Śruti* is presented as the final word on spiritual truth, beyond which there is nothing to be known or said. There is no religious idea anywhere, he claims, that cannot be found in the Vedas. All that needs to be done is to apply the dicta of the *śruti* to the changing needs and conditions of societies (*CW,* 3:248–250, 6:105).

At the beginning of this chapter, I presented Vivekananda's contention that the Vedas are the result of the direct perception of the *āptas* and that they are valid only because the *āptas* are competent persons. A clear contrast of emphasis with this view emerges from a scrutiny of his talks in India. Here, he insisted on the impersonal nature of Vedic authority and differentiated this sharply from the personal authoritative foundations of all other religious traditions:

> Excepting our own almost all the other great religions in the world are inevitably connected with the life of one or more of their founders. All their theories, their teachings, their doctrines, and their ethics are built round the life of a personal founder, from whom they get their sanction, their authority, and their power; and strangely enough, upon the historicity of the founder's life is built, as it were, all the fabric of such religions. If there were one blow dealt to the historicity of that life, as has been the case in modern times with the lives of almost all the so called founders of religion—we know that half of the details of such lives is not now seriously believed in, and the other half is seriously doubted—if this becomes the case, if that rock of historicity, as they pretend to call it, is shaken and shattered, the whole building tumbles down, broken absolutely, never to regain its lost status. (*CW,* 3:182–183)

In several ways, he contrasts this personal authority with what he now highlights as the impersonal character of Vedic authority. The Vedas, he says, are not the utterance of any persons and do not owe their authority to anybody. The authority of the Vedas, he now claims, is not even dependent on reasoning. Whereas he had formerly complained about the absoluteness of scriptural authority over even the incarnations, he now glorifies this fact: "That you obey your religion is not because it came through the authority of a sage, no, not even of an Incarnation. Krishna is not the authority of the *Vedas,* but the

Vedas are the authority of Krishna himself. His glory is that he is the greatest preacher of the *Vedas* that ever existed" (*CW,* 3:249). Vedānta, he stresses, is grounded in impersonal principles, for no human being can claim to have created the Vedas, only to have discovered their eternal truths. At the same time, he argues that these impersonal principles are not opposed to personalities but allow sufficient scope for them. The principles remain unaffected by the lack of historicity of particular persons (*CW,* 3:118–119, 183–184, 249–251, 279–280, 332).[31]

In his lectures in the West, whenever Vivekananda spoke about the concept of Vedic eternity, he usually drew an analogy with natural or scientific laws. The eternity of the Vedas, he pointed out on these occasions, did not mean the eternity of books composed of words and sentences. He identified the Vedas with spiritual laws and concluded that the concept of Vedic eternity meant the changeless and timeless nature of these laws (see, e.g., *CW,* 1:6–7).[32] This interpretation was also presented in India, but there were significant differences. In the first place, the idea of eternity was more frequently, elaborately, and emphatically stated. Second, he did not always manifestly distinguish between the Vedas as spiritual laws and as words and sentences. In fact, he seemed on occasion to be moving much closer to the traditional orthodox position.

In India, he voiced his skepticism about Western scholarship on the dating of the Vedas. The Vedas, he says, cannot and never have been dated because they are eternal (*CW,* 3:118–119). Hindus, he affirms, do not subscribe to the opinion that parts of the Vedas were produced at different times; rather, the consider that the Vedas were brought into being as a whole. They do not share the view that the Vedas were written by men in some remote age (*CW,* 3:230, 322, 456). His stress was on the unwritten and ahistorical nature of the Vedas. He advanced nonhistoricity as an argument in favor of their validity (*CW,* 3:334).[33]

The dissimilarities between Vivekananda's statements in India and in the West are important in any evaluation of his views on the Vedas. It appears that, whereas in his Western talks Vivekananda was at liberty to express his views unreservedly, in India there were constraints and concerns that did not allow the same freedom. The principal of these concerns, which I have already noted, was his passion for national unity and his conviction that this could be achieved only on the basis of religious unity. I have also remarked, in this respect, on his generalization of the common features of Hinduism and the prominence that he gave to the acceptance of Vedic authority as one of these features. In a tradition of such internal diversity and a plurality of authoritative sources, Vivekananda felt that a commonly accepted authority was indispensable. It could serve as both a focus of unity and a platform for the challenge and reform of objectionable religious practice.

There is another, even more important reason why Vivekananda's statements in the West could be seen as more truly representative of his position.[34] These statements are fully consistent with a central conviction of all his lectures and writings. This is the doctrine that religious truth is acquired only by an experience of direct perception or apprehension, not by inquiry into words and sentences of any revelatory text. This is a view that he unfailingly hammered and that may, with good reason, be said to constitute the pivot of his metaphysics. He was always consistent in this position and did not deviate in India. In one of his Indian lectures, he states,

> This is the *ṛṣi-hood,* the ideal in our religion. The rest, all these talks and reasonings and philosophies and dualisms and monisms, and even the *Vedas* themselves are but preparations, secondary things. The other is primary. The *Vedas,* grammar, astronomy, etc., all these are secondary; that is the supreme knowledge which makes us realize the Unchangeable One. Those who realized are the sages whom we find in the *Vedas:* and we understand how this ṛṣi is the name of a type, of a class, which every one of us, as true Hindus, is expected to become at some period of our life, and becoming which, to the Hindu, means salvation. Not belief in doctrines, not going to thousands of temples, nor bathing in all the rivers in the world, but becoming the ṛṣi, the *mantra-draṣṭā*—that is freedom, that is salvation. (*CW,* 3:254–255)

This issue emerges as the central and very radical point of departure between Vivekananda and Śaṅkara.

On the basis of Vivekananda's recorded statements, it is very difficult to find an unconditional rationale for the Vedas. This is not surprising in the light of his contention that conclusive and liberating knowledge is not gained by inquiry into the texts of the Upaniṣads. The closest he comes to a justification of such texts is in his view that they tell us of the spiritual findings of others and the processes by which we discover and verify such findings for ourselves. The difficulty is that, in some of his extreme assertions, he even denies them this limited value and function. This becomes apparent in his argument that the Vedas are properly understood only when one has lifted oneself to the same level of direct perception as its authors, that they were not written for the intellect and cannot be understood through reasoning. Such statements negate their preliminary value, which one assumes to depend on the possibility of some understanding of their claims and methods. If such an understanding cannot be sought through the faculty of intellectual reasoning, then scripture seems to be totally deprived of usefulness.

Chapter 3

KARMA, BHAKTI, AND *JÑĀNA* AS DIRECT AND INDEPENDENT WAYS TO *MOKṢA*

In chapter 2, my study of Vivekananda's understanding of the authority and functions of the Vedas revealed that he does not see the knowledge that is directly and immediately derived from those texts as liberating the individual. I noted the important distinction between *śruti*-derived knowledge and knowledge that he claims can be obtained by direct spiritual perception. While the content of both would be the same, it is the latter alone that carries absolute conviction and freedom from doubt. The Śaṅkara method of the fully qualified aspirant, inquiring into *śruti* with the aid of a teacher and following proper exegetical procedures, is nowhere presented by him as a means to freedom. We have seen his subordinate regard for the words and sentences of the *śruti* and his argument that, as a record of the experiences of others, these are of little avail. For Vivekananda, *śruti* is not a self-validating source of knowledge, and this is a very important area of contrast with Śaṅkara.

For the purposes of the discussion in the present chapter, however, it is necessary to point out the agreement between Śaṅkara and Vivekananda on the nature of the fundamental problem of *avidyā* (ignorance) and its resolution. It is only from this perspective that we can reasonably and justly evaluate Vivekananda's arguments for different, independent ways of accomplishing freedom.

In my study of the lectures and writings of Vivekananda, I find a clear consensus with Śaṅkara on the entirely notional problem of ignorance *(avidyā)*. This is the basis of Śaṅkara's contention that knowledge alone is freedom. Knowledge alone can be freedom only where bondage is only apparent and liberation has already been accomplished. Vivekananda affirms *avidyā* as the basic human problem and the source of all misery and evil (see *CW,* 1:53, 2:83–84, 3:128). Like Śaṅkara, he presents the primary manifestation of this ignorance as the erroneous identification of the self with the body. It is the assumption of the limitless to be limited: "All the different sorts of impressions have one source, ignorance. We have first to learn what ignorance is. All of us think, 'I am the body, and not the self, the pure, the effulgent, the ever blissful,' and that is ignorance. We think of man, and see man as body. This is the great delusion" (*CW,* 1:238; see also 2:257–258). Vivekananda follows Śaṅkara in presenting *avidyā* in the light of *adhyāsa* (superimposition) and illustrates it by employing Śaṅkara's vivid crystal-ball analogy. Like a crystal ball near a red or blue flower, the self appears to be impure or limited only by association. It is never so in reality (see *CW,* 2:439, 4:227). Bondage is, therefore, for Vivekananda, only the thought of being bound, and knowledge alone can confer freedom. Liberty involves nothing more than the destruction of ignorance, and it is this knowledge that is the goal of human endeavor. "This pure and perfect being, the soul, is one wheel, and this external hallucination of body and mind is the other wheel, joined together by the pole of work, of *karma.* Knowledge is the axe which will sever the bond between the two, and the wheel of the soul will stop—stop thinking that it is coming and going, living and dying, stop thinking that it is nature and has wants and desires, and will find that it is perfect, desireless" (*CW,* 2:281; see also 1:27, 333; 7:37).

In agreement with Śaṅkara, Vivekananda continuously asserts that freedom and perfection are not to be conceived as a new attainment. It is a matter of knowing or not knowing (*CW,* 2:350; see also 3:239). Whereas Śaṅkara often uses the story of the fictitious loss of the tenth man, Vivekananda employs a similar analogy to illustrate a notional loss through ignorance and a gain by knowledge. He frequently tells the story of a pregnant lioness who, in search of prey, died while in pursuit of a flock of sheep. She gave birth to a cub who lived with the flock and thought of itself as a sheep. It ate grass and bleated. Another astonished lion noticed this sheep-lion in the midst of the flock but could never get close because it fled in fear with the sheep. One day, however, he managed to isolate the sheep-lion and tried to convince it of its true identity. Not surprisingly, it refused to accept that it was a lion. As a last resort, the elderly lion took it to a nearby lake and pointed out the identity of their reflections. It immediately owned its original nature as a lion.

For both Śaṅkara and Vivekananda, the content of the knowledge that frees is the understanding of the limitless and unbound nature of the self. For Śaṅkara, this is the central theme of all the Upaniṣads; for Vivekananda, it is the progressive culmination of the teachings of these texts. Both men are, therefore, clearly in agreement on the fact of knowledge being equivalent to freedom and on the central content of this knowledge. Vivekananda, however, does not identify liberating knowledge with what is gathered from the exegetical analysis of the Upaniṣads. He is derisive about this knowledge and sees it as second-hand information, which is at best only provisionally valid. For him, it is only superficial intellectual knowledge. The claims of the Upaniṣads must be again directly discovered in the way in which he feels that they were originally apprehended by the authors of these texts. For the attainment of knowledge as he conceives it, Vivekananda proposes the four *yogas* of *karma, bhakti, jñāna,* and *rāja.*[1] He unequivocally affirms that the aim of all four *yogas* is the removal of ignorance: "There is no becoming with the Absolute. It is ever free, ever perfect; but the ignorance that has covered Its nature for a time is to be removed. Therefore the whole scope of all systems of *Yoga* (and each religion represents one) is to clear up this ignorance and allow the *ātman* to restore its own nature" (*CW,* 8:152). These four different paths, according to Vivekananda, converge at the same point, and he claims the support of the scriptures for the view that the attainment of knowledge is possible in a variety of ways. Even though he specifically mentions the *jñānakāṇḍa* as propounding this argument, he does not cite any texts (see *CW,* 4:432, 6:182).

It is important to note that Vivekananda sees each one of these methods as directly and independently capable of leading to knowledge and freedom. One frequently encounters statements of the following kind:

> You must remember that the freedom of the soul is the goal of all *Yogas,* and each one equally leads to the same result. By work alone men may get to where Buddha got largely by meditation or Christ by prayer. Buddha was a working *jñāni,* Christ was a *bhakta,* but the same goal was reached by both of them. . . . Each one of our *Yogas* is fitted to make man perfect even without the help of the others, because they have all the same goal in view. The *Yogas* of work, of wisdom, and of devotion are all capable of serving as direct and independent means for the attainment of *mokṣa.* (*CW,* 1:55, 93)

He does not see the different methods as being in conflict with or contradicting each other. His rationale for a plurality of means is derived from the variety of human personalities. Each one is adapted to a different nature and temperament. He generalizes the variety of human beings into four types. First of all, there is the active, energetic temperament, the worker, for whom is meant *karmayoga.* Second, there is the emotional person, who discovers his or her method in *bhaktiyoga.* Finally, *jñānayoga* is intended for the philosophical and rational mind, while *rājayoga* satisfies the mystically oriented person.[2]

We can now turn our attention to considering how Vivekananda understands these different methods and the way in which they lead to *jñāna* (knowledge). I am not concerned here with presenting all that he has to say about each method. I focus instead on the basic nature of each *yoga* as he understands it and assess particularly the connection that he establishes with the removal of *avidyā.* The validity of his claim that each method is a direct and independent path to *mokṣa* depends on his demonstration of the capability of each one to remove ignorance. The latter is, from his own standpoint, the fundamental problem.

Karmayoga

There is no single discussion in the lectures and writings of Vivekananda to which one can turn to find a clear and comprehensive statement of his understanding of *karmayoga.* What exactly constitutes *karmayoga* is, therefore, not as obvious and apparent as it is in Śaṅkara.

Vivekananda defines *karma* very broadly to refer to any kind of action, mental or physical (*CW,* 1:28–29).[3] He describes various personal motives from which individuals act. Among these are the desires for wealth, fame, power, and heaven. He suggests that higher than all these motives is work for work's sake, which he explains means working just for the good that comes out of it. Good, in this case, appears to indicate results that are beneficial to others (see *CW,* 1:31–32). As we search for his central definition of *karmayoga,* the concept that emerges most often, therefore, is the idea of unselfish action:

> It is the most difficult thing in this world to work and not to care for the result, to help a man and never think that he ought to be grateful, to do some good work and at the same time never look to see whether it brings you name or fame, or nothing at all. Even the most arrant coward becomes brave when the world praises him. A fool can do heroic deeds when the approbation of society is upon him, but for a man to constantly do good without caring for the approbation of his fellow men is indeed the highest sacrifice man can perform. (*CW,* 1:42–43; see also 1:62)

Although Vivekananda often speaks of *karmayoga* as an attitude of indifference to the results of action, one has to suppose that the unconcern is with personal selfish results only. A total unconcern with results will make even action for the sake of others impossible, for it is difficult to see how any action can be initiated without some end in view.

In addition to implying actions centered on the welfare and service of others, *karmayoga* also comprises a number of attitudes, two of which find frequent mention in Vivekananda. The first of these is the recognition of work as the privilege of worshiping God by serving God in all persons. The *karmayogī* serves others not because he or she views the service as being indispensable but because the occasions of service are opportunities for ridding oneself of selfishness and advancing toward perfection. The act of service is ultimately beneficial to the *karmayogī:*

> Blessed are we that are given the privilege of working for Him, not of helping Him. Cut out this word "help" from your mind. You cannot help; it is blaspheming. You are here yourself at His pleasure. Do you mean to say, you help Him? You worship. When you give a morsel of food to the dog, you worship the dog as God. God is in that dog. He is the dog. He is all and in all. We are allowed to worship Him. Stand in that reverent attitude to the whole universe, and then will come perfect non-attachment. This should be your duty. This is the proper attitude of work. This is the secret taught by *karmayoga.* (*CW,* 5:246; see also 1:84)

This attitude of work as worship, the giving up of all fruits of action to God, is one way, according to Vivekananda, by which the *karmayogī* achieves detachment from the results of action (see *CW,* 1:59–60, 102). One suspects, however, that, in order to emphasize the distinction between *karmayoga* and *bhaktiyoga,* Vivekananda insists that this detachment is also possible even for one who does not believe in *īśvara* (personal God). In this case, he insists that detachment be accomplished by force of will. He justifies this by a recourse to Sāṅkhya, where *īśvara* is not presupposed, and suggests that detachment is also possible by adopting the attitude that the world is a temporary place of abode, meant only for the education of the soul. Instead of identifying with nature, one should view it as a book to be read and then disposed of (*CW,* 1:56–57). Whether through the acceptance of *īśvara* or not, the *karmayogī*'s attitude is characterized by detachment from a concern with the personal rewards of action: "The *karmayogī* works because it is his nature, because he *feels* that it is good for him to do so, and he has no object beyond that. His position in this world is that of a giver, and he never cares to receive anything. He knows that he is giving, and does not ask for anything in return and, therefore, he eludes the grasp of misery. The grasp of pain, whenever it comes, is the result of the reaction of 'attachment' " (*CW,* 2:392). The view that *karmayoga* does not necessitate a belief in *īśvara* highlights an important difference between Śaṅkara and Vivekananda. With Śaṅkara, there seems to be hardly any distinction at all between *karmayoga* and *bhaktiyoga*. The form of detached activity that Śaṅkara conceives is that which is possible by the dedication of all actions to *īśvara* and the calm acceptance of results as coming from God. *Karmayoga* is not possible, therefore, without an appreciation of *īśvara* and of God as the dispenser of the fruits of action.[4]

The *karmayogī*'s attitude toward work is also characterized by an absence of fanaticism. He or she is nonfanatical because of a recognition of the limitations of all action. The *karmayogī* knows that, in spite of all efforts, the world will never be made perfect. Vivekananda often describes the world as a dog's curly tail, which always bends in spite of efforts to straighten it.[5] The *karmayogī* also escapes from fanaticism and self-importance by the awareness of his or her own dispensability.

In Vivekananda, as contrasted with Śaṅkara, one also notices the attempt to enlarge the concept of *karmayoga*. In most cases, however, his rationale for the inclusion of a particular concept within the framework of *karmayoga* is not sufficiently clear or justified. The result is that the *karmayoga* concept becomes unwieldly and almost all inclusive, blurring Vivekananda's aim of identifying it as a distinctive path to *mokṣa*. Without any development of argument, he claims, for example, that *karmayoga* has specially to do with the understanding of the three *guṇas* and their employment for success in activity. He also identifies *karmayoga* with the idea of variation in morality and duty according to life circumstances (*CW,* 1:36–37). In the course of the same discussion, he contends that the central idea of *karmayoga* is nonresistance: "The *karmayogī* is the man who understands that the highest ideal is non-resistance, and who also knows that this non-resistance is the highest manifestation of power in actual possession, and also what is called the resisting of evil is but a step on the way towards the manifestation of this highest power, namely, non-resistance" (*CW,* 1:39). Vivekananda supports this view with a very unusual interpretation of Arjuna's predicament in the first chapter of the Bhagavadgītā and Krishna's subsequent instruction to him. His argument is that Arjuna was terrified of the opposing army and masked his cowardly feelings by arguments about love. Krishna's goal was to lead him to the ideal of nonresistance, but this could not be accomplished without initiation into resistance to purge him of cowardice. Within the concept of *karmayoga,* Vivekananda also sees a natural place for the study and practice of rituals and "symbology" as well as for an understanding of the nature and force of words and other sound symbols and their use (see *CW,* 1:72–75).[6]

I have already drawn attention to Vivekananda's attempt to underline the distinctiveness of *karmayoga* from *bhaktiyoga* by arguing that the former does not necessarily depend on the acceptance of *īśvara.* Unselfish and detached action is possible without belief in God. For him, the essential factor about *karmayoga* as a path is its emphasis on work. It is meant for those whose minds cannot be applied on the plane of thought alone and whose natures demand some sort of activity. For such people, Vivekananda claims, *karmayoga* teaches where and how to work successfully. In order further to strengthen his claim for *karmayoga* as a direct and independent path to *jñāna,* Vivekananda distinguishes it—one supposes from *jñānayoga*—by describing it as being free from all doctrine and dogma. This a conclusion about *karmayoga* that he reiterates throughout his treatment of this path: "The *karmayogī* need not believe in any doctrine whatever. He may not believe even in God, may not ask what his soul is, nor think of any metaphysical speculation. He has got his own special aim of realizing selflessness; and he has to work it out himself. Every moment of his life must be realization, because he has to solve by mere work, without the help of doctrines or theory, the very problem to which the *jñāni* applies his reason and inspiration and the *bhakta* his love" (*CW,* 1:111; see also 1:93).[7]

This is a most puzzling conclusion, one that a critical examination of Vivekananda's statements on *karmayoga* finds very difficult to sustain. His views are clearly loaded with explicit and implicit doctrinal assumptions. These are clearly evident when his discussion presupposes *īśvara,* for there are definite concepts of the nature of God involved, but they are no less so when this standpoint is not presumed. The obvious fact is that one embarks on this path of detached activity only after certain conclusions about the nature of existence and the ultimacy of *mokṣa* as the goal of life. The lack of concern with the personal rewards of action is not absolute, for *karmayoga* is presented as a method adopted with a definite aim in mind. Through unselfish, detached action, the *karmayogī* hopes to be free. In spite of what Vivekananda says, therefore, the action of the *karmayogī* is not, and cannot be, an end in itself.

I should at this point make the observation that Vivekananda nowhere distinguishes between *karmayoga* as means and as end. One gets the impression that the possibility of selflessness is assumed from the beginning, without considering the very personal aim of the *karmayogī*. The distinction between *karmayoga* as means and as end is more clearly preserved in Śaṅkara, who appears to see the possibility of unselfish action only after the *karmayogī* has attained to the fullness of self that *brahmajñāna* confers. From the logic of Vivekananda's presentation of the problem of *avidyā,* it would appear that he must also accept that complete unselfishness is not possible without self-knowledge. The unresolved paradox is that, in his presentation of *karmayoga,* he assumes that one cannot attain self-knowledge unless one is perfectly selfless. In fact, in spite of the fact that he does not acknowledge it and that he claims that *karmayoga* as a path involves neither doctrine nor dogma, the *karmayoga* that he presents is intelligible only in the doctrinal context of Advaita. Its rationale is to be found there only. This is readily apparent in the following kind of discussion, which is common in his presentation of *karmayoga* and suffused with Advaita postulates and premises:

> Therefore *karmayoga* tells us to enjoy the beauty of all the pictures in the world, but not to identify ourselves with any of them. Never say "mine." . . . If you do, then will come the misery. Do not say "my house," do not say "my body." The whole difficulty is there. The body is neither yours, nor mine, nor anybody's.These bodies are coming and going by the laws of nature but we are free, standing as witness. The body is no more free than a picture or a wall. Why should we be attached so much to a body? If somebody paints a picture, he does it and passes on. Do not project that tentacle of selfishness, "I must possess it." As soon as that is projected, misery will begin. (*CW,* 1:100–101)[8]

In these kinds of passages, *karmayoga* appears to be more the result of self-knowledge, possible only through self-knowledge, rather than a means to it. If *karmayoga* is to be distinguished from *jñānayoga* by the absence of any doctrinal postulates, then Vivekananda has not at all proved this. The knowledge that is its declared aim to discover is already presupposed at the inception. Vivekananda's claim, therefore, that the *karmayogī* is or can be indifferent to doctrine cannot be sustained. As an independent path, it does not exist in a doctrinal vacuum and cannot be said to be unique on this basis. Vivekananda has nowhere defined what exactly he means by doctrine or dogma, but one wonders if his view is not somehow made explicable by proposing that the Advaita contentions have such an axiomatic character for him that they easily slip into his discussion as unquestionable propositions.

But perhaps the most problematic aspect of Vivekananda's discussion of this matter is the connection that he aims to establish between *karmayoga* and *mokṣa.* It is here also that other important contrasts with Śaṅkara are evident. In evaluating this connection, it is very important to bear in mind Vivekananda's consensus with Śaṅkara on the apparent nature of bondage through *avidyā* and the simple necessity of knowledge for its removal. Each different path, he claims, is an independent and direct means to this knowledge. It is clear, therefore, that he presents these *yogas* as having the same function that *śruti* as a source of valid knowledge has for Śaṅkara. They are supposed, in their distinct ways, to give rise directly to *brahmajñāna* and remove the notional bondage of the self.

In Śaṅkara, the function of *karmayoga,* as of all other methods, techniques, and disciplines apart from *jñana,* is the development of the requisite qualities of intellect and emotion, prior to inquiry into the Upaniṣads. The disciplines themselves never assume the function of sources of knowledge, for only the accepted valid *pramāṇas* (sources of knowledge) can give rise to knowledge. The disciplines, however, are necessary for mental purity *(citta-śuddhi).* Vivekananda also accepts that mental purification is the most important aim of *karmayoga.* Because he views *karmayoga* as a path of detached, selfless activity, mental purity is the attainment of unselfishness and indifference to personal reward: "We have seen already that in helping the world we help ourselves. The main effect of work done for others is to purify ourselves. By means of the constant effort to do good to others we are trying to forget ourselves; this forgetfulness of self is the one great lesson we have to learn in life" (*CW,* 1:84; see also 7:179).

Vivekananda's radical departure from Śaṅkara is his contention that this unselfishness and detachment directly bring about self-knowledge. He does not mention any intervening need for inquiry into a *pramāṇa* (source of valid knowledge):

> We must do the work and find out the motive power that prompts us; and, almost without exception, in the first years, we shall find that our motives are always selfish; but gradually this selfishness will melt by persistence, till at last will come the time when we shall be able to do really unselfish work. We may all hope that some day or other, as we struggle through the paths of life, there will come a time when we shall become perfectly unselfish; and the moment we attain that, all our powers will be concentrated and the knowledge which is ours will be manifest.

> To attain this unattachment is almost a life-work, but as soon as we have reached this point, we have attained the goal of love and become free; the bondage of nature falls from us, and we see nature as she is; she

> forges no more chains for us; we stand entirely free and take not the results of work into consideration; who then cares for what the results may be?
>
> This attainment does not depend on any dogma, or doctrine or belief. Whether one is a Christian, or Jew, or Gentile, it does not matter. Are you unselfish? That is a question. If you are, you will be perfect without reading a single book, without going into a single church or temple. (*CW,* 1:34–35, 59, 93)[9]

Ignorance is presented as somehow falling away with the cultivation of selflessness and detachment. I have already commented on the fallacy of Vivekananda's assertion that *karmayoga* is free from and does not necessitate any concern with doctrine or dogma. I have shown the presupposition and inextricable involvement of Advaita postulates throughout his discussion. Even if one were to grant that the selflessness and detachment of which Vivekananda speaks are possible without any Advaita presumptions, it is still difficult to grasp how their accomplishment leads to freedom in the Advaita sense. Within the context of Advaita, attachment and selfishness are the symptoms of *avidyā.* They are the expressions of *avidyā,* not the cause of it. Their overcoming, if possible, would still appear to leave the fundamental problem of *avidyā* and bondage unresolved.

The very few areas of discussion in Vivekananda where one encounters attempts to develop in more detail the relation between *karmayoga* and *mokṣa* are still not satisfactory. One always has to accept the supposition that *avidyā,* by some means or other, spontaneously falls away in the automatic manifestation of *brahmajñāna.* Very often, in making the connection between *karmayoga* and *mokṣa,* Vivekananda's language becomes hazy and imprecise, and there is a tendency to reformulate the nature of the problem and the goal to be attained. Selfishness, for example, rather than *avidyā,* is described as the root of bondage (*CW,* 8:153). The goal is presented as that of self-abnegation, and, by its emphasis on service to others, *karmayoga* leads to this by encouraging self-forgetfulness and humility. This is identified by Vivekananda with *nivṛtti* (renunciation):

> We become forgetful of the ego when we think of the body as dedicated to the service of others—the body with which most complacently we identify the ego. And in the long run comes the consciousness of disembodiedness. The more intently you think of the well-being of others, the more oblivious of self you become. In this way, as gradually your hearts gets purified by work, you will come to feel the truth that your own Self is pervading all beings and all things. Thus it is that doing good to others constitutes a way, a means of revealing one's own Self or *ātman.* Know

> this also to be one of the spiritual practices, a discipline for God-realization. Its aim is also Self-realization. Exactly as that aim is attained by *jñana* (knowledge), *bhakti* (devotion) and so on, also by work for the sake of others. (*CW,* 7:111–112; see also 1:84–87)

Again, however, one cannot but add that, from the Advaita point of view, *avidyā* is not simply a problem of exalting or humbling oneself. It is the erroneous apprehension of the self in the form of *adhyāsa* (superimposition). Humility, as a virtue that may be concomitant with the service of others, might be more conducive to *jñāna* than the arrogant exaltation of oneself above all others, but it is difficult to see how it can destroy *avidyā* and lead to the kind of self-understanding that *brahmajñāna* implies. Without any doctrinal presuppositions, the supposedly natural progression that Vivekananda postulates in the passage quote above from the service of others to a knowledge of the distinction of self and body, its nondual and all-pervasive nature, is difficult to understand. It is not at all clear how such far-reaching deductions can be made or how they are self-evident. A "feeling" of affinity with others through service is not the same as a knowledge of the nonduality of the self.

On another occasion, *mokṣa* is identified as "infinite expansion," claimed by Vivekananda to be the goal of all religious, moral, and philosophical doctrines. He identifies this "infinite expansion" with "absolute unselfishness" and claims that *karmayoga* leads to the former by bringing about the latter (*CW,* 1:109). Again, it is not at all clear whether this "infinite expansion" is the same as *brahmajñāna,* with its implications about the nondual nature of the self and its transcendence of spatial and temporal limitations. In Advaita also, one can speak only figuratively about the "infinite expansion" of the self. Being, by definition, limitless, such an "expansion" can be only in terms of gaining the knowledge of its infinity. The consistency of this argument and the preciseness of definition and language are not always preserved by Vivekananda in these discussions.

The picture of the relation between *karmayoga* and *mokṣa* in Vivekananda appears to become even more complicated when one encounters various statements that seem to deny and contradict the position that selfless activity leads directly to self-knowledge. All work is presented by him as presupposing ignorance, and one must infer, therefore, that work is incapable of leading directly to freedom: "The active workers, however good, have still a little remnant of ignorance left in them. When our nature has yet some impurities left in it, then alone can we work. It is in the nature of work to be impelled ordinarily by motive and attachment. . . . The highest men cannot work, for in them there is no attachment. Those whose soul is gone into the Self, those whose desires are confined in the Self, who have become ever associated with the Self, for them there is no work" (*CW,* 1:106). These are passages in which knowledge is affirmed over and above work as the only means of freedom: "Salvation means knowing the truth. We do not become anything; we are what we are. Salvation (comes) by faith and not by work. It is a question of *knowledge!* you must *know* what you are, and it is done" (*CW,* 1:512; see also 1:498).

On occasions, the connection between work and freedom is presented only as an indirect one, a position identical with that of Śaṅkara:

> *Question:* Can *Jīva-seva* (service to beings) alone give *mukti?*
>
> *Answer:* *Jīva-seva* can give *mukti* not directly but indirectly, through purification of the mind. But if you wish to do a thing properly, you must, for the time being, think that that is all-sufficient. (*CW,* 5:325)[10]

Are these two sets of statements, arguing, respectively, for a direct and an indirect connection between *karmayoga* and *mokṣa,* entirely opposed? Is Vivekananda adopting here a position identical with Śaṅkara's and implying a need for inquiry into *śruti* as *śabda-pramāṇa* (a source of valid knowledge)? To suggest this would be to go against the main lines of all his arguments about the functions of the *śruti* and the relation between *karmayoga* and *mokṣa.* Besides, even in these statements where he speaks of work as an indirect aid to *jñāna,* there is definitely no mention of any necessity for inquiry into *śruti* as a means of gaining the knowledge of *brahman.* What then are we to make of the suggestions in these passages? There is one significant occasion on which Vivekananda gives us a clue to his meaning in these passages (*CW,* 7:178–179). All work, Vivekananda says here, is useful only for removing the "veils" that obscure the "manifestation" of the *ātman.* After the "veils" have been removed, "the *ātman* manifests by Its own effulgence." In this sense, according to Vivekananda, work cannot be said to lead directly to *ātmajñāna.* Vivekananda cites Śaṅkara in support of this view, but Śaṅkara's position is entirely different. For Śaṅkara, there is no concept or question of the *ātman* manifesting in this manner, for it is never at any time unmanifest. As awareness, it is always self-revealing, and *manifesting* and *unmanifesting* would be misleading terms, although Vivekananda uses them quite frequently.

The fundamental problem, as far as Śaṅkara is concerned, is an incorrect apprehension of an ever-revealing *ātman*. *Śabda-pramāṇa* is necessary not for making its existence known but for correcting false notions about it. For Śaṅkara, however, the self-revelatory nature of the *ātman* does not imply or is not equivalent to a knowledge of its true nature, and he does not suggest that *brahmajñāna* is somehow spontaneously manifest without *pramāṇa* inquiry. In this discussion, Vivekananda does not distinguish between the so-called manifestation of the *ātman* and the knowledge of its nature. Again, there is a problem of terminological and conceptual clarity and consistency. For, if *manifestation* is identical with self-revelatory character, and if this again is equal to knowledge of *ātman*'s nature, there will never be a problem of *avidyā* for anyone at any time. If, on the other hand, *manifestation* is identical with the knowledge of the true nature of the self, how is this knowledge "manifested" by a self that, by definition, is free from and beyond all activity?

Although this particular passage helps clarify, to some extent, some of Vivekananda's apparently contradictory statements about the indirect nature of work, it does not, however, reconcile all such passages. Perhaps one must also take into consideration what appears to be a tendency in Vivekananda to idealize and extol each path as he describes it, without attempting to reconcile the contradictions arising from this approach. In his discussion, there is no attempt to relate the particularity and the possibilities of each method back to the presuppositions and implications of *avidyā* as the fundamental problem. The result is an obscurity of terminology and concept. Ultimately, we remain unconvinced about the connection between *karmayoga* as a path of detached, selfless activity and *mokṣa* as involving a knowledge of the nonduality of the *ātman*, its nature as ultimate reality, and its transcendence of spatial and temporal limitations.

Bhaktiyoga

Vivekananda provides several definitions of *bhaktiyoga*, showing that its singularity lies in love and worship and that its aim is also identity with the absolute:

> *Bhaktiyoga* is a real, genuine search after the Lord, a search beginning, continuing, and ending in love.
>
> *Bhakti* is a series or succession of mental efforts at religious realization beginning with ordinary worship and ending in a supreme intensity of love for *Īśvara*.

> *Bhaktiyoga* is the path of systematized devotion for the attainment of union with the Absolute. (*CW,* 3:31, 36; 6:90)

Vivekananda reminds us that love and worship directed only to *Īśvara* can be properly termed *bhakti.*[11] He makes it clear that love, as a relationship, cannot obtain with the impersonal, nondual *brahman,* free from all qualities *(nirguṇa).* As an attitude, therefore, *bhakti* is possible only in relation to *brahman* as personal God, possessed of qualities *(saguṇa).* The impersonal and the personal, however, are not conceived of as being distinct:

> *Brahman* is as the clay or substance out of which an infinite variety of articles is fashioned. As clay, they are all one; but form or manifestation differentiates them. Before every one of them was made, they all existed potentially in the clay, and, of course, they are identical substantially; but when formed, and so long as the form remains, they are separate and different; the clay-mouse can never become a clay-elephant, because, as manifestations, form alone makes them what they are, though as unformed clay they are all one. *Īśvara* is the highest manifestation of the Absolute Reality, or in other words, the highest possible reading of the Absolute by the human mind. Creation is eternal and so is *Īśvara.* (*CW,* 3:37; see also 3:42)

The worship of minor gods *(devas),* therefore, cannot be described as *bhakti.* This type of worship is interpreted by Vivekananda as ritualistic, aimed at producing some limited enjoyable result, but never *mokṣa.* In the early stages of *bhaktiyoga,* substitutes and images are necessary and useful, but *Īśvara* should never be completely identified with any of these. Their right role is only to serve as suggestions for the worship of *Īśvara,* who always remains the central focus. Even the lesser gods can, in this manner, function as suggestions for the worship of *Īśvara,* but the attitude is not *bhakti* when any of these are worshiped as ends in themselves (*CW,* 3:59–62).[12]

Whereas *karmayoga* is meant for the activity-oriented nature, *bhaktiyoga* is conducive to the largely emotional temperament who wants only to love and does not care for abstract definitions of God or philosophical speculation. Vivekananda often identifies *bhaktiyoga* with the attitudes and ideas of the Purāṇas and describes the method as a concession to the human weakness of dependence: "So long as there shall be the human weakness of leaning upon somebody for support, these *Purāṇas,* in some form or other, must always exist. You can change their names; you can condemn those that are already existing, but immediately you will be compelled to write another *Purāṇa*" (*CW,* 3:387). He constantly affirms the advantage of *bhaktiyoga* to be its naturalness and easiness as a method of attaining *mokṣa.*[13] This argument is linked with the possibility of renunciation, seen by him as a common demand of all paths. In *karmayoga,* renunciation is in the form of an indifference to the personal rewards of action. In *rājayoga,* it is accomplished by looking on nature as a school of experience, the purpose of which is to enable the soul to realize its eternal separation from matter. In *jñānayoga,* which, according to Vivekananda, is the most difficult, the individual must detach herself by the strength of her reason alone (*CW,* 3:70–71). The renunciation of the *bhakta,* however, is the smooth and spontaneous consequence of his intense love for *īśvara:* "The renunciation necessary for the attainment of *bhakti* is not obtained by killing anything, but just comes in as naturally as in the presence of an increasingly stronger light, the less intense ones become dimmer and dimmer until they vanish away completely. So this love of the pleasures of the senses and of the intellect is all made dim and thrown aside and cast into the shade by the love of God Himself" (3:72; see also 3:77–79, 6:90, 7:198).[14] In *bhaktiyoga,* the various human passions and feelings are not viewed as being essentially wrong; instead, they are given a new orientation in relation to *īśvara.* Pleasure and pain, for example, should be responses not to the gain or loss of wealth but to the realization or nonrealization of love.

Unlike Vivekananda's discussion of *karmayoga,* where one finds no descriptions of a progressive development of method, in his discussion of *bhaktiyoga* we are provided with details of qualifications required by both student and teacher.[15] As far as the student is concerned, six preparatory qualities are repeatedly mentioned. The first of these is *viveka,* which, following Rāmānuja, he interprets primarily as discrimination in matters of food.[16] Food can be impure as a result of three factors. First, certain kinds of food—meat, for example—are impure by nature. So also are some types of stimulating foods. Food can also be rendered unsuitable by the presence of external impurities, such as dust or dirt. Finally, food is also affected by the character of the person who prepares or serves it. The idea seems to be that, by some means or other, the personality of the individual transmits itself through the food. This emphasis on food is the result of a link that Vivekananda sees between the quality of thoughts and the nature of food.

The second qualification required of the *bhakta* is *vimoha,* or freedom from desires. All other ideals and objects in life are useful, not as ends in themselves, but to the extent that they lead to the attainment of *bhakti.* The third qualification is *abhyāsa,* or practice. There must be a continuous effort to restrain the mind from the habit of contemplating objects of enjoyment and to fix its attention instead on *īśvara.* Here Vivekananda emphasizes the value of music. The fourth qualification is *kriyā,* or good activities. These embrace the daily study of religious texts, the making of offerings to departed ancestors, the worship of God, and the service of human and nonhuman beings. The fifth qualification is *kalyāṅa,* or purity, which is realized in attitudes and acts of truthfulness, straightforwardness, compassion, noninjury, and charity. A gloomy mind, according to Vivekananda, is incapable of love. At the same time, he cautions against excessive merriment, associated with fickleness and unsteadiness of mind. The right attitude is one of calm cheerfulness.

In his discussion of *bhaktiyoga* as a path to *mokṣa,* Vivekananda stresses the role of the *guru* and the necessity of faith, humility, and submission toward the teacher. The ideal teacher, by whom he appears to mean the *avatāra* (incarnation), is self-evident and is immediately recognized by the student: "When the sun rises, we instinctively become aware of the fact, and when a teacher of men comes to help us, the soul will instinctively know that truth has already begun to shine upon it. Truth stands on its own evidence, it does not require any other testimony to prove it true, it is self-effulgent" (*CW,* 3:47–48). One can, however, adds Vivekananda, also benefit from lesser teachers, but these must be evaluated by certain criteria. Three such norms are supplied by him. First, the teacher should know the secret of the scriptures, and Vivekananda distinguishes this from a knowledge of syntax, etymology, and philology.[17] To be a *bhakta,* for example, according to Vivekananda, there is no need for conclusive historical knowledge of the date of the Bhagavadgītā or the details of Krishna's life: "You only require to *feel* the craving for the beautiful lessons of duty and love in the *Gītā*" (*CW,* 3:50; see also 4:24–26).[18] Second, the teacher of *bhakti* must be sinless, for only one of impeccable moral stature can communicate spiritual truths. Finally, his motive for teaching must be only love for his disciple. *Bhakti* grows only in the relationship between a genuine teacher and a fully qualified aspirant.

Vivekananda presents *bhaktiyoga* as progressing through two stages. The first of these is *gauṇī,* or the preparatory stage, when there is still a necessity for myths, symbols, forms, rituals, and the repetition of names. All these are associated with the observance of the formal or ceremonial aspects of religion and are necessary, he says, for the purification of the soul. From the preparatory stage, one moves on to *parābhakti,* or supreme devotion. Vivekananda, however, does not delineate the details of this transition. Although *parābhakti* is inexpressible, it could, he claims, be described by analogy with human relationships of increasing emotional intensities (*CW,* 3:93–99). The first of these is *śānta,* or the peaceful relationship, just above the ceremonial or ritual aspects of worship and lacking in intensity of feeling. Higher than this is *dāsya,* or the servant attitude, the perception of *īśvara* as master and of oneself as servant. Next comes *sakhya,* or the relationship of friendship. Here *īśvara* is viewed as the beloved friend who is always near and to whom one's heart is open. It is almost a relationship of equals, and God is sometimes viewed as a playmate. Still higher, however, is the *vātsalya* attitude, or looking on God as one's child. It is a relationship intended to remove the association of power from our concept of God: "To conceive God as mighty, majestic, and glorious, as the Lord of the universe, or as the God of gods, the lover says that he does not care. It is to avoid this association with God of the fear-creating sense of power that he worships God as his own child. . . . This idea of loving God as a child comes into existence and grows naturally among those religious sects which believe in the incarnation of God" (*CW,* 3:95–96). The highest relationship, however, is the *madhura* (sweet), in which God is viewed as the husband and the *bhakta* as the wife. Sometimes even the analogy of illicit and obstructed love is employed to characterize its intensity.

Parābhakṭi is most commonly represented by Vivekananda as a triangle of three vital characteristics (see *CW,* 2:47–49; 3:86–90, 391–392; 6:70–71). Its first feature is the absence of all bargaining. No real love, he points out, is possible in the expectation of some return. In *parābhakti,* there is not even the hope for salvation. It is the ideal of love for love's sake; *īśvara* is loved because God is lovable and the *bhakta* cannot help loving. The second characteristic is the absence of all fear. God is not loved or worshiped from fear because both are incompatible with love. The worship of God through fear of punishment, says Vivekananda, is the crudest expression of love. God's role as rewarder or punisher is not important at this level of devotion. Finally, the love of God is always the highest ideal. The most intense love is possible only when its object is our highest ideal.

Along with these three characteristics, *parābhakti* is also distinguished by responses of reverence, pleasure, and misery. Everything associated with the beloved, such as temples, pilgrimage sites, and teachers, is revered. The *bhakta*'s delight in God is as intense as the pleasure of the sensualist in objects of enjoyment. The devotee is miserable because of not having attained the ideal of love and dissatisfied with anything that draws attention away from God. Ultimately, life is of value only because of this love. There are many very beautiful and inspiring passages in Vivekananda's description of *parābhakti.* The ideal is attained when the *bhakta* transcends the need for all symbol and forms and when all thoughts and emotions effortlessly center themselves on God. In and through a love for God as the universal, the *bhakta* comes to love everything in the universe: "In this way everything becomes sacred to the *bhakta,* because all things are His. All are His children, His body, His manifestation. How then may we hurt any one? With the love of God will come, as a sure effect, the love of everyone in the universe. The nearer we approach God, the more do we begin to see that all things are in Him. When the soul succeeds in appropriating the bliss of this supreme love, it also begins to see Him in everything" (*CW,* 3:82; see also 3:76, 92). In this state of intense, all-absorbing love, the *bhakta* is completely resigned to the will of God. The incomparable peace of this resignation is the result of welcoming all experiences, pleasurable and painful, as coming from the beloved.

There are obviously few difficulties with Vivekananda's comprehensive account of the prerequisites and characteristics of *bhaktiyoga.* In this detailing, he acknowledges his dependence on Rāmānuja and other *bhakti* writers (*CW,* 4:3, 3:35, 38). Rāmānuja, of course, fiercely challenged many of the conclusions of Advaita, and his concepts of *brahman, ātman,* and *mokṣa* differ sharply from both Śaṅkara's and Vivekananda's. Vivekananda, however, presents *bhaktiyoga* as leading directly to the conclusions and goal of Advaita: "Those who have faith in the Personal God have to undergo spiritual practices holding on to that idea. If there is sincerity, through that will come the awakening of the lion of *brahman* within. The knowledge of *brahman* is the one goal of all beings but the various ideas are the various paths to it" (*CW,* 7:192; see also 1:440; 3:28, 32, 282; 7:121). One imagines that, by "the awakening of the lion of *brahman* within," Vivekananda really means the gain of the knowledge of *brahman,* for there is no question of an arousal of *brahman.* In my analysis of *karmayoga,* however, I remarked on the terminological imprecision at the same point in his discussion and the tendency to reformulate the fundamental problem, which is one of ignorance of an ever-available *brahman.*

Vivekananda's entire presentation of *bhaktiyoga* is descriptive, and, while he claims that the method leads directly to *brahmajñāna,* there is very little discussion of how this is brought about. To this effect, two suggestions emerge from his writings. The first is that the final removal of *avidyā* and the freedom of nonduality is effected, for the *bhakta,* by the grace of *Īśvara:*

> That love of God grows and assumes a form which is called *parā bhakti* or supreme devotion. Forms vanish, rituals fly away, books are superseded; images, temples, churches, religions and sects, countries and nationalities—all these little limitations and bondages fall off by their own nature from him who knows this love of God. Nothing remains to bind him or fetter his freedom. A ship, all of a sudden, comes near a magnetic rock, and its iron bolts and bars are all attracted and drawn out, and the planks get loosened and freely float on the water. Divine grace thus loosens the binding bolts and bars of the soul, and it becomes free. (*CW,* 3:72–73; see also 1:13, 3:42–43, 78)[19]

Passages like these, however, provide no details about the nature of the freedom so gained, and they are contradicted by the view, expressed elsewhere, denying the dependence of salvation on grace:

> *Question:* Can salvation *(mukti)* be obtained without the grace of God?
>
> *Answer:* Salvation has nothing to do with God. Freedom already *is.* (*CW,* 5:317)

There are other passages in Vivekananda that suggest a natural progression toward freedom through *parābhakti.* One can do no better than cite one such example:

> We all have to begin as dualists in the religion of love. God is to us a separate Being, and we all feel ourselves to be separate beings also. Love then comes in the middle, and man begins to approach God, and God also comes nearer and nearer to man. Man takes up all the various relationships of life, as father, as mother, as son, as friend, as master, as lover, and projects them on his ideal of love, on his God. To him God exists as all these, and the last point of his progress is reached when he feels that he has become absolutely merged in the object of his worship. We all begin with love for ourselves, and the unfair claims of the little self make even love selfish. At last, however, comes the full blaze of light, in which this little self is seen to have become one with the Infinite. Man himself is transfigured in the presence of this Light of Love, and he realizes at last the beautiful truth that Love, the Lover, and the Beloved are One. (*CW,* 3:100; see also 3:86, 8:221, 258)

That the movement from the duality of *bhaktiyoga* to nonduality is a natural and inevitable progression is not at all clearly demonstrated in these passages. In fact, these passages seem to occur only in the context of his general presupposition that all religious quests will eventually end in nonduality and in the context of the progressive development of doctrine that he claims to be able to trace in the Vedas (see chap. 2 above). Unless this presupposition is accepted, then the inexorable movement from duality to nonduality is not clear from his discussion of *bhaktiyoga*. The discovery of nonduality occurs at the stage of *parābhakti,* but, from his own descriptions, even at this level there is a clear distinction between worshiper and worshiped. One cannot assume this discovery to be in terms of knowledge derived from the Upaniṣads, for, as in *karmayoga,* he stresses the lack of necessity for doctrines in *parābhakti.* Without *śabda-pramāṇa,* therefore, the transition from the love and worship of God to a knowledge of the limitlessness and reality of one's own self remains open to question.

Jñānayoga

It may appear to be very surprising that, of all the paths to *mokṣa* examined in the present chapter, Vivekananda offers the least details on *jñānayoga.* It is true that most of his lectures and writings elaborate Advaita theories about the nature of God, the human being, and the universe and could, in this sense, be said to be concerned with *jñāna.* He does not provide, however, any clear outline of the method of *jñānayoga* as a path to *mokṣa.* One suspects that the difficulty here is that, even from Vivekananda's standpoint, *jñāna* is the goal for which all other paths are means. In proposing *jñānayoga* as a path among other direct paths, *jñāna* becomes a means to *jñāna.* If at the very inception one has the knowledge that is the object of the quest, then there seems to be no further need to search for that knowledge. In Śaṅkara, this difficulty is obviated by the fact that knowledge gained from the *śruti* is both means and end. Śaṅkara does not suggest that this knowledge must, in some way or other, be further applied or employed as a means of gaining the same knowledge. In Vivekananda's case, however, any knowledge derived from *śruti* inquiry is not final knowledge, and this is an important contrast with Śaṅkara. Final, liberating knowledge is derived only through the direct verification afforded by a special experience. Only in this sense does *jñānayoga* as a means to *jñāna* appear understandable. Even so, Vivekananda does not demonstrate how this initial, but inconclusive, knowledge is further applied to arrive at the same, but conclusive, knowledge.

In Vivekananda's writings, we are given only vague suggestions about what constitutes the distinctiveness and development of *jñānayoga* as a path among other paths. We can bring together the suggestions that find frequent mention. He presents *jñānayoga* as a method suitable only for the highest and most exceptional minds, the brave, strong, and daring. It is the way of the minority. In contrast with other paths, it is the most difficult, but it also brings the quickest results: "The object of *jñānayoga* is the same as that of *bhakti* and *rājayoga,* but the method is different. This is the *Yoga* for the strong, for those who are neither mystical nor devotional, but rational" (*CW,* 8:3; see also 1:98, 3:11, 7:198). While selfless activity seems to be the chief distinctive feature of *karmayoga* and loving worship that of *bhaktiyoga,* Vivekananda presents "pure" reason and reliance on will as the singular characteristics of *jñānayoga.* He describes it as the rational and philosophical side of *yoga:*

> As the *bhaktiyogī* works his way to complete oneness with the Supreme through love and devotion, so the *jñānayogī* forces his way to the realization of God by the power of pure reason. He must be prepared to throw away all old idols, all old beliefs and superstitions, all desire for this world or another, and be determined only to find freedom. Without *jñāna* (knowledge) liberation cannot be ours.
>
> The *jñānī* is a tremendous rationalist; he denies everything. He tells himself day and night, "There are no beliefs, no sacred words, no heaven, no hell, no creed, no church—there is only the *ātman.*" When everything has been thrown away until what cannot be thrown away is reached, that is the Self. The *jñānī* takes nothing for granted; he analyses by pure reason and force of will, until he reaches *nirvāṇa* which is the extinction of all relativity. (*CW,* 8:3, 11; see also 3:17, 8:10)

Occasionally, the path of *jñānayoga* is briefly alluded to as the negative way, *neti, neti* (not this, not this), but the exact nature of this negative reasoning is not developed (see, e.g., *CW,* 1:98). In one place, it is described as a method of mind control or destruction, after which the real discloses itself (*CW,* 5:300). Elsewhere, his description suggests that it is a denial of the nonself and an assertion of the self (*CW,* 6:464, 8:4). Among other characteristics of *jñānayoga,* Vivekananda twice describes it as "creedlessness." It is, according to him, the end to which all creeds should aspire, but it is above and beyond creeds (*CW,* 5:272, 8:8). Perhaps this statement must also be seen in the light of Vivekananda's general low estimation of what he regards as doctrine.

The most common definition of *jñānayoga* in Vivekananda is his description of it as a method of pure reason and will. This definition, however, raises a number of problems within the context of his overall views. In describing *jñānayoga* to be of this nature, he does not indicate the source of the propositions on which the *jñānī* exercises his reason or whether these propositions are arrived at by reason itself. One is left wondering, therefore, about whether *śruti* is to be understood as the source. If we assume that the original propositions are derived from *śruti,* then the utility or even the possibility of reasoning on these statements seems to be undermined by some of Vivekananda's own contentions. I have already noted his view that, as the product of an experience transcending reason, *śruti* cannot be understood by reason. He has also argued that, as a record of other people's experiences, *śruti* is of little benefit to the new aspirant. We shall also later see his claim that reason is possible only after experience, that it does not precede it.

It appears that, in order to understand and evaluate Vivekananda's definition of *jñānayoga* as a path to knowledge through pure reason, we must take a broader look at the nature and functions of reason in his writings. We also need to look at specific examples of the kinds of reasoning that he employs and the claims that he makes for these.

In spite of his characterization of *jñānayoga* as a path of pure reason, Vivekananda, like Śaṅkara, argues for the limited nature of reason. Its activity, he says, is confined only to a narrow sphere; beyond this it cannot reach. The most that reason can do in relation to ultimate questions is to adopt a position of agnosticism, for the answers to these questions lie outside its field (*CW,* 1:150, 181).[20] According to Vivekananda, the highest demonstration of reasoning in any branch of knowledge can make a fact only probable: "The truths of religion, as God and Soul, cannot be perceived by the external senses. I cannot see God with my eyes, nor can I touch Him with my hands, and we also know that neither can we reason beyond the senses. Reason leaves us at a point quite indecisive; we may reason all our lives, as the world has been doing for thousands of years, and the result is that we find we are incompetent to prove or disprove the facts of religion" (*CW,* 1:232).

The chief limitation of reason, therefore, as a faculty of deriving knowledge about God is its dependence on sense perception for its data. It can run, he contends, only within the bounds of perception, for one reasons only on data gathered through the senses. This constitutes its essential weakness and binds it to the realms of time and space. He sees reason as classified and stored perception, preserved in memory (*CW,* 8:20). As an intellectual process, it comes into being only after perception. This is true for both secular and spiritual knowledge:

> All argument and reasoning must be based upon certain perceptions. Without these, there cannot be any argument. Reasoning is the method of comparison between certain facts which we have already perceived. If these perceived facts are not there already, there cannot be any reasoning. If this is true of external phenomena, why should it not be so of the

> internal. The chemist takes certain chemicals and certain results are produced. This is a fact; you see it, sense it, and make that the basis on which to build all your chemical arguments. So with physicists, so with all other sciences. All knowledge must stand on perception of certain facts, and upon that we have to build our reasoning. (*CW,* 2:162)

This argument that reason becomes possible only after perception seems to undermine Vivekananda's own claim about *jñānayoga* as a path of reason. If reason is the chief tool that the aspirant has to employ from the inception, then it appears impossible to do so without a direct perception of spiritual truths. If, on the other hand, one perceives these truths directly, then, from the logic of Vivekananda's own arguments, reason is redundant.

Śaṅkara shares the view that the primary limitation of inferential reasoning is its reliance on perception. In Śaṅkara, however, the problem of the limitations of reason is overcome by the acceptance of *śruti* as a *pramāṇa*. *Śruti* is the only source of *brahmajñāna*. For Śaṅkara, reason is the tool that we employ in understanding, interpreting, and reconciling the words and sentences of the *śruti*. As a *pramāṇa* in the form of words, these must be understood accurately, for the meanings of words are not always obvious.[21]

The contrast in the role ascribed to reason by Śaṅkara and Vivekananda is clearly highlighted in their respective interpretations of an important *śruti* text, Kaṭha Upaniṣad 1.2.7–9, which is concerned with the problems of expounding the *ātman* and the limits of reason: "The wisdom that you have, O dearest one, which leads to sound knowledge when imparted only by someone else (other than the logician), is not to be attained through argumentation. You are, O compassionable one, endowed with true resolution. May our questioner be like you, O *Naciketa*" (Ka.U 1.2.9). Vivekananda interprets this text as proscribing the application of all kinds of reasoning to the attainment of *brahmajñāna* (*CW,* 2:162–163, 7:167). Śaṅkara, on the other hand, sees it as forbidding only independent reasoning, conjured by one's own intellect and having no basis in the *śruti*. He does not deny the futility of all reasoning (see Ka.U = B 1.2.7–8, pp. 137–141).

Unlike Śaṅkara, Vivekananda posits the overcoming of the limitations of reason through a transcendental or superconscious state of mind. The knowledge that Śaṅkara gains from the *śruti* is imparted, for him, by an experience that goes beyond reason. It is a faculty, he claims, that all people possess (*CW,* 1:150, 183, 197, 262–263; 2:61). Generally speaking, because of the overriding importance that Vivekananda places on this special experience as a source of knowledge, he ascribes much less importance and esteem to reason than Śaṅkara does. He groups reason with theories, documents, doctrines, books, and ceremonies, as an aid to religion. In relation to the superconscious experience, the role of reason is merely preparatory (*CW,* 1:232). Vivekananda does not elaborate on this function, but it appears to be largely negative. It checks and prevents crude errors and superstition: "The intellect is only the street-cleaner, cleansing the path for us, a secondary worker, the policeman; but the policeman is not a positive necessity for the workings of society. He is only to stop disturbances, to check wrong-doing, and that is all the work required of the intellect" (*CW,* 2:306; see also 2:307; 5:283; 7:60, 91–92). In the light of Vivekananda's argument that reason cannot operate before perception, it is not clear how it can accomplish even this negative role. There is no clear indication of the nature and source of the information on which the aspirant exercises his reason and no suggestion of the principles that should guide reason in this preperception stage.

My attempt to study the wider significance of reason in Vivekananda seems, therefore, to question and raise several unresolved issues about his definition of *jñānayoga* as the method of pure reason. These doubts are also supported by a consideration of specific examples of his own reasoning. The nature of his reasoning can be studied in what is, perhaps, one of his most interesting lectures, "Reason and Religion" (*CW,* 1:366–382).[22] Religions, argues Vivekananda, have very often assumed the superiority of their claims over the findings of the secular sciences and refused to be justified by the latter. The unfortunate result of this has been a perpetual struggle between religion and secular knowledge, with the claims of the former being gradually eroded. If religion is to survive, it must, according to Vivekananda, justify itself in the light of rational investigation and the findings of secular knowledge:

> Are the same methods of investigation, which we apply to sciences and knowledge outside, to be applied to the science of Religion? In my opinion this must be so, and I am also of the opinion that the sooner it is done the better. If a religion is destroyed by such investigations, it was then all the time useless, unworthy superstition; and the sooner it goes the better. I am thoroughly convinced that its destruction would be the best thing that could happen. All that is dross will be taken off, no doubt, but the essential parts of religion will emerge triumphant out of this investigation. Not only will it be made scientific—as scientific, at least, as any of the conclusions of physics or chemistry—but will have greater strength, because physics or chemistry has no internal mandate to vouch for its truth, which religion has. (*CW,* 1:367)[23]

Vivekananda then proceeds to enumerate two principles of reasoning or knowledge that, he claims, conclusively establish certain Advaita propositions to be scientifically valid. The first principle of reasoning is that movement in knowledge is from the particular to the general, and from the general to the more general, until the universal is reached. He sees the notion of law or species of beings as applications of this principle of generalization (*CW,* 1:369–370). The second principle of reasoning is that the explanation of a thing must come from the inside, not from the outside: "This tendency you will find throughout modern thought; in one word, what is meant by science is that the explanation of things are in their own nature, and that no external beings or existences are required to explain what is going on in the universe" (*CW,* 1:371). Vivekananda sees the concept of evolution as a demonstration of this principle. He understands evolution as signifying the reproduction of the cause in the effect or the full presence of the potentialities of the cause in the effect. He also sees the concept of the personal, extracosmic deity as creator of the universe as having failed to satisfy this scientific demand for an internal explanation. Vivekananda sees the *brahman* concept of Advaita as satisfying both these scientific principles.

> We have to come to an ultimate generalization, which not only will be the most universal of all generalizations, but out of which everything else must come. It will be of the same nature as the lowest effect; the cause, the highest, the ultimate, the primal cause, must be the same as the lowest and most distant of its effects, a series of evolutions. The *brahman* of the *Vedānta* fulfils that condition, because *brahman* is the last generalization to which we can come. It has no attributes but is Existence, Knowledge, and Bliss—Absolute. Existence, we have seen is the very ultimate generalization which the human mind can come to. (*CW,* 1:372)

Brahman also satisfies the need for an internal explanation, for it has nothing outside itself. It is identical with the universe, and the latter could, therefore, be described as self-creating, self-manifesting, and self-dissolving. As identical with *brahman,* the universe is its own explanation. For purposes of clarification, it should be stated that *brahman* is not identical with the universe in the sense of having undergone a real transformation to become the universe. The universe is only an appearance in *brahman,* brought about by *māyā. Māyā* is identical with *brahman* and cannot be defined as either real or unreal. *Brahman*'s nature is never lost, and it is not limited by the appearance of the universe.

In order to evaluate the achievements of these kinds of arguments in Vivekananda, it is better, at this point in the discussion, to view them in the much wider context of his general attempt to present Advaita as scientific. *Karma*- and *bhaktiyoga* are described, respectively, as the science of work and love (*CW,* 1:99, 3:73). It is obvious that, in drawing this parallel, Vivekananda was working with a certain concept of science. This attempt to harmonize science and religion is not, by any means, original to Vivekananda; it was an important strand of thought in the Brahmo Samaj movement, particularly in its early phases, in thinkers like Akshaykumar Dutt, Ishwarchandra Vidyasagar, and Brajendranath Seal.[24] To found and justify their religion on rational and scientific grounds was fundamental to their approach. Religion and science were seen not as incompatible but as two sides of the same quest for truth, and the "science of religion" was an expression often used in their writings. As one who moved in the milieu of the Brahmo Samaj during the earlier years of his life, Vivekananda was undoubtedly influenced by this line of thinking, and many of these ideas are later echoed by him.

The difficulty of arriving at the root of his concept of science is that he never formulated it clearly in any particular lecture or writing. Certain general ideas, however, find repeated mention, and these serve as the clue to the scientific concept that he was using to draw a parallel with religion. The most important idea, for him, linking science and religion was that of unity. The aim and end of scientific method, according to Vivekananda, was to find unity, the one out of which the manifold is being manifested. As soon as any science found such a unity, it would come to an end, for it would have reached the highest point beyond which it could not proceed (see, e.g., *CW,* 1:14–15). He represented science as having already discovered the physical oneness of the universe, in telling us that everything is a manifestation of energy, the sum total of all that exists. The difference between Advaita and science, he says, is that the former had discovered this oneness much earlier by its search into internal nature while the latter had discovered it through investigating the external. The corollary, of course, is that the discovery of this common goal makes Advaita scientific:

> Physics would stop when it would be able to fulfil its services in discovering one energy of which all the others are but manifestations, and the science of religion become perfect when it would discover Him who is the one life in a universe of death, Him who is the constant basis of an ever-changing world. One who is the only Soul of which all souls are but delusive manifestations. Thus is it, through multiplicity and duality, that the

ultimate unity is reached. Religion can go no farther. This is the goal of all science. (*CW,* 1:14–15)

The issue here is whether the aim and method of science can be defined by the search for unity. If, for the sake of argument, one were to accept this as being so, the question as to whether a religion that proposes a goal of oneness is justified in being described as scientific still remains open. If drawn into this controversy, the scientist will most certainly contend that his discipline cannot be defined only by its general aim, even provided that this could be agreed on. There is the vital question of its methodology, the most important aspect of which is its agreed means and standards of verification.

Although Vivekananda is not explicit on this point, it seems that he uses the concept of science to refer to any rational system that proposes a goal and outlines a "practical" method for its accomplishment. *Scientific* is equated, by him, with that which is internally consistent and practical. It appears that he also describes the four *yogas* as being scientific in this sense. This strikes one, however, as a loose application of the term. It is perhaps more accurate and meaningful to describe such a system as rational rather than scientific. We have already noted his identification of the method of generalization and the search for an internal explanation as other features of science.

The search for unity, the movement from the particular to the general, and the attempt to explain all phenomena by reference to their own natures are perhaps broad features of scientific method, although science does not necessarily proceed on the assumption of the existence of any final unity. It is another matter, however, to describe as scientific any system that proposes unity as the ultimate reality, that proceeds from the particular to the general, and that offers an internal explanation.[25] In spite of Vivekananda's attempt to show that the method of generalization and the criterion of an internal explanation render Advaita scientific, it is obvious that this aim is not achieved. While Advaita might proceed by moving from the particular to the general, and while *brahman* as a universal encompasses everything, these features do not make Advaita scientific in the same sense as other conclusions of the physical sciences are. This is also true for the argument that the universe must be explained with reference to its own internal nature. These kinds of reasoning perhaps demonstrate Advaita to be in line with certain general trends in scientific thinking, but they are not independently conclusive arguments. They add a certain plausibility to the propositions of Advaita and reveal them as not being inconsistent with some forms of scientific thinking, but one cannot contend that these explanations scientifically demonstrate the validity of Advaita. In this sense, Vivekananda's reasoning is not different in its achievement from what Śaṅkara conceives to be the possibility of reason in relation to *śruti*. This conclusion raises further questions about his definition of *jñānayoga* as a method of pure reason and his belief that religion must be fully justified by the standpoint of reason (see *CW,* 2:335, 390).

This conclusion can be further demonstrated by looking at one more example of his reasoning. One of his favorite and most frequently employed forms of reasoning is to draw parallels between the microcosm and the macrocosm.[26] In observing the microcosm, Vivekananda says, the pattern is that everything begins from certain seedlike or fine forms and then becomes grosser and grosser. Things develop in this way for some time, before subsiding and reverting back to their fine forms. The manifest or gross is the effect and the finer form the cause, but the effect is simply a reproduction of the cause in a different form. The effect is not different from the cause. His second conclusion is that all forms in the microcosm are cyclically rising and falling. Third, the grosser forms do not immediately emerge from the finer ones. Their emergence is preceded by a period of unmanifest activity. Finally, we never observe anything in the microcosm being produced out of nothing. Vivekananda extends these conclusions to the nature of the macrocosm. The universe, as a whole, has its cause in *brahman,* from which, as an effect, it is not different. It has also emerged out of a finer form to which it will again revert, and this process a cyclic one. Like the other argument that we have considered, this is also not independently conclusive. While certain generalizations can be made from observation of the microcosm, one cannot infallibly make inferences from these about the nature of the macrocosm. As an assumption, the uniformity of nature may not have been refuted, but it is only an assumption nevertheless. This argument, however, can add some credence to the cosmological views of Advaita.

Close scrutiny of Vivekananda's arguments show that they are all constructed on implicit premises from the *śruti.* He does not directly acknowledge this, and, in the manner in which his arguments are presented, the *śruti*-derived propositions are not always obvious. We can illustrate this by citing an interesting example from his writing:

> The *ātman* is the only existence in the human body which is not material. Because it is immaterial, it cannot be a compound, and because it is not a compound, it does not obey the law of cause and effect, and so it is immortal. That which is immortal can have no beginning because everything with a beginning must have an end. It also follows that it must be

> formless; there cannot be any form without matter. . . . But the Self having no form, cannot be bound by the law of beginning and end. It is existing from infinite time; just as time is eternal, so is the Self of man eternal. Secondly, it must be all-pervading. It is only form that is conditioned and limited by space; that which is formless cannot be confined in space. So according to *Advaita Vedānta,* the Self, the *ātman,* in you, in me, in everyone, is omnipresent. (*CW,* 2:254–255)

This excerpt is a splendid example of a logically formulated argument, constructed from successive inferences. Its movement is swift and complex, but it is all composed on the premise of the immateriality of the *ātman.* The validity of all subsequent inferences depends on this. This premise, however, is not arrived at through any kind of inference, and we must therefore conclude that its origin is in the *śruti.*

Vivekananda's writings reveal that his principal concern in elaborating the four *yogas* as direct and independent means to *mokṣa* was to highlight what he saw as the liberal and universal claims of Vedānta. He wished to contrast this with the exclusivism, particularly of Christianity, that proclaimed only one way to freedom. It is not within the scope of this discussion to present a detailed analysis of Vivekananda's theories of religious diversity, but it is important to understand his motivation in arguing for different ways to *mokṣa.* He saw religious strife as the result of the adoption by each religion of a narrow, self-righteous position. It was a special concern of his, and his first speech before the Parliament of Religions in 1893 was on the theme of sectarianism and bigotry. Vivekananda's own solution was to propose the concept of a universal religion. By *universal religion* he does not mean religious uniformity or the triumph of one particular tradition over all others. He saw certain failure in such attempts (*CW,* 1:24, 2:363). Universal religion, for him, seems synonymous with the absence of exclusiveness. In this connection, he distinguishes between the terms *religion* and *sect.* The former is indicative of an all-embracing attitude, whereas the latter is exclusive. He makes the same distinction between religion and creed and refuses to use the former appellation to designate Christianity because of its antagonistic features.[27] By *universal religion* Vivekananda means, more than anything else, a particular outlook on religious diversity. A number of attitudes constitute this outlook. The natural necessity of variation must be recognized and accepted: "Just as we have recognized unity by our very nature, so we must also recognize variation. We must learn that truth may be expressed in a hundred thousand ways, and that each of these ways is true as far as it goes. We must learn that the same thing can be viewed from a hundred different standpoints and yet be the same thing" (*CW,*

2:382–383). In spite of this diversity of expression, religions are to be seen as manifestations of a common struggle toward God, and each should strive to assimilate the spirit of others while preserving its own individuality.

In Vivekananda's formulation of the concept of universal religion, two Hindu ideas have an extended function in the interpretation of diversity and the development of a spirit of understanding. The first of these is the idea of the *avatāra* or the incarnation of God in the human world. The application of the idea in this context would result in the recognition of the falsity of the assertion that any single prophet is alone true. He saw each religious founder as representing and emphasizing a great ideal. The second idea centers around the principle of the *iṣṭadeva,* or the freedom to choose a concept or representation of God and a means of worship consistent with one's own needs and preferences. There is no necessity to impose one's preferences on others.

It is in the light of his ideal of universal religion and what he considered to be its central characteristics that one must look at Vivekananda's argument for Advaita as fulfilling this ideal. There are several grounds on which he sought to justify this role. We have already noted his argument that, whereas all other traditions are based on the life of a founder and therefore susceptible to any doubts of historicity, Vedānta is founded on impersonal principles. Within this impersonal framework, however, it has, in the ideas of *avatāra* and *iṣṭa,* a wide scope for the play of personalities. He has argued that it is easier to share a common vision on principles rather than on personalities. Among other characteristics, he sees the idea of tolerance as being well rooted and the harmony of its propositions with the findings of secular knowledge. He also considers the spiritual oneness of the universe advocated in Advaita as a better foundation for ethics than personal authority. It is in this context that he proposes the methods of *karma-, bhakti-, jñāna-,* and *rājayoga* as being wide enough to embrace the active, emotional, philosophical, and mystical temperaments. He sees these four paths within a single tradition as overcoming the one-sided nature of other religions.

In the present chapter, however, I have tried to show that he does not conclusively demonstrate *karmayoga* and *bhaktiyoga,* as he formulates them, to be direct and independent paths to *mokṣa.* With regard to these two methods, my principal line of argument has been that, in the context of the Advaita definition of *avidyā* and the nature of bondage as well as its conception of *mokṣa, karmayoga* and *bhaktiyoga* raise and leave unanswered many questions. There is no clear formulation of the nature of *jñānayoga* as a distinct method, and his characterization of it as a method of pure reason cannot be sustained in the light of a wider examination of the functions that he assigns to reason. In fact, his own claim that these *yogas* are independent paths to *brahmajñāna* appears to break down when, as we shall see in the next chapter, he argues that *rājayoga* is the only means through which one can gain the unique experience that directly validates religious truth. In the light of this claim, all other methods appear preparatory for *rājayoga* rather than the self-sufficient means that he presents them as. Throughout his discussion of *karmayoga* and *bhaktiyoga,* there is the hint or suggestion of these methods suddenly culminating in an experience of some kind, which, by itself, eliminates *avidyā*. It is to a consideration of his innumerable references to this experience that we must now turn our attention.

Chapter 4

THE MEANING AND AUTHORITATIVENESS OF *ANUBHAVA* IN VIVEKANANDA

IN CHAPTER 2, I sought to present Vivekananda's understanding of the nature, role, and authority of the Vedas. It clearly emerged that Vivekananda does not posit the knowledge derived from the Upaniṣads as having any immediate or self-sufficient validity for the aspirant. At best, such knowledge stands only as a possibility, testifying to the spiritual discoveries of others and the methods by which these have been made. To be free from all doubts and incontestable, the declarations of the Upaniṣads, according to Vivekananda, must be personally verified by each individual through some sort of direct perception of their claims. It is only knowledge derived through this direct apprehension that he considers to be ultimately valid and capable of liberating from *avidyā* (ignorance). He seems to think that knowledge obtained from any other source is secondhand and will always lack certitude and conviction. In considering the methods of *karma, bhakti,* and *jñāna* in chapter 3, we repeatedly encountered suggestions of the progression to a final experience in which the knowledge of *brahman* spontaneously manifests and *avidyā* is overcome. In this connection, I pointed to a certain obscurity in Vivekananda's discussion and to difficulties in reconciling the nature of *mokṣa* (liberation) with the peculiarities and assumptions of the methods suggested. In the present chapter, I seek to draw together and evaluate Vivekananda's many statements on the nature of the experience, which, he asserts, leads to valid knowledge of *brahman*.

The Rationale and Significance of Anubhava

One cannot overestimate the importance of the experience of direct perception in Vivekananda's philosophy of religion. It is this that he signifies by the frequently used expression *realization* and that may, with good reason, be said to constitute the central and most outstanding feature of his religious thought. It is an idea that he unfailingly labors in almost every one of his lectures. In his first major address at the Parliament of Religions in 1893, for example, he presented this idea as "the very center, the vital conception of Hinduism":

> The Hindu does not want to live upon words and theories. If there are existences beyond the ordinary sensuous existence, he wants to come face to face with them. If there is a soul in him which is not matter, if there is an all-merciful Soul, he will go to Him direct. He must see Him, and that alone can destroy all doubts. So the best proof a Hindu sage gives about the soul, about God, is: "I have seen the soul; I have seen God." And that is the only condition of perfection. The Hindu religion does not consist in struggles and attempts to believe a certain doctrine or dogma, but in realizing—not in believing, but in being and becoming. (*CW,* 1:13)

In his quest for the common bases of the diverse traditions within Hinduism, he again and again presented this idea of religion as realization or direct perception, as belonging to every one of them:

> The mighty word that came out from the sky of spirituality in India was *anubhūti,* realization, and ours are the only books which declare again and again: "The Lord is to be seen." Bold, brave words indeed, but true to their very core; every sound, every vibration is true. Religion is to be realized, not only heard; it is not in learning some doctrine like a parrot. Neither is it mere intellectual assent—that is nothing; but it must come into us. Ay, and therefore the greatest proof that we have of the existence of a God is not because our reason says so, but because God has been seen by the ancients as well as by the moderns. (*CW,* 3:377–378)

Why does realization or the possibility of a direct perception of religious claims occupy such an unmistakably prominent focus in Vivekananda's thought? What was his primary interest in arguing for its necessity and reality? It emerges from his lectures and writings that he was anxious to find an essential point of reference or appeal, by virtue of which the profound issues and claims of religion could be placed on the level of fact. He was concerned that all the crucial and significant issues of religion, such as the existence and nature of God and the soul, could never be finally and satisfactorily established by any form of argument or process of reasoning.[1] In chapter 2, I sufficiently emphasized his disdain for "theoretical" religion, doctrine, and dogma. Vivekananda wanted to demonstrate that religious propositions can, and must, be certified by a process of verification not unlike that employed by the physical sciences.[2]

All knowledge, contends Vivekananda, is based on and derived from experience.[3] Inferential knowledge, for example, has its basis in sense experience. The appeal of the physical sciences, according to Vivekananda, lies in the fact that claims can be referred to particular experiences of all human beings: "The scientist does not tell you to believe in anything, but he has certain results which come from his own experiences, and reasoning on them when he asks us to believe in his conclusions, he appeals to some universal experience of humanity. In every exact science there is a basis which is common to all humanity, so that we can at once see the truth or fallacy of the conclusions drawn therefrom" (*CW,* 1:125).[4] The problem of religion, argues Vivekananda, is that it is generally presented as founded on faith and belief and as lacking central and universal experiences by reference to which its claims can be verified. He strongly denies this, affirming that religious beliefs are also derived from certain generic experiences. All religions, according to Vivekananda, make the claim that their truths originate from the experiences of certain persons:

> The Christian asks you to believe in his religion, to believe in Christ and to believe in him as the incarnation of God, to believe in a God, in a soul, and in a better state of that soul. If I ask him for a reason, he says he believes in them. But if you go to the fountain-head of Christianity, you will find that it is based upon experience. Christ said that he saw God; the disciples said they felt God; and so forth. Similarly, in Buddhism, it is Buddha's experience. He experienced certain truths, saw them, came in contact with them, and preached them to the world. . . . Thus it is clear that all the religions of the world have been built upon that one universal and adamantine foundation of all our knowledge—direct experience. (*CW,* 1:126; see also 2:60–61)[5]

The unfortunate fact, argues Vivekananda, is the claim in the present time that these experiences were unique to certain people and are no longer possible and that religious conviction must now be founded on faith. His strong contention is that any experience in a particular branch of knowledge must be repeatable.

Rājayoga is the method proposed by Vivekananda for enabling us to attain direct perception of religious truths. In fact, he claims that this is the method advanced by all schools of Indian philosophy for gaining *mokṣa* (see *CW,* 1:122, 127).[6] In his discussion of *rājayoga,* we also find the declaration that it is "as much a science as any in the world" (*CW,* 8:36), with its own unique methods for producing results when properly applied. Like his claim for the method of *karmayoga,* he emphasizes that no faith or belief is necessary (*CW,* 1:128, 131;

8:36). This, one assumes, is linked to his urge to demonstrate this method to be scientific. We must now concern ourselves with the outline and steps of *rājayoga* as presented by Vivekananda.

The Method of Rājayoga

Rājayoga, based primarily on the Yoga-sūtras of Patañjali, comprises eight disciplines. We shall look briefly at how Vivekananda understands each of these procedures.

The first steps are the ethical and moral disciplines of *yama* and *niyama. Yama* incorporates nonkilling, truthfulness, nonstealing, celibacy, and the nonreceiving of gifts. *Niyama* comprises cleanliness, contentment, austerity, study, and self-surrender to God. These disciplines, according to Vivekananda, are the very basis of the successful practice of Yoga (*CW,* 1:137). The second step is *āsana* (posture). Vivekananda explains that a comfortable posture is necessary for the daily execution of physical and mental exercises. The posture that is easiest should be chosen, as long as the spinal column is kept erect.

The practice of *prāṇāyāma* follows facility in *āsana.* It is one of the procedures of *rājayoga* discussed at length by Vivekananda. He is most concerned to refute the popular view that *prāṇāyāma* is essentially a routine aimed at the control of breathing. The universe, according to Vivekananda, is composed of two basic materials, *ākāśa* and *prāṇa. Ākāśa* is the original substance out of which everything possessing form or produced as a result of combination evolved. It is, in other words, conceived by Vivekananda as the basic, subtle stuff of the universe. *Prāṇa,* on the other hand, is the power by which *ākāśa* is manufactured into a diversity of forms. Out of *prāṇa* emerges everything called force or energy, and among its manifestations are motion, gravitation, and magnetism (*CW,* 1:147–148). Vivekananda explains, therefore, that *prāṇāyāma* is really the knowledge and control of *prāṇa.* In the human body, adds Vivekananda, the most ostensible demonstration of the activity of *prāṇa* is the rhythmic motion of the lungs in breathing. *Prāṇa* is responsible for this movement, not vice versa. *Prāṇāyāma* is a vast attempt, through the mastery of the breathing process, to gain control of all conscious and unconscious activity in the body.[7]

The next three processes in *rājayoga* are the largely mental disciplines of *pratyāhāra, dhāraṇā,* and *dhyāna. Pratyāhāra* is the continuous process of restraining and controlling the mind by curbing its attachment to the internal and external organs of perception. *Pratyāhāra* is followed by *dhāraṇā,* the practice of focusing the mind's attention on certain fixed points. One may center attention, for example, exclusively on some parts of the body (*CW,* 1:171–178). *Dhyāna* follows directly from this exercise: "When the mind has been trained to remain fixed on a certain internal or external location, there comes to it the power of flowing in an unbroken current, as it were, towards that point. This state is called *dhyāna*" (*CW,* 1:186; see also 1:181, 270). It is through the steady practice of *dhyāna* that the aspirant eventually attains to *samādhi,* the culmination of all the disciplines of *rājayoga.* The entire procedure, claims Vivekananda, is designed to bring us scientifically to this all-important state:

> From the lowest animal to the highest angel, some time or other, each one will have to come to that state, and then, and then alone, will real religion begin for him. Until then we only struggle towards that stage. There is no difference now between us and those who have no religion, because we have no experience. What is concentration good for, save to bring us to this experience? Each one of the steps to attain *samādhi* has been reasoned out, properly adjusted, scientifically organized, and when faithfully practised, will surely lead us to the desired end. Then will all sorrows cease, all miseries vanish; the seeds for actions will be burnt, and the soul will be free for ever. (*CW,* 1:188)

Samādhi is the result, attests Vivekananda, of the awakening of the *kuṇḍalinī.*[8] This is the single way, he says, of attaining spiritual knowledge through direct perception. He sees all religious disciplines as leading consciously or unconsciously to this end and proclaims *rājayoga* as "the science of religion, the rationale of all worship, all prayers, forms, ceremonies, and miracles": "Thus the rousing of the *kuṇḍalinī* is the one and only way to attaining Divine Wisdom, superconscious perception, realization of the spirit. The rousing may come in various ways, through love for God, through the mercy of perfected sages, or through the power of the analytic will of the philosopher" (*CW,* 1:165). Although the concept of the *samādhi* experience is derived by Vivekananda from the Yoga-sūtras of Patañjali, Patañjali does not refer to the *kuṇḍalinī.* The idea of the *kuṇḍalinī* appears to have been unknown to him and belongs to the schools of Tantra.[9]

Samādhi occupies, for Vivekananda, the same function and status as a source of knowledge for *brahmajñāna,* which Śaṅkara ascribes to the Vedas as *śabda-pramāṇa* (a source of valid knowledge). In fact, he presents *samādhi* as the only satisfactory source of *brahmajñāna.* It is important, therefore, that we seek to understand the exact manner in which he sees knowledge as occurring in this state.

The Nature of Samādhi *as a Source of Knowledge*

Samādhi *as the Highest Level of Mental Activity*

Vivekananda very often describes the nature of *samādhi* by distinguishing three gradations of mental activity. The lowest of these is the level of instinctive behavior, most highly developed among animals. Here, according to Vivekananda, thought is largely unconscious, and actions are unaccompanied by any feelings of egoism or self-awareness. Instinctive activity includes all reflex actions. Although he describes instinct as the lowest instrument of knowledge, he speaks of it as being almost infallible. The impulse of an animal rarely fails (*CW,* 2:389, 446). The problem with instinct, however, says Vivekananda, is the limited sphere of knowledge and activity within which it operates. Its responses are mechanical and incapable of dealing readily with anything new or uncharted.

Reason is a more highly developed instrument of knowledge than instinct. It is conscious mental activity, most efficient in humans, and accompanied by a sense of egoism and self-awareness (*CW,* 1:150, 180). It is the level of thought and judgment, gathering facts, and generalizing. Even though its sphere of operation, says Vivekananda, is much wider than the confines of instinct, it is nevertheless very limited.[10] In contrast with the accuracy of instinct, Vivekananda describes reason as being slower and more liable to error.

Higher than unconscious instinct and conscious reason is the superconscious state of mind, or *samādhi.* It is described by Vivekananda as the most elevated plane on which the mind can function, and here it completely transcends the limits of reason and instinct and apprehends facts inaccessible to these. He characterizes the superconscious as being infallible and far more unlimited in its scope than reason. The superconscious, according to Vivekananda, shares with instinct the quality of being free from the sense of egoism, but the two levels are completely opposed. He admits the danger and difficulty of mistaking instinct for inspiration and suggests a set of criteria by which these two could be distinguished. Using sleep as an example of unconscious mental activity, he points out the primary difference from *samādhi:*

> When a man goes into deep sleep, he enters a plane beneath consciousness. He works the body all the time, he breathes, he moves the body, perhaps, in his sleep, without any accompanying feeling of ego; he is unconscious, and when he returns from his sleep, he is the same man who went into it. The sum total of the knowledge which he had before he

> went into the sleep remains the same; it does not increase at all. No enlightenment comes. But when a man goes into *samādhi,* if he goes into it a fool, he comes out a sage. (*CW,* 1:180; see also 4:213)

The second norm for distinguishing the superconscious from instinct, according to Vivekananda, is that the former never contradicts reason. If it ever does, he argues, it cannot be the superconscious, and reason has to be the basis for making this distinction. The explanation, adds Vivekananda, lies in the fact that these three states progressively evolve: "There are not three minds in one man, but one state of it develops into the others. Instinct develops into reason, and reason into the transcendental consciousness; therefore, not one of these states contradicts the others. Real inspiration never contradicts reason, but fulfils it" (*CW,* 1:185; see also 2:390, 4:59).[11] The third standard proposed by Vivekananda has to do with the integrity of the individual who claims to be inspired. Such a person should be seen to be perfectly unselfish, not motivated by any desire for fame or material gain, and the content of the experience should be for the good of all. It is Vivekananda's view that, although the state of superconsciousness is attained by few, it is possible for all.

Samādhi *as a Method of Concentration*

As a means of knowing the self, *samādhi* is usually presented by Vivekananda as a method of concentration or meditation. This is again clearly associated with his concern to present *rājayoga* as a scientific method of gaining *brahmajñāna.*

To do this, Vivekananda speaks in universal terms about the acquisition of different kinds of knowledge. The process of acquiring knowledge, he contends, begins with the gathering of facts through observation. On the basis of these facts, we then generalize and deduce conclusions (*CW,* 1:129). Vivekananda emphasizes observation or concentration as the primary and paramount act in the operation of acquiring any knowledge. In the physical sciences, it is a question of concentrating the mind on external phenomena: "There is only one method by which to attain this knowledge, that which is called concentration. The chemist in his laboratory concentrates all the energies of his mind into one focus, and throws them upon the materials he is analyzing, and so finds out their secrets. The astronomer concentrates all the energies of his mind and projects them through his telescope upon the skies; and the stars, the sun, and the moon, give up their secrets to him" (*CW,* 1:130; see also 2:390–391, 5:299).[12]

No real science, continues Vivekananda, is possible without this power of concentration, and it is similarly presented by him as the key to the knowledge of the essential nature of the human being. In this case, however, the observation is internal: "The power of the mind should be concentrated and turned back upon itself, and as the darkest places reveal their secrets before the penetrating rays of the sun, so will this concentrated mind penetrate its own innermost secrets. Thus will we come to the basis of belief, the real genuine religion. We will perceive for ourselves whether we have souls, whether life is of five minutes or of eternity, whether there is a God in the universe or none. It will be all revealed to us" (*CW,* 1:131). Internal observation, admits Vivekananda, is not as easily attained as the observation of external nature in science, but he sees in *rājayoga* a method of developing this capacity.[13] The common quality, identified by Vivekananda, of deriving knowledge through observation is one of the principal arguments used by him in seeking to show *rājayoga* to be scientific. Because it derives its facts simply by observing, says Vivekananda, there is no necessity for reliance on faith or blind belief (*CW,* 1:130–131, 135).

The uniqueness and chief characteristic of *rājayoga* as a method of procuring knowledge through observation is that the object of study as well as the instrument is the mind (*CW,* 1:129, 131). It is the study of the contents of the mind that reveals to us our true natures. Sometimes, without distinguishing between mind and soul, Vivekananda speaks of the necessity for analyzing or anatomizing, by observation, the nature of the soul. Through this method alone, he attests, does one discover its immortality and omnipresence (*CW,* 2:163, 413).[14]

Vivekananda's conception of *rājayoga* as a mode of acquiring knowledge through concentration of the mind has to be seen in the context of his repeated assertion that all knowledge, secular or spiritual, is within. No knowledge, he contests, ever comes from outside. Using the terms *mind* and *soul* interchangeably, he describes both as repositories of infinite knowledge (*CW,* 1:28, 3:130, 2:339–340). Past, present, and future knowledge, he says, is inherent in the human being and preexisting through eternity. The entire process of knowing, according to Vivekananda, is more accurately described as one of discovery or unveiling, for knowledge is never really created: "We say Newton discovered gravitation. Was it sitting anywhere in a corner waiting for him? It was in his own mind; the time came and he found it out. All knowledge that the world has ever received comes from the mind; the infinite library of the universe is in your own mind" (*CW,* 1:28).

Vivekananda describes the external world as simply the suggestion or stimulus that drives one to study the contents of one's own mind.

He affirms that knowledge is never to be found in insentient matter. Vivekananda, however, still justifies the necessity for the spiritual teacher by proposing a similar argument. While never compromising his stand that every kind of knowledge is inherent, he contends that this inborn knowledge can be called out or made manifest only by another knowledge: "Dead, insentient matter never calls out knowledge; it is the action of knowledge that brings out knowledge. Knowing beings must be with us to call forth what is in us, so that these teachers were always necessary. The world was never without them, and no knowledge can come without them" (*CW,* 1:216-217). In all these discussions, his emphasis is on the teacher within who really teaches and without whom all teachers are useless. Vivekananda claims the support of the Bhagavadgītā for this view and speaks of the imperative for getting the knowledge contained in the Upaniṣads from within oneself (*CW,* 1:439; see also 7:71).[15] In fact, Vivekananda presents this argument about the innate nature of all knowledge as a doctrine of Vedānta, and describes all spiritual disciplines, including *karmayoga, bhaktiyoga* and *jñānayoga,* as being meant only for its awakening (*CW,* 4:431-432, 5:366).

Through *samādhi,* contends Vivekananda, is this intrinsic knowledge directly gained. He goes to the extent of claiming that *samādhi* is the means of spiritual knowledge in every religious tradition. In all cases, according to Vivekananda, where religious teachers claimed to have received knowledge "from beyond," the source has always been within themselves. Knowledge is often described as coming from the outside because individuals can stumble on the *samādhi* state without understanding its nature (*CW,* 1:183-184). The accidental discovery of *samādhi,* and its interpretation according to different levels of belief and education, is Vivekananda's explanation for the quaint mixture of truth and superstition in religion (*CW,* 1:184).[16]

Samādhi *as the Death of the Mind and the Absence of Duality*

So far in this study of Vivekananda's description of the nature of *samādhi* as a source of knowledge, the impression is that he identifies the state with a particular level of mental activity. Even in what he defines as the superconscious condition, the mind still appears to be operative. This description, however, seems to be modified, if not contradicted, by several passages in which he repeatedly affirms that *samādhi* is consequent on the death of the mind and that it is characterized by a total absence of all mental functions. There is a constant tension in Vivekananda's writings between his portrayal of *samādhi* as a state in which the mind still obtains and one in which it ceases to exist.

Vivekananda describes the goal of *rājayoga* as the total suppression of all thought forms in the mind. He speaks of the necessity to curb each thought as it enters into the mind, making the mind a vacuum (*CW,* 1:188, 212–213). A disciple is advised by him to "kill the mind" (*CW,* 7:196). He repeatedly contends that the knowledge of the *ātman* naturally and spontaneously follows the extinction of the mind. In fact, he presents *ātmajñāna* as being dependent on this extinction:

> Yoga is the science by which we stop *citta* from assuming, or becoming transformed into, several faculties. As the reflection of the moon on the sea is broken or blurred by the waves, so is the reflection of the *ātman,* the true self, broken by the mental waves. Only when the sea is stilled to mirror-like calmness can the reflection of the moon be seen, and only when the "mind-stuff," the *citta* is controlled to absolute calmness is the self to be recognized.
>
> The mind has to be divested of all modifications *(vṛttis)* and reconverted into a transparent lake, so that there remains not a single wave of modification in it. Then will *brahman* manifest itself. (*CW,* 8:40, 7:195)[17]

There are several occasions on which Vivekananda enthusiastically professed that even a momentary cessation of the mind leads to the full knowledge of the self.[18]

There are not many descriptions in Vivekananda's writings of the actual state of *samādhi.* He describes it as being "sensationless" and characterized by the cessation of all mental modifications (*CW,* 7:140, 8:36). All duality disappears and the knower and known become one (*CW,* 5:336, 6:89, 7:196). We are afforded, however, two personal accounts of the *samādhi* state by Vivekananda, both strikingly similar. On the basis of Vivekananda's own discussions, we can consider the first account, where even his ego sense disappeared, to be truer to the *samādhi* ideal. The confession of his inability to recollect anything in the absence of his ego consciousness is significant: "One day in the temple-garden at Dakshineswar Shri Ramakrishna touched me over the heart, and first of all I began to see that the houses —rooms, doors, windows, verandahs—the trees, the sun, the moon —all were flying off, shattering to pieces as it were—reduced to atoms and molecules—and ultimately became merged in the *ākāśa.* Gradually again, the *ākāśa* also vanished, and after that, my consciousness of the ego with it; what happened next I do not recollect" (*CW,* 5:392).[19]

Samādhi *as Direct Perception or Objective Knowledge*

The analogy almost invariably used by Vivekananda to describe the gain of ultimate knowledge in *samādhi* is *pratyakṣa* (direct perception). He argues throughout for the possibility of a direct perception of religious truths. He fervently asserts that this alone can be convincing and satisfactory proof of the verity of religious claims.[20] This direct perception is always particularly distinguished by him from intellectual assent or dissent and belief in doctrine. He derides the latter kind of religious commitment, classifying it as not being different from atheism. The goal is always affirmed to be direct perception, which alone constitutes real knowledge. This perception is, of course, not described by him to be the same as ordinary sense perception. He is clear that normal sense perception cannot apprehend religious truth. What is required is superconscious or "superfine" perception. This similarity lies in what he sees as the immediate verification that perception of both kinds affords:

> What is the proof of God? Direct perception *pratyakṣa.* The proof of this wall is that I perceive it. God has been perceived that way by thousands before, and will be perceived by all who want to perceive Him. But this perception is no sense-perception at all; it is supersensuous, superconscious, and all this training is needed to take us beyond the senses.
>
> Facts have to be perceived, and we have to perceive religion to demonstrate it to ourselves. We have to sense God to be convinced that there is a God. We must sense the facts of religion to know that they are facts. Nothing else, and no amount of reasoning, but our own perception can make these things real to us, can make my belief firm as a rock. That is my idea, and that is the Indian idea.
>
> Religion is based upon sense contact, upon seeing, the only basis of knowledge. What comes in contact with the superconscious mind is fact. *Āptas* are those who have "sensed" religion. (*CW,* 1:415, 4:167, 7:64; see also 4:34)[21]

The notion of realization, which we have noted to be a prominent feature of Vivekananda's thought, is equivalent to this direct perception. He makes the proof of the very existence of the *ātman* dependent on perception (*CW,* 5:318). The possibility of coming into direct contact with the facts of religion is seen by him as putting the basis of verifying religious truth on the same level with science (*CW,* 8:233). This direct encounter occurs in the state of *samādhi:* "The highest grade of *samādhi* is when we see the real thing, when we see the material out of which the whole of these grades of beings are composed, and that one lump of clay being known, we know all the clay in the universe" (*CW,* 1:159). He makes the same point with reference to the movement of the *kuṇḍalinī:* "It is supersensuous perception. And when it reaches the metropolis of all sensations, the brain, the whole brain, as it were, reacts, and the result is a blaze of illumination, the perception of the self" (*CW,* 1:164). The image of a flash or "blaze of illumination" is quite frequently employed by Vivekananda to describe the gain of knowledge in *samādhi.* He describes inspiration as the process of gaining knowledge "by flashes" (*CW,* 4:58). Purification and preparation through Yoga and meditation make clearer the "flashes or realization" (*CW,* 8:12). The conception of monism "flashes" into the human soul, and on one occasion he describes as "the full blaze of light" the moment in which "this little self is seen to have become one with the Infinite" (*CW,* 3:100; see also 3:282, 6:97, 7:92).

Although it has been alluded to in this discussion, it is important specifically to emphasize the self-valid status that Vivekananda ascribes to knowledge gained through this process of direct perception. His disdain for dogma, doctrine, theory, books, and intellectual assent and dissent is directly related to this view of the self-valid nature of knowledge gained through realization. Throughout his writings, he upholds the supreme value of realization in contrast with all these:

> Talking is one thing, and realizing is another. Philosophies, and doctrines, and arguments, and books, and theories, and churches, and sects, and all these things are good in their own way; but when that realization comes, these things drop away. For instance, maps are good, but when you see the country itself, and look again at the maps, what a great difference you find! So those that have realized truth do not require the ratiocinations of logic and all other gymnastics of the intellect to make them understand the truth; it is to them the life of their lives, concretized, made more tangible. (*CW,* 2:284)[22]

He affirms that the superconscious state never makes an error and that inspiration requires no external test but is immediately recognized (*CW,* 7:60, 8:45). It is only through this kind of experience that all doubts finally vanish. What is intellectually grasped, he declares, may be dislodged, but what is directly perceived can never be supplanted (*CW,* 1:128, 2:165, 4:128, 7:77). He has stated positively on many occasions that only through realization can there be any reality in religious life or any genuine moral values.

A Critical Overview of Rājayoga *as a Means to* Brahmajñāna

My attempt to bring together the various dimensions of Vivekananda's conception of *rājayoga* as a means to the direct knowledge of *brahman* highlights certain problematic and unresolved aspects of his argument. Many of these are closely connected to crucial contrasts with Śaṅkara's understanding of the nature of *brahmajñāna* and the means of its attainment. It is on these issues I now focus discussion.

In chapter 3, we considered some of the reasons behind Vivekananda's proposal of distinct direct paths to *mokṣa.* We saw his argument that the *yogas* of *karma, bhakti,* and *jñāna* were each independently capable of leading to freedom. We encountered difficulties, however, in reconciling the details of these methods with the nature of *mokṣa* as understood in Advaita. Vivekananda's rationale for *rājayoga* also appears to undermine this central argument of his. Here, he professes that direct perception is the only acceptable way of ascertaining religious truth and that this is attained solely through *samādhi,* the culmination of the discipline of *rājaygoa.* We have seen that "all worship consciously or unconsciously leads to this end" and that *rājayoga* is "the science of religion, the rationale of worship, all prayers, forms, ceremonies and miracles." In the face of these paramount and exclusive claims for *rājayoga* as the means par excellence, what are we to make of the view that *karma, bhakti,* and *jñāna* lead directly to the desired end? Are we to understand now that these approaches are really only preparations for *rājayoga,* even as Śaṅkara argues for the relation between other methods and *jñāna?*

In his discussion of these paths, however, Vivekananda does not make any mention of the necessity for a subsequent undertaking of the disciplines of *rājayoga.* He presents them as self-sufficient means for the gain of *mokṣa.* If *samādhi* is the only valid source of religious knowledge, and if *karma, bhakti,* and *jñāna* are not to be understood as merely preparatory to *rājayoga,* then it would seem that we ought to comprehend these as also leading to *samādhi.* We have seen, however, Vivekananda's claims that the different steps of *rājayoga* are designed to lead the aspirant scientifically to the state of *samādhi.* He has also argued about the dangers of accidentally encountering this state without following the prescribed procedures of *rājayoga.* One is likely to be deranged, the source of knowledge will be misunderstood, and with knowledge will come superstition: "To get any reason out of the mass incongruity we call human life, we have to transcend our reason, but we must do it scientifically, slowly by regular practice, and we must cast off all superstition. We must take up the study of the superconscious state just as any other science" (*CW,* 1:184–185). If these dangers can be averted only by understanding and adopting the scheme of *rājayoga,* are they not present as real possibilities for the aspirant in *karma, bhakti,* and *jñāna,* where Vivekananda does not make *rājayoga* imperative? Will there not also be errors in knowledge and, therefore, nonattainment of *mokṣa?* Vivekananda's arguments for the independence and self-sufficiency of these other means seem now to be called into question.

I have referred from time to time in this discussion to Vivekananda's attempts to equate the gain and verification of knowledge through *rājayoga* with the methods employed in science. The grounds, however, on which he draws his parallels leave many questions unanswered.[23] Vivekananda's analogy with science is basically an analogy between religious experience and sense perception. The assumption is that both are verifiable in the same way. Almost all his examples, as well as his terminology, are drawn from the world of sense perception. There appear, however, to be very important differences between sensory experience and religious experience. Sense perception is not as simple as Vivekananda assumes, and it is certainly not always self-validating. The possibilities of sense illusion and deception are very well accepted. Even though these may not be readily apparent, there are definite criteria that are employed in validating sense experience. It might be argued that definite criteria are also available for verifying religious experience. But the problem here is reaching agreement on those criteria. In the case of sense perception, the criteria are widely accepted, but the criteria for evaluating religious experience in any particular community of shared beliefs may not be considered reliable in a community with different traditions.

In drawing the analogy between sense experience and religious experience, Vivekananda's comparison usually rests on the sense of sight alone. The fact, for example, that there are five distinct organs operating in a combined way, reinforcing and correcting each other, is not taken into account. In the case of his common example of the wall, sight could be reinforced by touch and sound. The absence of anything to compare with this in religious experience must be taken into account whenever a parallel is drawn with sense perception. Agreement within a religious community on the criteria to be used in evaluating spiritual experience may be valid and genuine. There is always, however, the possibility that such agreement may be the result of a lack of awareness of alternatives, the sharing of erroneous beliefs, or the use of the same techniques to produce similar results.[24] We have seen Vivekananda's acceptance of the possibility that instinct could be mistaken for the superconscious.

As I have noted earlier, Vivekananda suggests three criteria by which we could distinguish the *samādhi* experience from anything involving the unconscious or instinct. Out of *samādhi,* says Vivekananda, one emerges with wisdom. This, however, does not help us very much unless there is some prior agreement on what constitutes wisdom. It is these very truth claims that need to be evaluated. If we try to apply his second criterion that the experience must be in accord with reason, other problems emerge. What are the agreed-on forms or premises of reason to be applied? Where are these to be derived from? How can reason be employed in validating claims to which reason has no direct access and is incapable of apprehending? If the validity of the experience is dependent on its conformity to reason, providing that such standards of reasoning could be agreed on, this would seem to elevate reason to a status above that of the experience. It would also challenge Vivekananda's argument about the self-valid nature of the experience and its infallibility.

In seeking to present *rājayoga* as conforming to the methods of science, Vivekananda is constrained to modify considerably, if not misrepresent, the scientific process of gaining knowledge. He uses the word *experience* in the most general sense possible, when he speaks of all knowledge as being derived from experience. He does not specify the uniqueness and complexity of the "experience" through which knowledge is gained and corroborated in the physical sciences. The claims of science are not always as easily verified in the experiences of ordinary people as Vivekananda suggests. In the same way, Vivekananda speaks of all religious traditions as being founded on "experience," without taking into account the great diversity among and within religious traditions about their origins and the nature of their authoritative sources. But perhaps the most significant point about his loose use of the word *experience* is the fact that, with respect to *samādhi,* he is making claims for a singular and unique experience, one totally unlike any other. He speaks generally about science and all other religious traditions as being founded on experience and, ignoring all diversity and differences, slips into making assertions about the distinctive experience of *samādhi.* Another very clear example of Vivekananda's oversimplification of the methodology of science in order to underline parallels with *rājayoga* is his highlighting of observation or concentration as the only formula for gaining knowledge. As important as this quality of mind is in most fields of endeavor, one cannot assert that the insights gained by the scientist in the laboratory are simply the results of concentration or that the latter is the chief element of the scientist's methodology.

Vivekananda's analogy between *samādhi* and sense experience provokes another crucial question. We have seen that he speaks repeatedly about the necessity for a direct perception of the *ātman* if its very existence is to be certified beyond any doubt. Perception, however, whether ordinary or supersensuous, involves knowledge gained through objectification. It also implies a duality between the knower and the known. In Advaita, the definition of the *ātman* as the ultimate and only knower, incapable of being objectified by any faculty, is a fundamental tenet.[25] There is no other knower for whom the *ātman* can become an object. To suggest that the *ātman* must be known through a form of objective perception is to posit the existence of some other knower. The objectification of the *ātman* by another knowing entity would also signify its limitation, for only a delimited thing can be objectified. Thus, a suggestion about acquiring knowledge of the *ātman* through any kind of perception appears to deny its very nature. Vivekananda himself argues this position very lucidly.

> You cannot by any possibility say you know Him; it would be degrading Him. You cannot get out of yourself, so you cannot know Him. Knowledge is objectification. For instance, in memory you are objectifying many things, projecting them out of yourself. All memory, all things which I have seen and which I know are in my mind. The pictures, the impressions of all these things, are in my mind, and when I would try to think of them, to know them, the first act of knowledge would be to project them outside. This cannot be done with God, because He is the essence of our souls; we cannot project Him outside ourselves. . . . He is one with us; and that which is one with us is neither knowable nor unknowable, as our Self. You cannot know your own Self; you cannot move it out and make it an object to look at, because you *are* that and you cannot separate yourself from it. Neither is it unknowable, for what is better known than yourself? It is really the center of our knowledge. In exactly the same sense, God is neither unknowable nor known, but infinitely higher than both; for He is our real Self. (*CW,* 2:133–134; see also 3:422)

Vivekananda's proposal, through *rājayoga,* of the necessity and possibility of *ātmajñāna* by a direct perception of the existence and nature of the *ātman* cannot be reconciled with the fundamental Advaita position that he unequivocally formulates in the passage quoted above. It is difficult to make sense of his call for analyzing or anatomizing, by observation, the nature of the *ātman.* I have stated before that he draws a parallel between *rājayoga* and the method of science by asserting that both depend on observation or concentration. In the case of *rājayoga,* the observation is supposed to be internal. I fail to see, however, how full knowledge of the *ātman* can be gained by any kind of observation, internal or external. As awareness *(cit),* it is the very content and basis of the observer and therefore not available as an object of observation. If, as Vivekananda also suggests, the content of the mind is the object of observation in *rājayoga,* it is not at all clear how this can afford us knowledge of the self, the very witness of all mental processes. We gain knowledge through observation only when an object is available for scrutiny.

Vivekananda's concern for positing the possibility of a direct perception of religious truth is undoubtedly motivated by what he thinks to be the drawbacks of other arguments and approaches. The basis of his attempt to do this involves the creation of a sharp dichotomy between experience and doctrine, accepting, in doing so, the possibility of a pure, uninterpreted experience. We have already noted, from many different standpoints, his belittling of everything that he considers to be doctrine and dogma. This attitude is directly related to the fact that he presupposes the existence of a pure self-interpretative experience. Recent studies of mysticism and religious experience have brought into sharp focus the flaws of this assumption and highlighted the complexity of the interplay between experience and doctrinal interpretation.[26]

In Vivekananda's view, a clear experience is followed later by the recording, in words, of its implications and significance. This is how he conceives, for example, the origin of the Vedas.[27] The assumption is that having an experience is distinct from giving it expression in language. In reality, however, no such dichotomy can be easily demonstrated, for language and experience are inseparable. Language does not merely provide labels for describing but, in fact, makes experience possible. It broadens the range of experience. Simply to describe an experience as "religious" involves a tremendous interpretative process. Anyone, for example, unfamiliar with the language, imagery, or theology of a religion cannot describe herself as having a "religious" experience. The simplest interpretation of experience in religious terms takes for granted the complex doctrinal claims with which it is heavily laden. In fact, it would seem that an "uninterpreted experience" is a contradiction in terms. An experience always belongs to someone who is never free from a belief system of some kind. Experience, therefore, seems to imply interpretation and never occurs in a vacuum. Even in the case of science, from which Vivekananda draws most of his analogies, an uninterpreted experience is not usually a means of objective knowledge. It is only when the "simple" experiences of the physical world are seen in wider theoretical frameworks that meaningful conclusions are drawn. It seems reasonable to suggest that experience, of itself, is not knowledge but that it puts one in a position where knowledge can be increased.

There are many passages in Vivekananda's own writings that suggest a far more dynamic and intricate interplay between experience and doctrine than the simple one for which he argues in *rājayoga*. In considering his treatment of *karmayoga,* we noted that, in spite of his claim that this method required no belief in doctrine, his entire discussion was suffused with Advaita postulates and premises. Vivekananda also makes the same claim for the method of *rājayoga* as part of his plea for its scientific character. His writings on *rājayoga,* however, are permeated particularly with doctrinal postulates of the Sāṅkhya school. The entire system of discipline is unfolded with a specific view of the nature of the ultimate goal of the human being: "The aim, the end, the goal, of all this training is liberation of the soul. Absolute control of nature, and nothing short of it, must be the goal. We must be the masters, and not the slaves of nature; neither body nor mind must be our master, nor must we forget that the body is mine, and not I the body's" (*CW,* 1:140).

Very important questions are raised by the fact that Vivekananda turns to the *rājayoga* system of Patañjali to find the veridical experience on which he places all his emphasis. The Patañjali's system derives its interpretative framework almost entirely from Sāṅkhya, and both exhibit fundamental doctrinal differences with Advaita. Vivekananda was not unaware of these differences (*CW,* 1:251, 253, 361; 2:454–462).[28] The culminating experience of *samādhi* carries for the follower of Patañjali totally different doctrinal implications from what Vivekananda proposes. It is strange—and significant—that the implications of this are not considered by Vivekananda at those points in his discussion of *rājayoga* where he deals with matters of Sāṅkhya doctrine. If different conclusions can be inferred from an identical experience, this would seem to suggest that the experience is not self-interpretative. The meaning of the experience would depend on the prior doctrinal stand of the aspirant. Vivekananda clearly seems to think that the experiences of mystics in all religious traditions are the same (*CW,* 6:81, 7:43). What their radical differences tell us about the self-valid nature of the experience is not fully explored by him. His suggestion, discussed earlier, that the nature of *samādhi* is easily misunderstood by someone not properly trained in its method and meaning only reinforces the argument that the experience is not self-explanatory.

Other questions about the nature of *samādhi* as a self-valid source of knowledge are raised by Vivekananda's own descriptions of the experience. I have already referred to the tension between his portrayal of *samādhi* as a state in which the mind is actively existent, even if at a higher level, and one in which it ceases to exist. Arguing from Vivekananda's own standpoint, we are obliged to accept that the latter description is more accurate if *samādhi* is to be conceived as a state wherein one is identical with the nondual reality of the universe. The difficulty, however, is that a state in which the differences between the knower, the object known, and the process of knowing are transcended cannot be described as involving any kind of perception. Even the word *experience,* suggesting duality, is an inappropriate description. If knowledge is an activity and affirmation of the mind, how can such a state be described as one involving the gain of knowledge? Who is there to perceive, to know anything, to be enlightened? As the Bṛhadāraṇyaka Upaniṣad (2.4.14) defines the nondual *ātman:*

> Because when there is duality, as it were, then one smells something, one sees something, one hears something, one thinks something, one knows something. [But] when to the knower of *brahman* everything has become the Self, then what should one smell and through what, what should one see and through what, what should one hear and through what, what should one speak and through what, what should one think and through what, what should one know, and through what? Through what should one know That owing to which all this is known—through what, O Maitreyī, should one know the Knower?

Chāndogya Upaniṣad (7.24.1) offers a similar definition: "Wherein one sees nothing else, hears nothing else and understands nothing else, —that is the *Infinite;* wherein one sees something else, hears something else, and understands something else,—that is *Finite.*" If there is any possibility of a return from the state of *samādhi,* there is also the difficulty of explaining how the conscious mind can make any affirmation or inferences about an experience that involved its total transcendence. In this context, Vivekananda's inability to recall much of his own experience is perhaps significant.

Chapter 5

VIVEKANANDA AND ŚAṄKARA

In chapter 4, I outlined the method proposed by Vivekananda for the attainment of *anubhava* and critically evaluated his arguments for this experience as an infallible source of liberating knowledge. His descriptions of *anubhava* and the epistemological status that he grants to it present, as we have seen, many difficulties.

Throughout my discussion, I have drawn attention to areas of crucial difference between Vivekananda and Śaṅkara. My aim in the present chapter is to draw together and highlight these contrasts. I begin, however, with a brief outline of Śaṅkara's understanding and justification of the *śruti* as the authoritative means of knowledge for *brahman*. With the help of this outline, the scope and nature of the differences between Vivekananda and Śaṅkara will be made clearer.[1]

The Vedas as a Source of Valid Knowledge in Śaṅkara

Śaṅkara's general justification for a special means of knowledge like the Vedas is that it provides knowledge of those things that cannot be known through any other sources of knowledge. The two categories of knowledge, according to Śaṅkara, attained exclusively through the Vedas are *dharma* and *brahman*. The knowledge of *dharma* (merit) and *adharma* (demerit) is derived solely from the Vedas since these are supersensual truths that can be neither perceived nor inferred. In addition, claims Śaṅkara, *dharma* and *adharma* vary with time and place, and these changing applications cannot be known except through the Vedas.

The knowledge of *dharma* is gained from the first sections of the

Vedas, which deal with ritual action *(karmakāṇḍa)*. The final sections of the Vedas, referred to variously as the *jñānakāṇḍa,* the Vedāntavākyas, or the Upaniṣads, reveal the nature of *brahman.*

For Śaṅkara, the *śruti* is the valid means of knowing *brahman* because, by the very nature of *brahman,* it is the logical means. *Brahman* cannot be known through a sense organ since it has no characteristics like sound, touch, form, smell, or taste through which it can be apprehended. It also cannot be objectified. As awareness, it illumines all things and has as its object the entire universe, including the mind, the body, and the senses. *Brahman,* the subject and knower of everything, can never itself be objectified for scrutiny and analysis. If sense perception cannot give us knowledge of *brahman,* other ways of knowing, like inference, that depend on information from the senses cannot inform us conclusively about *brahman.*

Śaṅkara buttresses his argument that the nature of *brahman* renders its knowledge impossible through any means but the words of the *śruti* with the claim that this knowledge is an adequate solution for the basic human problem of ignorance *(avidyā).* In Śaṅkara's view, *śruti* is not necessary to produce *brahman* or to reveal its existence. As awareness, the content and basis of the "I" or ego notion, *brahman* is self-revealed and always manifest (BS = B 1.1.1, p. 11). The basic problem is the erroneous identification of *brahman* with the limited qualities of the body, mind, and senses. The task of the *śruti,* therefore, is not the production or revelation of an unknown entity but the imparting of correct knowledge about a limitless, but misunderstood, self. Where the problem is one of ignorance, argues Śaṅkara, the knowledge gained by proper inquiry into the words of the *śruti* can be an adequate solution.

For Śaṅkara, action *(karman)* is a right and appropriate solution where the problem involved is the accomplishment of something unaccomplished. Knowledge *(jñāna)* is adequate where the problem is one of ignorance about an already attained entity, and it is clear that Śaṅkara conceives the attainment of *brahman* to be of this kind.

Śaṅkara's arguments for the appropriateness and adequacy of the *śruti* as a source of valid knowledge about *brahman* are underlined by his emphasis on the fruitfulness of this knowledge. He reiterates the immediate results of the knowledge derived from the sentences of the Upaniṣads. Even as the comprehension of the sentence "This is a rope, not a snake" can at once eliminate the fear of someone who mistakenly takes a rope for a snake, the knowledge gained from the sentences of the *śruti* directly and immediately removes the ignorance, grief, and fear associated with erroneously taking oneself to be the finite body and mind. The fruitfulness of this knowledge is apparent in the transformed life of one who appreciates the nature of the self.

It is Śaṅkara's repeated contention that, for the qualified aspirant, equipped with *sādhana-catuṣṭaya, mokṣa,* the fruit of *śruti*-derived knowledge, is simultaneous with the gain of knowledge. No intervening action between the two is necessary (BS = B 1.1.4, p. 28). Clearly, Śaṅkara does not understand the *śruti* as according only a provisional or hypothetical knowledge awaiting confirmation, as does Vivekananda. In fact, from the standpoint of Śaṅkara, it is not even accurate to say that *mokṣa* is the effect of knowledge. *Mokṣa,* being identical with *brahman,* is always accomplished and eternal. The knowledge revealed in the *śruti* enables us to appreciate the liberated self.

Śruti sentences, in Śaṅkara's view, fulfill their purpose in being properly understood. In this way, they are different in intent from sentences in the first sections of the Vedas, where certain actions are necessary above and beyond understanding for bringing about previously nonexistent results. Even as in our everyday world a form is revealed as soon as it is properly illumined in light, similarly *avidyā* and its effects are negated through the proper comprehension of the word of the *śruti.* In Śaṅkara's understanding, the relation obtaining between *brahman* and *śruti* is one between an existent but misunderstood reality and the appropriate means for knowing it. It is not the creation or attainment of anything new but the right knowledge of something always there.

The Distinction between the Karmakāṇḍa *and the* Jñānakāṇḍa

In the matter of Vedic exegesis, we can draw an important contrast between Śaṅkara and Vivekananda. Śaṅkara sees the subject matter of the Vedas as divided into two broad sections. The first or the ritual section *(karmakāṇḍa)* informs us of approved means for attaining desirable but yet unaccomplished ends. The second or knowledge section *(jñānakāṇḍa)* comprises the Upaniṣads and informs us of the nature of absolute reality *(brahman).* These two sections are clearly distinguishable, according to Śaṅkara, in four ways:[2]

1. *Viṣaya* (subject matter). *Karmakāṇḍa* is concerned with the revelation of *dharma,* while the *jñānakāṇḍa* has *brahman* for its subject.
2. *Adhikārī* (aspirant). The aspirant pursuing the goals of the *karmakāṇḍa* is one who has not yet grown to understand the defects of any result attained by *karma.* The aspirant of the *jñānakāṇḍa* has appre-

ciated the limitations of *karma*-accomplished ends and seeks a limitless gain.[3]

3. *Phala* (result). The *karmakāṇḍa* has prosperity and worldly and heavenly enjoyment as its aim. The result of the *jñānakāṇḍa* is *mokṣa*.

4. *Sambandha* (connection). The knowledge that is revealed in the *karmakāṇḍa* informs us of an end that is not yet in existence. It can be realized only by an appropriate action. Knowledge is not an end in itself. The *jñānakāṇḍa,* on the other hand, reveals an already existent *brahman.* Knowledge of *brahman* is an end in itself. The connection here is between a revealed object and a means of revelation. *Jñānakāṇḍa* fulfills itself in its knowledge-dispensing role, while the *karmakāṇḍa* drives one to action.

Vivekananda adopts the same two divisions (namely, *karmakāṇḍa* and *jñānakāṇḍa*) and distinguishes them in several ways (*CW,* 1:450–454). He identifies the ideal of the *karmakāṇḍa* as the attainment of enjoyment here and in the hereafter. The goal is not complete freedom from *karma.* Vivekananda enumerates four important differences between both sections:

1. The Upaniṣads posit a belief in God and God's unity.
2. Although the Upaniṣads accept the operation of the law of *karma* and human bondage to it, they do not accept that it is absolutely inescapable and suggest a way out.
3. The Upaniṣads condemn rituals and sacrifices, particularly those involving the slaying of animals, and point out the limitations of what can be achieved through sacrifices. The gains are short lived.
4. Finally, the Upaniṣads enjoin renunciation rather than enjoyment.

While it is clear that the differences pointed out by Vivekananda coincide with those indentified by Śaṅkara on the points of aspirant, subject matter, and fruit or result, Vivekananda never mentions the difference of connection *(sambandha)* to which Śaṅkara repeatedly alludes. This appears to me to be an extremely significant omission. Śaṅkara sees the *karmakāṇḍa* as providing us with knowledge about ends that are not yet in existence. These must be brought into being by some appropriate action. In other words, knowledge is not an end in itself. The knowledge revealed in the *jñānakāṇḍa,* however, is centered in an already existent *brahman.* Knowledge, here, is an end in itself, and the connection is between a revealed entity and the appropriate means of knowing *(pramāṇa).*

I am suggesting that this is an extremely important point of divergence, for, along with everything discussed in the earlier chapters, it demonstrates that Vivekananda does not see the knowledge that is gained by inquiry into the words and sentences of the Upaniṣads as an end in itself. We have noted his description of these as theoretical or secondhand religion and his call for their claims to be verified by a form of direct perception.

The Self-Sufficiency and Validity of Upaniṣadic Knowledge

For Śaṅkara, the necessity of the Vedas as a valid source of knowledge about *brahman* is explained by the inapplicability of all other means of knowing. The senses, for example, are naturally capable of grasping and revealing their special objects. Sound, sensation, form, taste, and scent are their respective spheres of functioning. *Brahman,* however, has neither sound, touch, form, taste, nor smell. It is without qualities *(nirguṇa)* and, therefore, outside the domain of the senses (BS = B 1.1.2, p. 17, and 1.1.4, p. 22). A *brahman* that is known through the senses would, in any case, be a contradiction since to become an object of sense-knowledge it must be finite and *brahman* is limitless. It is impossible for *brahman,* the unchanging subject of all sense knowledge, to be made an object of the senses or mind. If perception is thus limited, so are all the other means of knowledge, dependent as they are on perception for their data. The Vedas, then, for Śaṅkara, are the valid source for our knowledge of *brahman* since they generate immediate and fruitful knowledge. This capacity is intrinsic and self-evident and does not depend on inferential verification (Ch.U. = B 6.8.7, p. 367).

From Śaṅkara's position, the Vedas, in fact, would not fulfill the criterion of being a source of valid knowledge *(pramāṇa)* unless they were capable of producing a unique and self-valid knowledge. Any defect-free *pramāṇa* can independently generate knowledge, and this knowledge does not have to be authenticated by another *pramāṇa.* Such knowledge is not of a provisional nature, awaiting confirmation. As a source of valid knowledge in the forms of words *(śabda-pramāṇa),* the Vedas, therefore, for Śaṅkara, can generate knowledge of *brahman* independent of any other means. For our knowledge of *brahman,* according to Śaṅkara, nothing beyond the words and sentences of the Upaniṣads is necessary. Actions may facilitate the gain of knowledge from the texts but do not themselves constitute direct sources of liberating knowledge.

Scrutiny of Vivekananda's statements on the Vedas and scriptural revelation, in general, reveals a point of view that is unqualifiedly opposed to Śaṅkara's position. We have examined several analogies used by Vivekananda (e.g., map, almanac), all of which illustrate the contents of the Vedas as a poor substitute. He has argued that the assertions of the Vedas are to be considered only provisionally true and that they become valid knowledge only when verified by direct apprehension. His distinction between knowledge afforded by the *śruti* and realization reinforces this argument, and so does his emphasis on the necessity of going beyond the *śruti.* He speaks, as we have seen, of the scriptures as "theoretical religion" and as one of the nonessential aspects of religion. The Vedas, he contends, cannot give us knowledge of the *ātman.*

All this stands in unmistakable and remarkable contrast to Śaṅkara's view of the self-valid status of scriptural knowledge and his related arguments. Vivekananda sees the Vedānta as a method for attaining superconscious perception rather than as a *pramāṇa,* and it is revealing that nowhere in his writings does one find any detailed consideration of the concept of *pramāṇa.* In fact, the term itself was never employed directly by him, except on the one occasion of his commentary on the Yoga-sūtras of Patañjali, to which I have referred.

The Transcending of the Vedas

Like Vivekananda, Śaṅkara also speaks of an ultimate transcending of the Vedas, but in an entirely different sense and context. For Śaṅkara, the Vedas are transcended in the sense that, after producing valid knowledge of *brahman,* they are no longer necessary as a *pramāṇa* for the one who has gained that knowledge. Directives to act or to refrain from action are relevant to one who is in search of appropriate means for gaining some desirable object or avoiding an undesirable one. Vedic injunctions appear superfluous to the knower of *brahman* who has no unfulfilled personal wants. The *śruti*'s tribute to the one who has attained her ideal is to liberate this person from dependence on scripture (Ai.U. = B, introduction, p. 8; see also BG = B 2.46, p. 69).

The fact that the knower of *brahman* transcends the necessity for the *śruti* does not in any way detract from its indispensability as a source of knowledge. The point is that, having successfully given rise to knowledge, a *pramāṇa* is no longer needed for that purpose. Its value is not thereby reduced, and that it is no longer needed does not suggest that this knowledge can be attained in some other fashion.

The Vedas are also transcended, for Śaṅkara, in the sense that, for the knower of *brahman,* their reality is only empirical. Śaṅkara ascribes to the Vedas the same empirical *(vyāvahārika)* level of reality as he does to the world, for he admits that the Vedas, like the world, are negated in the knowledge of the nondual *brahman* (BS = B 4.1.4,

p. 821). Śāṅkara nowhere speaks, like Vivekananda, of transcending the Vedas in the sense of pointing to an alternative and superior *pramāṇa*. This is a very important point of difference.

The Personal and Nonpersonal Authority of the Vedas

Like the Pūrva-Mīmāṁsā tradition, Sankara admits that the Vedas are authorless *(apauruṣeya)*.[4] He understands authorlessness, however, to mean the revelation of the Vedas by God *(Īśvara)* in the same linguistic form at the beginning of each cycle of creation. It is extremely important to note, however, that Śaṅkara does not seek to establish the authority of the Vedas from the fact of God's omniscience. The reason is that he finds it impossible to prove the existence of God by any kind of independent reasoning. In the absence of such a proof, all arguments become helplessly circular, "omniscience being proved from the authority of the scriptures and the [authority of the] scriptures being proved from the knowledge of the omniscience of the author" (BS = B 2.2.38, p. 436).

Vivekananda, on the other hand, advances a personal authoritative basis for the Vedas derived from the competence and reliability of the *āptas*. The authority of scripture is derived from the personal authority of the *āpta*. These *āptas* are the authors of the sacred scriptures, and the latter are proof only because of this fact. *Śruti* was not authoritative, for Śaṅkara, because it embodied the experience and discoveries of the ṛṣis. Its uniqueness lay in the fact that its authority was not personal or derived.

With respect to the direct apprehension of religious truths by the *āptas,* Vivekananda does not suggest any role for God as revealer. His analogy is that of the scientific discovery of natural laws. Śaṅkara ascribes to God the role of revealing the Vedas. In Śaṅkara, the emphasis is on the *ṛṣis* receiving rather than discovering (BS = B 1.3.29, p. 217; see also 1.3.30, p. 219). Consistent with his scientific analogy, Vivekananda often defines the eternity of the Vedas as an eternity of natural spiritual laws, the existence of which is independent of their discovery. Śaṅkara, on the other hand, conceives of Vedic eternity in the sense of a fixed body of knowledge. This transmission is initiated in each creation cycle by God.

Alternative Ways to the Attainment of Mokṣa

Vivekananda proposed the methods of *karma-, bhakti-, jñāna-,* and *rājayoga* as direct and independent means to liberation. In relation to this claim, I have argued that, in the context of the Advaita definition of ignorance *(avidyā)* and the nature of bondage, Vivekananda's thesis leaves us unconvinced and with many unanswered questions. In his characterization of these methods, however, further contrasts with Śaṅkara are evident.

For Śaṅkara, the function of *karmayoga,* as of all other methods, techniques, and disciplines other than direct inquiry into the words of the Upaniṣads, is the development of the appropriate qualities of intellect, emotion, and will for this inquiry.[5] The disciplines themselves never replace the valid sources of knowledge and are not *pramāṇas.* These disciplines help engender mental purity *(citta-śuddhi).* While Vivekananda accepts that mental purity is the most important aim of *karmayoga,* he departs radically from Śaṅkara in claiming that this purity directly brings about self-knowledge. He does not mention any need for subsequent inquiry into the Upaniṣads.

This contrast was also obvious in Vivekananda's treatment of *sādhana catuṣṭaya.*[6] Whereas Śaṅkara argues for *sādhana catuṣṭaya* as a preparation for inquiry into the Upaniṣads, Vivekananda argues that the cultivation of these qualities is all that is required. Similarly, although the disciplines of *bhaktiyoga* are founded on dualistic presuppositions, they are supposed somehow to lead to nondualism. The movement from dualism to nondualism, however, is not argued by Vivekananda in convincing detail.

Vivekananda characterizes the path of *jñānayoga* as a way to *mokṣa* through the application of pure reason. Here also we found many contradictions, including his admission of the limitations of reason. Śaṅkara also admits the limitations of reason as an instrument for gaining conclusive knowledge of *brahman.* These limitations, however, are overcome by the revelations of the Vedas. For Vivekananda, on the other hand, the limitations of reason are overcome through a transcendental experience. This experience is supposed to provide the insights that, for Śaṅkara, come only from the Vedas.

Samādhi *as a Source of* Brahmajñāna

Significant points of contrast with Śaṅkara also emerge from Vivekananda's description of *rājayoga* as a path to *mokṣa.* The most obvious is, of course, Vivekananda's insistence on *samādhi* as the authoritative source of the knowledge of *brahman (brahmajñāna).* This is in radical contrast to Śaṅkara's entire justification of *śruti* as the only conceivable medium of this knowledge. Related to this fundamental disagreement over the source of *brahmajñāna* are other very interesting dissimilarities.

Along with Vivekananda's plea for *samādhi* as the only self-valid source of knowledge, one gets the impression that he conceives of *mokṣa* as obtaining only in that state:

> When a man reaches the superconscious state, all feeling of body melts away. Then alone does he become free and immortal.
>
> That is the goal—the superconscious. Then, when that state is reached, this very man becomes divine, becomes free. (*CW,* 6:125, 5:250)[7]

In fact, Vivekananda uses the word *liberation (mokṣa)* as synonymous with *samādhi* (*CW,* 6:456).[8] This state is attained, as we have seen, when the conscious mind is completely transcended. Vivekananda emphasizes that religion and spirituality do not belong to the field of the senses or the intellect; they belong to the supersensuous (*CW,* 6:132–133; see also 3:1, 72). With Vivekananda, the mind overcomes its inherent limitations to apprehend truth independently, by transcending itself or even dying. There is also another significant feature of his characterization of *mokṣa* that emerges from his discussion of *rājayoga*. This appears to be associated with his view of *mokṣa* as obtaining only in *samādhi*. Vivekananda mentions that the goal is the real separation of the self from the body and from all nature (*CW,* 1:160, 255; 4:226). It is also described as being attained only when the self achieves complete mastery over internal and external nature (*CW,* 1:133, 172, 257, 412). Such conclusions are clearly different from Śaṅkara's understanding of what constitutes *mokṣa* and seem more congenial in the Sāṅkhya-Yoga doctrinal context than in Advaita.[9]

There is no evidence in the commentaries of Śaṅkara to suggest that he conceived *brahmajñāna* as occurring only through a transcendence of the ordinary level of mental functioning. On the other hand, the overwhelming evidence of the manner in which he understands the problem of *avidyā* and its resolution through inquiry into the *śruti* indicates that he saw *brahmajñāna* as occurring only in and through the mind.[10] It is important to note that, for Śaṅkara, the *śruti* is not needed for revealing the existence of the self *(ātman)*. As awareness, the self is always evident and not completely unknown. *Śruti* is needed for correcting erroneous knowledge about the self. This is in contrast to Vivekananda, who sees the superconscious experience as necessary for establishing both the existence and the nature of the self.

The problem of ignorance, therefore, for Śaṅkara, is one of incomplete and erroneous knowledge of an ever available and manifesting *ātman,* arising out of the inability to distinguish it from the nonself. At the individual level, ignorance is a mode or modification *(vṛtti)* of the mind, where the problem of false knowledge lies and where alone it can be corrected. For this, another mental mode, truly coinciding with the entity to be known, has to be produced by an adequate source of knowledge. For Śaṅkara, the *śruti* is this source of knowledge. Although Śaṅkara shares with Vivekananda the view that the reasoning processes of the mind are independently incapable of arriving at a true knowledge of the *ātman,* he proposes that these limitations can be overcome by recourse to *śruti* as a source of valid knowledge. He nowhere advances that these limitations can be surmounted by the mind transcending itself or entering a higher state in the sense in which Vivekananda submits. Because reason is an important tool that we employ in understanding the meaning of the *śruti,* in removing, as far as possible, all doubts, and in dealing with contradictory views, it appears to have a much more positive and valued role in Śaṅkara with respect to the gain of *brahmajñāna.*[11] There is an impassioned derogation and belittlement of the human intellect in Vivekananda, which is not at all to be found in Śaṅkara.

It is very significant to know that some of the texts of the Upaniṣads that Vivekananda identifies as describing the superconscious experience are interpreted by Śaṅkara as *śruti* attempts to define *brahman.*[12] "There the eyes cannot reach nor speech nor mind" (Ke.U. 1.3) is seen by Śaṅkara as the *śruti*'s definition of *brahman* as subject or knower of the eyes, the organ of speech, and the mind. It expresses, for him, the impossibility of knowing *brahman* as an object of cognition. Śaṅkara sees "We cannot say that we know it, we cannot say that we do not know it" (Ke.U. 2.2) as identical in purport to "It is different from the known and is also above the unknown" (Ke.U. 1.4). *Brahman*'s difference from the known is seen by Śaṅkara as again denying the availability and nature of *brahman* as one of the objects of the world. That *brahman* is also different from the unknown points, for Śaṅkara, to its nature as the self:

> When it is affirmed that It is different from the unknown, it amounts to saying that It is not a thing to be obtained. It is for the sake of getting an effect that somebody acquires something different from himself to serve as a cause. For this reason too, nothing different from the Self need be acquired to serve any purpose distinct from the knower (Self). Thus the statement that *brahman* is different from the known and unknown, having amounted to *brahman* being denied as an object to be acquired or rejected, the desire of the disciple to know *brahman* (objectively) comes to an end, for *brahman* is non-different from the Self. For nothing other

> than one's own Self can possibly be different from the known and the unknown. Then it follows that the meaning of the sentence is that the Self is *brahman*. (Ke.U. = B 1.4, pp. 50–51)

"Whence words fall back with the mind without reaching it" (Ta.U. 2.9.1) expresses, for Śaṅkara, the difficulty of defining *brahman* through the generally accepted forms of word usage (see Ta.U. = B 2.9.1, pp. 385–386).[13]

The Nature of the Jīvanmukta

Vivekananda's identification of *mokṣa* with the state of *samādhi* leaves us with a certain ambiguity as far as his attitude towards the concept of the *jīvanmukta* is concerned. In the *Advaita* tradition, the *jīvanmukta* is the person who continues to live in the body after coming to a knowledge of the self. Except for fundamental differences in the way knowledge is gained, there are occasions when Vivekananda formulates the concept of the *jīvanmukta* in agreement with Śaṅkara (see, e.g., *CW,* 1:365, 3:10, 55). On these occasions, he explains that the body is retained after knowledge of *brahman* because of the persistence of unused *karma*. Because of the person's knowledge of the self, however, the world can no longer cause any misery or grief. Elsewhere, Vivekananda speaks of the impossibility of any return to bodily existence from the state of *samādhi:* "The conclusion of the *Vedānta* is that when there is absolute *samādhi* and the cessation of all modifications, there is no return from that state" (*CW,* 7:83).

Only *avatāras,* explains Vivekananda, who retain desires for the good of the world, return from *samādhi*. This position seems to negate the possibility of the *jīvanmukta* unless one proposes that every *jīvanmukta* is an *avatāra*. There is no evidence, however, that Vivekananda equates both concepts.

If one sticks rigidly to Vivekananda's contention, one will have to admit that only the *avatāra* can be a teacher and transmitter of *brahmajñāna,* for no one else would survive the gain of knowledge in *samādhi*. If anyone else did, his or her experience and knowledge would have to be considered incomplete. Perhaps this stand of Vivekananda's has to be seen in relation to the view, noted earlier, that freedom involves a real detachment or separation of the self from the body and all nature. If this occurs only in *samādhi,* then any other state is bondage.[14]

With Śaṅkara, on the other hand, where the problem of *avidyā* is defined as superimposition *(adhyāsa),* the presence of the body or the world does not constitute or imply bondage. The limitation of the self is always only notional, and the *jīvanmukta* becomes possible with the removal of ignorance.[15]

In support of his claim that there is no return from the state of *samādhi,* Vivekananda simply cites, "There is no return for released souls on the strength of the Upaniṣadic declaration" (BS 4.4.22).[16] Śaṅkara, however, sees this *śutra* as affirming the nonreturn to the world of transmigration of two classes of aspirants. Those who have attained the world of the creator *(brahma-loka)* dwell there until the dissolution of the creation, after which they are no longer subject to rebirth. The verse, according to Śaṅkara, also affirms freedom for those who have attained *brahmajñāna* here and for whom *mokṣa* is an already accomplished fact (see BS = B 4.4.22, pp. 911–912).

The Mind as a Source of Brahmajñāna

Vivekananda's argument that knowledge of the self can be gained through independent internal observation by the mind of its own contents has no parallel in Śaṅkara. Śaṅkara's entire rationale for the *śruti* is centered on the argument that the knowledge of *brahman* that it affords cannot be obtained in any other way.

There is also no view in Śaṅkara corresponding to Vivekananda's assertion that knowledge of the self spontaneously follows the concentration or silencing of the mind. In fact, it is difficult to know what exactly Vivekananda means when he speaks of *brahman* as becoming manifest when mental modifications are eliminated. That *brahman* is not always manifest and available would imply some form of limitation. While it is clear in Śaṅkara that what is to be attained is *brahmajñāna* and not *brahman,* with whom identity already exists, Vivekananda often leaves us wondering.

He does not always distinguish the necessity for gaining *brahmajñāna,* as opposed to *brahman.* Śaṅkara specifically refutes the system of Yoga and its disciplines as direct means to *mokṣa.* He specifically rebuts the argument that *mokṣa* can be obtained through concentration of the mind.[17] This clearly undermines Vivekananda's assertion that *rājayoga* is the method advocated by all schools of Hinduism for gaining *mokṣa.* Śaṅkara's position is that the purity and steadiness of mind discovered through the practices of Yoga are indirect aids to the gain of knowledge but cannot themselves give rise to knowledge.

Vivekananda's view that knowledge naturally follows the silencing of the mind has to be connected with his belief that all knowledge is already within the individual. It appears to me that, while it is feasible to argue that all knowledge occurs in the mind, it is difficult and different to assert that all knowledge is already there. Vivekananda's view is contradictory to Śaṅkara's position that the knowledge of *brahman* springs from inquiry into the words of the Upaniṣads. Vivekananda's view that the role of the teacher is only to arouse an inherent knowledge is also opposed to the function of the teacher in Śaṅkara.[18] It is the teacher who, through his or her exegesis of the *śruti* and skillful handling or words, generates a hitherto unknown knowledge. The teacher is not merely a stimulus or suggestion.[19] Vivekananda's view that this doctrine represents the position of the Vedānta is difficult to sustain. It is also difficult to find the support that he claims for this doctrine in the Bhagavadgītā.[20]

Chapter 6

THE LEGACY OF VIVEKANANDA

IN CHAPTER 5, I outlined Śaṅkara's arguments for the *śruti* as a source of valid knowledge about *brahman* and highlighted several important areas of contrast with Vivekananda on the nature and attainment of *brahmajñāna*. The differences are substantial in that they concern the very means for the attainment of *mokṣa*. My aim in the present chapter is to highlight and assess important aspects of the legacy of Vivekananda's methods and interpretations to contemporary Vedānta and, more broadly, the Hindu tradition. I also identify important areas for further investigation.

Vivekananda as a Reformer

Vivekananda's attitude toward the authority of scripture was molded in an atmosphere where the most progressive movement of the day, the Brahmo Samaj, of which he was a member for a short time, had unequivocally rejected the ultimate authority of the *śruti*. This is undoubtedly one of the most significant and dramatic developments in the recent history of Hinduism and one that has played a major part in influencing the contemporary understanding of the *śruti*. The environment of Vivekananda's youth was surcharged with a skepticism and mistrust of the authority and value of scriptural texts, voiced particularly by the very popular and influential Keshub Chandra Sen. Indeed, opinion among the leading reformers and thinkers was virtually unanimous, and there can be little doubt that Vivekananda's own approach to scriptural authority was affected.

Paradoxically, the resolution to revoke the supreme authority of the Vedas as the source of Hinduism came in response to Christian missionary invective against the doctrine of Vedic infallibility. Adherence to the authority of the Vedas became a cause for positive embarrassment to the Brahmo Samaj. In responding to missionary censure, the Samaj utilized arguments and doctrines derived from Unitarian Christianity and also found there congenial suggestions about alternative sources of religious knowledge. In particular, they seized on the concepts of intuition and nature and sought, with very little success, to construct a theology on the basis of what could be known through these means. The consequence was that, while the movement initiated and contributed to various social reform measures, minimal theological development occurred. This is reflected in the failure to establish and maintain a regular theological school. The absence of any theological originality or uniqueness that the Samaj might have creatively derived from its Hindu roots is further demonstrated by the fact that it could accept the training of its teachers at a Unitarian institution in England.

While the roots of many of Vivekananda's ideas could be traced back to the Brahmo Samaj, there is an essential difference that explains Vivekananda's wider appeal. The Brahmo Samaj openly ridiculed many of the doctrines and practices of Hinduism and was not generally concerned to preserve a Hindu identity. Keshub Chandra Sen, in fact, consciously sought to terminate links between the Brahmo Samaj of India and the wider Hindu tradition. The influence and example of Ramakrishna distinguished Vivekananda's approach to Hinduism from that of the Brahmo Samaj.

In Ramakrishna, Vivekananda perceived someone who, without any of the Western learning that characterized most of the Brahmo leaders, had attained the pinnacle of Hindu spirituality by adopting many of the beliefs and practices vehemently condemned by the reformers. In Ramakrishna's eclectic vision, an explanation and justification was found for almost everything that had become a part of Hinduism. In nearly every one of his major public addresses in India, Vivekananda scathingly denounced many reformist views and deliberately disassociated himself from their methods. The following example reflects the intensity of his disapproval of certain reformist approaches, especially those that were inspired by European models:

> For nearly the past one hundred years, our country has been flooded with social reform proposals. Personally, I have no fault to find with these reformers. Most of them are good, well-meaning men, and their aims too are very laudable on certain points; but it is quite a patent fact that this one hundred years of social reform has produced no permanent and valuable result appreciable throughout the country. Platform

> speeches have been made by the thousand, denunciations in volumes have been hurled upon the devoted head of the Hindu race, and its civilization, and yet no practical result has been achieved; and where is the reason for that? The reason is not hard to find. It is in the denunciation itself. (*CW,* 3:194–195; see also 3:450)

While he did not reject the urgent necessity for change and innovation in Hinduism, Vivekananda subtly emphasized that what he desired was "growth" and "expansion" rather than "reformation." Describing himself as a nonbeliever in reform, he defined the reformist method as one of "destruction," whereas his was an attempt at "construction" (*CW,* 3:195, 213–220). This delicate and astute distinction enabled Vivekananda to be critical of the Hindu tradition while never alienating himself from it. He struck a very fine and original balance between an aggressive defense of Hinduism and a vociferous cry for transformation. This fact provides the most important clue to understanding Vivekananda's popularity and the nature of the reinterpretation that he formulated. Vivekananda also distinguished himself from his Brahmo contemporaries by his linking of Hindu revival with Indian nationalism and patriotism and his greater appeal to these sentiments. The way in which his presentation of Hinduism was shaped by this identification of religion and nationalism needs more detailed study.

The Use of a Scientific Model

The general orientation of the Brahmo Samaj toward scriptural authority provided a strong stimulus to Vivekananda's reinterpretation of the nature and basis of the authority of the *śruti.* From this source also he might have derived suggestions about an alternative source of spiritual knowledge, but he sought to locate this within the Hindu tradition and, in particular, in the tradition of Yoga. The crucial difference is that Vivekananda sought the elements of his reinterpretation within Hinduism.

If one had to seek for a single model in the light of which Vivekananda attempted to formulate his view of the *śruti* and the process of gaining *brahmajñāna,* one must turn to his understanding of the nature of the scientific method. It is his use of this model, however, that also gives rise to many of the problems presented by his formulation. Science as a method of attaining knowledge about human beings and the universe and as the key to human progress was enjoying considerable prestige among the Bengali intelligentsia in the nineteenth century.[1] It was widely felt that all systems of human thought, including religion, had to be validated by the scrutiny of science and reason.[2] This prompted attempts within the Brahmo Samaj to seek a reconciliation of their religious views with what they understood to be the propositions and methods of science. A. K. Datta, for example, suggested that God should be approached through the study of the natural sciences, and Keshub Chandra Sen tried to justify his views in the name of science.

The impact of science on Vivekananda's views and the esteem with which it was regarded are evident in his lectures and writings. He continuously seeks to demonstrate the compatibility of Advaita with the findings of science and presents this as one of the principal arguments in favor of this system. His understanding of science is the paradigmatic basis on which he constructs a view of the *śruti* and the method of attaining knowledge of *brahman.* His interpretations are most readily explained in this context. The frequent attempts in contemporary studies to draw analogies between Advaita and the methods of science are a reflection of Vivekananda's continuing influence. While Vivekananda's concern to express his views in relation to science might have been partially influenced by certain approaches within the Brahmo Samaj, the resulting synthesis was an original one.

It is important, therefore, to venture a brief reconstruction of Vivekananda's thought against the background of what he understood to be scientific method. The influence of this method is evident primarily in his aim to demonstrate that the validity of religious propositions need not depend on what he considered to be the weak foundation of faith and belief. Vivekananda represented the Vedas as a collection of spiritual laws, often emphasizing that they were not books. These spiritual laws are portrayed as similar to the natural laws governing our physical universe in that they have an existence that is independent of human apprehension. The doctrine of Vedic eternity, therefore, can now be represented as the timelessness of impersonal laws rather than of a word revelation. Even as scientists do not create physical laws but only discover these by the application of proper methods, Vivekananda portrays the *āptas* as the "discoverers" of spiritual laws. Like a scientific manual, the Vedas, as books, are just the written records of these spiritual laws, discovered by different people at different times.

The representation of the Vedas as records or reports of spiritual findings and of the ṛṣis as discoverers provides the foundation for the deepening and development of the scientific paradigm. One is not obliged, according to Vivekananda, to accept scientific propositions as valid because of faith in the individual scientist. As a method of gaining knowledge, he sees science as being distinguished by the fact that it offers the possibility of verification. One can personally confirm the findings of a scientist by the application of proper methods. In the same way, according to Vivekananda, the spiritual aspirant is not condemned to establishing his or her convictions on the basis of faith in the *āpta* or in the reports recorded in scripture. Neither the scientist nor the *āpta* is genuine, says Vivekananda, if a claim is made for a unique access to knowledge.

In the Vedas, just as in the report of a scientist, the *āpta* has the right to tell us only what has been discovered and the methods that were employed. If we have confidence in the *āpta* and the scientist, we may accept their claims as provisionally true. These claims, however, especially in the case of the spiritual aspirant, can never have any ultimately convincing validity unless they are personally rediscovered and verified by an application of the same methods. In the case of the Vedas, Vivekananda emphasizes not only the possibility of verification but also its necessity. The foundation of knowledge, therefore, for Vivekananda, is not the authority of the Vedas as a word revelation since the texts indicate only a method for the direct apprehension of spiritual facts.

It is within this context of his endeavor to reconstruct the process of attaining *brahmajñāna* in Advaita on the model of scientific method that we can best see and understand Vivekananda's version of the significance of the *śruti. Śruti,* he affirms, may stimulate a desire for firsthand knowledge, but it is in itself only "theoretical" or secondhand knowledge. *Śruti* is not, as in Śaṅkara, a *pramāṇa* for the knowledge of *brahman;* rather, it is a method for the direct and independent discovery of spiritual facts. While in spiritual childhood we may rely on the *śruti,* we must eventually transcend it and certify its claims. Even as a scientific experiment can be repeated if we wish to verify its results personally, so too is the discovery of *brahmajñāna* by one person evidence of the necessity and competence of every other human being to attain it by the same method.

The scientific analogy continues and is further elaborated by Vivekananda when he details the method by which *brahmajñāna* is gained. He very consciously sets out to demonstrate that this method is like the process of attaining and verifying knowledge in the physical sciences. It is very significant that Vivekananda finds this method in the Yoga system of Patañjali and not in the Upaniṣads on which Śaṅkara bases his interpretation of the tradition. We have examined the enormous difficulties presented by the method of *rājayoga* in relation to Vivekananda's attempts to identify it with the procedures of science.

The parallels that he makes are possible only through a radical simplification of scientific method. The scientific analogy revolves around his key concept of "experience" *(anubhava).*

In designating "experience" as the common basis of knowledge in both Yoga and science, Vivekananda overlooks the complexity of the so-called experience through which knowledge is gained in the sciences. The scientific technique is further simplified in the interests of superficial similarities when he argues for observation or concentration as its chief feature. The self-valid quality that he posits of both sense perception and religious experience disregards the difficulties that both present. In the case of religious experience, it presumes a self-interpretativeness that glosses over the influence of doctrinal assumptions on interpretation, an influence strongly demonstrated in Vivekananda's own writings. In fact, it is indeed strange that, as an Advaitin, Vivekananda argues so strongly for the immediate validity of sense perception. Advaita contends that the universe that is apprehended through the senses is an inexplicable appearance of *brahman.* In positing that *brahman* is in reality free from the characteristics possessed by objects of the universe, Advaita questions the ultimate validity of the impressions that we form of the world on the basis of sense perception.

The problems of using *rājayoga* as the method of attaining *brahmajñāna* are not confined simply to drawing dubious analogies with science. The approach is also undermined by serious problems originating mainly from two sources. The first of these relates to the fact that *rājayoga* and its culminating experience of *samādhi* have their doctrinal basis in the system of Sāṅkhya, which differs from Advaita on crucial issues concerning the nature of the *ātman* and *mokṣa.* In spite of his awareness of these divergences, Vivekananda neglects their significance in proposing *samādhi* as the authoritative source of *brahmajñāna.* I have specified another set of problems deriving from Vivekananda's very definition of *samādhi* and his claims for it as a state and source of knowledge. Not only is it contradictory to speak of a state of nonduality as involving "perception," but it is also untenable, within the context of Advaita, to propose a direct perception of the *ātman* in *samādhi.* Such a proposition presupposes another self for which the *ātman* must become a limited object of knowledge.

Many Paths to the Same Goal?

Vivekananda's claim that *karmayoga, bhaktiyoga, jñānayoga,* and *rājayoga* can be direct and independent ways to the attainment of *mokṣa* is closely linked to his reinterpretation of the significance of the *śruti* and his upholding of the *samādhi* experience as the ultimately valid source of *brahmajñāna*. For Śaṅkara, who advocates the *śruti* as the unique source of this knowledge, inquiry into the words of the texts, with the help of a teacher, is the means of attaining knowledge of *brahman*. There are disciplines and aids for helping the inquirer gain and assimilate the knowledge generated by the *śruti*, but there is no substitute for *śruti* as the valid source. For Vivekananda, who endorses an experience (namely, *samādhi*), rather than *śruti*, as the valid source of knowledge, it is perhaps more plausible to posit different ways of attaining this experience. This is what Vivekananda sets out to do in his elaboration of the methods of *karmayoga, bhaktiyoga, jñānayoga,* and *rājayoga*.

The thesis that there are four different paths to the attainment of *mokṣa* was partly employed by Vivekananda to demonstrate the superiority of Hinduism in its capacity to cater to different spiritual needs and temperaments. Today, like so many of the interpretations popularized by Vivekananda, it has become a standard argument in Hindu apologetic writing and even in scholarly studies produced by both Hindus and non-Hindus. When Vivekananda's arguments are subjected to close scrutiny in relation to basic Advaita propositions about the nature of *avidyā* and *mokṣa,* they are not convincing. There is no attempt carefully to relate the nature of each method to the assumptions of *avidyā* as the fundamental problem. At crucial points in his discussion, where it is necessary clearly to demonstrate the connection between a particular method and the attainment of *mokṣa* in the Advaita sense, Vivekananda becomes vague and obscure in his terminology and concepts.

In the case of *bhaktiyoga,* for example, he claims, but fails to establish, that the movement from the dualism of worship to the unity and identity of *brahmajñāna* is a natural one. He argues for *jñānayoga* as a method of pure reason but presents a wider view of the limitations of reason that nullifies this argument. While arguing that belief in doctrines is dispensable, his characterization of each method is permeated with doctrinal assumptions. We appear to have to accept that *avidyā* vanishes inexplicably.

Ultimately, Vivekananda contradicts his own thesis that each of the four paths can lead independently to *mokṣa* when he argues that the *samādhi* experience afforded by the disciplines of *rājayoga* is the only valid source of *brahmajñāna*. While the assertion about different ways of attaining *mokṣa* has a certain liberal appeal and is often used to argue apologetically for the inclusiveness of Hinduism, it requires far more than this to be rationally convincing, and there is no evidence that the many difficulties were carefully considered by Vivekananda.

The Divorce of Scholarship and Spirituality

Vivekananda's championing of an experience *(anubhava)* as the ultimate source of spiritual knowledge contributed to the divorce of scholarship from spirituality in modern Advaita and Hinduism. This effect can be best demonstrated by contrast with the classic approach and methods of Śaṅkara. For Śaṅkara, *śruti* is the definitive source of *brahmajñāna,* and the immediate result of this knowledge is *mokṣa.* As a *pramāṇa, śruti* is composed of words, and these must be correctly understood. Scriptural learning, study, and exegesis, therefore, become very important, along with such disciplines as grammar and etymology that aid interpretation. Proper principles for arriving at the meaning of texts are necessary.

It is very important to note that the acceptance of *śruti* as an authoritative *pramāṇa* did not mean the abandonment of a very significant role for reason. Reason is important in deciding between different interpretations of particular passages and in reconciling conflicting ones. Reason also has a major role to play in demonstrating that the affirmations of *śruti* are not inconsistent with what we know about the world and ourselves from other *pramāṇas.* It also plays a crucial role in assessing and responding to rival views. Śaṅkara obviously takes doctrinal differences very seriously, and, in responding to the claims of rival systems that do not accept the authority of the *śruti,* he is constrained to try to demonstrate the validity of Advaita on the basis of the reasonableness of its propositions. Opposing views are carefully outlined by Śaṅkara, and the significance and development of doctrinal and philosophical argument are evident in his commentaries.

The decline of the significance of the *śruti* during the ascendancy of the Brahmo Samaj and Vivekananda's own characterization of it as secondhand religion contributed to a low estimation of the value of scriptural scholarship. Because *śruti* is no longer seen as the definitive source of *brahmajñāna,* its study, exegesis, and right interpretation are not of the utmost importance. The intellectual disciplines that aid interpretation are also less valued. In examining Vivekananda's attitude toward the Vedas, we have seen how he fervently and repeatedly denounces the value of scriptural study, learning, and scholarship in the quest for *mokṣa.* These are contemptuously dismissed as activities at a theoretical and intellectual level, and Vivekananda even classifies scripture as belonging among the nonessentials of religion. The full impact of this attitude on contemporary Hinduism has not attracted sufficient attention.

The Devaluation of Reason

The upholding of the *samādhi* experience, instead of the *śruti,* as the self-valid source of *brahmajñāna* is also connected to the low value accorded reason. For Śaṅkara, conclusive knowledge is gained by the application of one's reason to the analysis, with the help of a qualified teacher, of the valid source of knowledge (namely, the *śruti*). Since knowledge occurs in the mind and is mediated through reason, the demands of the latter, as far as possible, must be satisfied.

With Vivekananda, on the other hand, knowledge is gained not by the mediation of reason but by its transcendence. This transcendence is, in fact, the very condition for gaining that knowledge. In Vivekananda, therefore, reason, argument, and intellectual activity, in general, assume more of an obstructive character in relation to attaining *brahmajñāna.* Since conclusive knowledge can be attained only through a special experience, doubts can never be resolved through rational argument.

Paradoxically, it would seem that, where, as in Śaṅkara, faith *(śraddhā)* in the *śruti* as a valid means of knowledge is necessary to attain liberating knowledge, reason has a much more positive role in clarifying, explaining, and defending the propositions of the *śruti.* On the other hand, where an attempt is made, as in Vivekananda, to supersede the necessity of faith in the interest of being more rational, reason becomes less significant, and so does philosophical argument. The lack of development in contemporary Hinduism of philosophical argument must be connected to the emphasis on an experience as the ultimate source of knowledge, and this link needs to be studied more closely.

The Insignificance of Doctrinal Differences

Vivekananda's derision of scholarship, his ridicule of dogma and doctrine, and his belittling of reason are reflected in his treatment of doctrinal differences. On the whole, he attaches little importance to the reality and implications of these. This attitude is most evident in his discussion of *karma-, bhakti-, jñāna-,* and *rājayoga* as means to the attainment of *mokṣa.*

His outline of the method of *bhaktiyoga,* for example, is almost entirely derived from Rāmānuja, yet he unhesitatingly glosses over the import of Rāmānuja's many doctrinal differences with Śaṅkara and affirms that the method naturally culminates in nonduality. He extracts the *sāmadhi* experience from the Sāṅkhya Yoga system and presents it as the authoritative source of knowledge in Advaita, overlooking the implications of crucial philosophical differences between both schools.

It would seem that, because Vivekananda posits the gain of valid knowledge only through an experience transcending the rational mind, he is able to dismiss the importance of differences born out of and existing at this level of the mind. He has not proved, however, that this experience is a self-valid one and that its meaning is independent of doctrinal influence and interpretation.

Vivekananda's minimizing and underplaying, in contrast to Śaṅkara, of the significance of the deep doctrinal differences among schools of Indian philosophical thought must also be related to his concern to emphasize the common basis of the Indian spiritual tradition. This again has to be seen in the context of his wider concern for Indian national unity. It is an example of political considerations influencing the shape of theology.

It is only by overlooking and dismissing the importance of different doctrinal and philosophical claims that one can so easily assert, as Vivekananda does, that all spiritual paths lead to the same goal. This argument, which owes its elaboration to Vivekananda and which, in its various formulations, has become a standard claim in contemporary Hindu rhetoric, has to be seen and evaluated in the light of his approach to epistemology and his scant regard for divergent doctrinal claims. In view of the importance of this argument in the contemporary Hindu attitude toward other religions, it is well worth a more detailed study and appraisal.

It is true that, in the quest for *mokṣa,* the value of scholarship and learning has to be placed in proper perspective. Scholarship is only a means and never an end in itself. Viewed as an end, it can easily degenerate into sterile pedantry. *Śruti* affords a knowledge that leads to the attainment of *mokṣa,* and scholarship is chiefly an aid to its proper understanding. It is more important to the individual who aims to be a teacher.

Muṇḍaka Upaniṣad 1.2.12 mentions proficiency in the meaning of the *śruti* as one of the two qualities necessary for the teacher. The other is establishment in the knowledge of *brahman.* In view of Vivekananda's influence on modern Hinduism, it is unfortunate that he did not adopt a more balanced view of the value of scholarship in the quest for *mokṣa.* The decline of scholarship and its dissociation from spirituality is one of the most lamentable trends in the recent history of Hinduism. Its reflection in the poor state of theological education in Hinduism needs more study.

There is also a need for an examination of the Upaniṣadic ideal of the nature, qualifications, and functions of the teacher and a contrast of this with Vivekananda's presentation of Ramakrishna as the model teacher in Hinduism. How far the emphasis on the gain of spiritual knowledge through an experience, rather than through *śruti,* has altered the understanding of the nature of the *guru* needs to be studied, as does its connection with the confusing proliferation of teachers in contemporary Hinduism. We need to examine the claim that the modern teacher makes on behalf of his own authority, along with the expectations that the student has of the teacher. All this should be interestingly related to the functions and expectations of the teacher when *śruti* is maintained as the authoritative source of knowledge.

In an age of skepticism, we can readily understand and perhaps even identify with Vivekananda's compelling desire to propose a means to the attainment of *mokṣa* that did not depend on faith in the *śruti* as a *pramāṇa.* He felt that this means offered the possibility of doubtless knowledge, as objective and verifiable as knowledge gained by the application of scientific methods. This is the motive that partly explains his radical divergence from Śaṅkara and his attempts to reinterpret the significance of the *śruti* and to suggest alternative means for the attainment of *brahmajñāna.*

It is clear, however, that his reconstruction of the basis of knowledge in Advaita is far from successful. Although many elements of his synthesis have been uncritically adopted into Hinduism, it presents innumerable problems, leaves many questions unanswered, and, on several crucial issues, contradicts fundamental Advaita propositions. His aim to suggest a more convincing source for the knowledge of *brahman* remains unaccomplished.

There is little continuity between Vivekananda and Śaṅkara with respect to the relation between *śruti* and *brahmajñāna.* His reconstruction represents a radical break rather than a continuation. In an age when science, in the enthusiasm and arrogance of its youth, seemed ready to subject all areas of human knowledge to its criteria and methods, Vivekananda felt that faith in the *śruti* as the source of *brahmajñāna* was irrational. He sought to posit a process of attaining *brahmajñāna* that he felt had satisfied the demands of science. Not only does it fail to do this, but, in a much wider perspective, his analysis is unconvincing and unsatisfactory. It is true that faith in the *śruti* as a *pramāṇa* is indispensable for Śaṅkara, but this faith is not one that proscribes the use of reason.

Vivekananda lived at a time of tumult and trauma in the history of Hinduism resulting from the impact of the West. In his reformulation of Advaita, he responded to and incorporated many of the diverse influences that were exerting themselves on Hinduism. The turbulence of his times is reflected in the synthesis that he attempted. In a very short career, he injected a a spirit of confidence into Hinduism, and his many positive achievements must be acknowledged. The assessment of his reinterpretation of the authority of the Vedas, undertaken here, is not intended to be a denial of these achievements. One of his most progressive concerns was to elicit from Advaita the justification for a life of commitment to the service of society. He also sought to challenge the widespread indifference of Hindu society to poverty and suffering.

It is understandable, but unfortunate, that his presentation of Advaita was not more critically appraised during his lifetime so that he could have responded to many of its problems and contradictions. Such an approach, however, cannot be condoned today, in view of the many inconsistencies of his interpretation.

In this light, the challenge must now be taken up by those who are the direct heirs of Vivekananda's legacy, and broadly by those movements and interpreters who have come under his influence, to provide a consistent and coherent account of the synthesis that he attempted. All the significant elements of this synthesis that have been uncritically incorporated into the contemporary formulation of Hinduism must be evaluated. These include arguments for the scientific character of Hinduism, the claim of many paths to the same goal, the nonessential character of doctrine, and the devaluation of reason. Vivekananda's reliance on *anubhava* as the authoritative source for the knowledge of *brahman* must, in particular, be critically evaluated. The significant divergences that have been established in this study between Vivekananda's interpretations and those of Śaṅkara must be addressed by those who argue for a continuity between neo-Vedānta and its classical roots and who see no deviation between Vivekananda and Śaṅkara. The task of such critical studies must not be limited to evaluation but must also undertake to place the contemporary Advaita tradition on secure epistemological and philosophical foundations.

Notes

Introduction

1. The term *anubhava* (experience) is widely used by neo-Vedānta interpreters to refer to what they consider to be the common experiential source of all religions. The use of the term, however, is generally imprecise. As we will see, while Vivekananda also used the term loosely, he identifies *anubhava* with the *samādhi* experience of the Yoga tradition. For a discussion of the contemporary and traditional use of the term, see Wilhelm Halbfass, *India and Europe* (Albany: State University of New York Press, 1988), chap. 21.

2. T. M. P. Mahadevan, *Swami Vivekananda and the Indian Renaissance* (Coimbatore: Sri Ramakrishna Mission Teachers College, 1965), p. 52.

3. R. S. Srivastava, *Contemporary Indian Philosophy* (Delhi: Munshiram Manoharlal, 1965), p. 43.

4. For other examples of uncritical identification of Vivekananda with Śaṅkara, see D. S. Sarma, *Renascent Hinduism* (Bombay: Bharatiya Vidya Bhavan, 1966), pp. 171–172; D. R. Kinsley, *Hinduism* (Englewood Cliffs, N.J.: Prentice-Hall, 1982), p. 22; R. C. Zaehner, *Hinduism* (London: Oxford University Press, 1966), p. 168; and S. N. Dhar, *A Comprehensive Biography of Swami Vivekananda,* 2 vols. (Madras: Vivekananda Prakashan Kendra, 1975–1976), 1:741.

5. Anantanand Rambachan, *Accomplishing the Accomplished: The Vedas as a Source of Valid Knowledge in Śaṅkara,* Monographs of the Society for Asian and Comparative Philosophy, no. 10 (Honolulu: University of Hawaii Press, 1991).

6. Swami Satprakashananda, "The Buddha, Śrī Śaṅkarācārya, and Swami Vivekananda," in *Parliament of Religions* (Calcutta: Swami Vivekananda Centenary Committee, 1965), pp. 39, 24.

7. See *The Complete Works of Swami Vivekananda* (hereafter *CW*), 8 vols. (Calcutta: Advaita Ashrama, 1964–1971), 8:351, 7:32, 6:201–224.

8. See Halbfass, *India and Europe,* p. 240. As Halbfass (p. 393) correctly points out, in the *Vivekacūḍāmaṇi* and other hymns attributed to Śaṅkara,

there is greater emphasis on emotions and personal experience than there is in a work like Śaṅkara's commentary on the Brahma-sūtra. It is clear, however, that Vivekananda's knowledge of Śaṅkara was not derived merely from secondary sources. As a result of Vivekananda's early exposure to the influence of Ramakrishna and the latter's emphasis on the authority of personal experience, it is quite likely that his understanding of Śaṅkara was influenced by questionable works like *Vivekacūḍāmaṇi* that were more in congruence with Ramakrishna's teachings. At the same time, Ramakrishna's influence, the prevailing attitudes toward scriptural authority in the Brahmo Samaj, and Vivekananda's own concern to demonstrate what he considered to be the scientific character of Hinduism may have led him to ignore Śaṅkara's emphasis on the *śruti* as the source of knowledge about *brahman*. The championing of scriptural authority, as we will see, was not at all popular in Bengal in the nineteenth century.

9. Ninian Smart, "Swami Vivekananda as a Philosopher," in *Swami Vivekananda in East and West,* ed. Swami Ghanananda and Geoffrey Parrinder (London: Ramakrishna Vedanta Centre, 1968), pp. 82–83.

10. A. L. Basham, "Swami Vivekananda: A Moulder of the Modern World," in *Swami Vivekananda in East and West,* p. 210.

11. Agehananda Bharati, "The Hindu Renaissance and Its Apologetic Patterns," *Journal of Asian Studies* 29 (1970): 278.

12. Halbfass, *India and Europe,* p. 228.

13. Using the dates given in the *Complete Works,* and with the help of biographical sources, I attempted to arrange and read the material in chronological order. I was, however, unable to detect any significant development of Vivekananda's thought on the relation between *śruti* and *anubhava*. Nevertheless, others have attempted to trace developments in his thought as a consequence of his assimilation of Western ideas. D. H. Killingley has argued that Vivekananda's view of ancient Indian evolutionary theory was modified by ideas picked up in the West, and Paul Hacker contends that the idea of the ethical applicability of the *tat tvam asi* doctrine was suggested to Vivekananda by P. Deussen (see D. H. Killingley, "*Yoga-Sūtra* IV, 2–3 and Vivekananda's Interpretation of Evolution," *Journal of Indian Philosophy* 18 [1990]: 151–179; and, for a summary of Hacker's views, Halbfass, *India and Europe,* pp. 238–241).

Chapter 1: Attitudes toward Scriptural Authority and Revelation from Rammohun Roy to Ramakrishna

1. K. M. Panikkar, *Hinduism and the West* (Chandigarh: Panjab University Publications Bureau, 1964), p. 4.

2. For a brief but good discussion of the reasons behind the failure of the *bhakti* movements, see C. H. Heimsath, *Indian Nationalism and Hindu Social Reform* (Princeton, N.J.: Princeton University Press, 1964), pp. 28–38.

3. Ibid., p. 37.

4. For Spencer's influence, see ibid., pp. 49–50.

5. David Kopf's excellent study, *British Orientalism and the Bengal Renaissance* (Berkeley: University of California Press, 1969), is still authoritative.

6. Wilson is quoted in ibid., p. 176.

7. Ibid., p. 284.

8. See R. C. Majumdar, *History of the Freedom Movement in India*, 3 vols. (Calcutta: Firma K. L. Mukhopadhyay, 1962–1963), 1:259–260.

9. I am not aware of any study that has examined, in detail, the effects of this period of change on the authority of these texts.

10. For a critical study of the growth and development of the Brahmo Samaj, see David Kopf, *The Brahmo Samaj and the Shaping of the Modern Indian Mind* (Princeton, N.J.: Princeton University Press, 1979). For a specific discussion of the legacy and wide influence of the movement, see chap. 2.

11. In 1943, Debendranath Tagore changed the name of the Brahmo Sabha to Brahmo Samaj.

12. See S. K. Das, *The Shadow of the Cross: Christianity and Hinduism in a Colonial Context* (Delhi: Munshiram Manoharlal, 1974), p. 64. Das is of the opinion that Roy mixed up the issues of religion and nationalism, the inevitable result of the colonial context in which he operated. According to him, the use of the texts as a medium of instruction was primarily the result of nationalistic sentiment.

13. See B. G. Ray, *Religious Movements in Modern Bengal* (Santiniketan: Visva-Bharati, 1965), p. 13.

14. Sisirkumar Mitra, *Resurgent India* (Delhi: Allied Publishers, 1963), p. 66; see also p. 65.

15. See D. Killingley, "Rammohun Roy's Interpretation of the Vedānta" (Ph.D. thesis, School of Oriental and African Studies, University of London, 1977), pp. 342–344. As an example of this tendency, Killingley cites Roy's explanation that those parts of the Vedas that teach the worship of figured gods represent an inferior view for the benefit of worshipers incapable of grasping the higher truths. Roy justified this interpretation as the only way of preserving the consistency of the text.

16. This attempt to suggest a different view relies a great deal on Killingley's study. His work is concerned primarily with contrasting the interpretations of Śaṅkara and Rammohun Roy, but it also provides significant clues for ascertaining Roy's attitude toward the authority of the Vedas. For an excellent discussion of Rammohun Roy, see Halbfass, *India and Europe*, chap. 12. Halbfass, however, is concerned less with Roy's attitude toward scriptural authority and more with the complexity of Roy's context and hermeneutics.

17. Rammohun Roy quoted in Killingley, "Rammohun Roy's Interpretation of the Vedānta," p. 341. Roy's significant writings appeared in both Bengali and English. For a view on the hermeneutical significance of his use of English, see Halbfass, *India and Europe*, pp. 203–204.

18. Rammohun Roy quoted in Killingley, "Rammohun Roy's Interpretation of the Vedānta," p. 341.

19. Ibid., pp. 328–336.

20. Ibid., pp. 349-351. As Halbfass points out, Roy was silent on those passages in Śaṅkara's commentary on the Brahma-sūtra that affirm the *adhikāra* doctrine (see *India and Europe,* pp. 205-206).

21. Killingley, "Rammohun Roy's Interpretation of the Vedānta," p. 343.

22. Sivanath Sastri, *History of the Brahmo Samaj,* 2d ed. (Calcutta: Sadharan Brahmo Samaj, 1974), p. 47.

23. Keshub Chunder Sen, "The Brahmo Samaj or Theism in India," in *Discourses and Writings* (Calcutta: Brahmo Tract Society, 1904), pp. 70-71. This appears to be a fair summary of Roy's attitude. On the universalistic ideals of the church, see p. 72.

24. It is strange that such a consequential decision has not received any detailed treatment in recent works discussing the movement under Debendranath Tagore. David Kopf (*The Brahmo Samaj,* p. 51), makes only brief mention of it. Kopf's concern is more with the sociological dimensions of the movement. For a brief discussion of Tagore's attitude toward scriptural revelation, see Halbfass, *India and Europe,* pp. 223-224.

25. See Mitra, *Resurgent India,* pp. 79-82.

26. D. K. Biswas, "Maharshi Debendranath Tagore and the Tattvabodhini Sabha," in *Studies in the Bengal Renaissance,* ed. A. K. Gupta (Calcutta: National Council of Education, 1958), pp. 33-46.

27. See Sastri, *History of the Brahmo Samaj,* p. 63.

28. Quoted in ibid., pp. 63-64. Sastri is of the opinion that this article was penned by Rajnarain Bose, who had then recently joined the Brahmo Samaj. Mitra *(Resurgent India)* attributes this piece of writing to Debendranath Tagore.

29. For a good summary of Datta's views, see Kopf, *The Brahmo Samaj,* pp. 49-54.

30. Sastri, *History of the Brahmo Samaj,* p. 65.

31. Ibid. See also Ray, *Religious Movements in Modern Bengal,* pp. 13-14.

32. It is unfortunate that there are no records of the details of the argument on both sides of the question or of the nature of the studies and inquiries undertaken by Debendranath Tagore and his emissaries at Benares. These would have thrown great light on the nature of the debate and the propositions that led Tagore to concede to Datta.

33. See Killingley, "Rammohun Roy's Interpretation of the Vedānta," p. 349.

34. The eleven authentic Upaniṣads mentioned here are probably those commented on by Śaṅkara.

35. Debendranath Tagore quoted in Das, *The Shadow of the Cross,* pp. 70-71.

36. See J. N. Farquhar, *Modern Religious Movements in India,* Indian ed. (Delhi: Munshiram Manoharlal, 1977), pp. 71-73; see also p. 41.

37. Debendranath Tagore, *Brahmo Dharma,* trans. Hem Chandra Sarkar (Calcutta: H. C. Sarkar, 1928), p. 73.

38. Ibid., pp. 119-120.

39. Debendranath Tagore quoted in Mitra, *Resurgent India,* p. 85. Halbfass points to the influence of various European sources on Tagore's search for personal experience (see *India and Europe,* p. 396).

40. On Sitanath Tattvabhusan and the theology of the Brahmo Samaj, see Kopf, *The Brahmo Samaj,* pp. 79–83.

41. K. C. Sen, "The Living God in England and India" (sermon delivered at Mill-Hill Chapel, Leeds, 28 August 1870), in *Discourses and Writings,* p. 5.

42. Sastri, *History of the Brahmo Samaj,* p. 149.

43. I am not aware of any work that specifically studies and analyzes Sen's thought. There are a few texts containing surveys of a very general kind only.

44. K. C. Sen, "Great Men" (lecture delivered at the Town Hall, Calcutta, 28 September 1866), in *Lectures and Tracts by Keshub Chunder Sen,* ed. S. D. Collet (London: Strahan, 1870), pp. 53, 56. Regarding God's self-evident manifestation in nature, one is reminded of the same argument in Rammohun Roy. In Sen, the arguments are worked out in more detail.

45. K. C. Sen, "The Religious Importance of Mental Philosophy" (two lectures delivered to the students of the Calcutta Brahmo School, 5 and 12 May 1867), in *Lectures and Tracts,* p. 184.

46. Sen, "Great Men," pp. 57–58.

47. The Brahmo Samaj has consistently rejected the orthodox theory of the *avatāra.*

48. See Sen, "Great Men," pp. 71–74.

49. Ibid., p. 86.

50. Ibid., p. 88.

51. K. C. Sen, "Regenerating Faith" (sermon preached on the occasion of the thirty-eighth anniversary of the Brahmo Samaj, 24 January 1868), in *Lectures and Tracts,* p. 110.

52. K. C. Sen, "The Brahmo Samaj," p. 73.

53. Sen, "The Living God," pp. 9–11.

54. K. C. Sen, "Primitive Faith and Modern Speculations" (substance of an anniversary lecture at the Town Hall, Calcutta, 23 January 1872), in *Discourses and Writings,* p. 46.

55. K. C. Sen, "The Existence of God" (substance of an unpublished lecture at Albert Hall, Calcutta, 29 January 1879), in *Discourses and Writings,* p. 58.

56. See Kopf, *The Brahmo Samaj,* chap. 9; and also Sastri, *History of the Brahmo Samaj,* pp. 163–186.

57. The idea of *ādeśa* was noted in connection with Debendranath Tagore.

58. K. C. Sen, "Apostles of the New Dispensation" (lecture delivered at the Town Hall, Calcutta, 22 January 1881), quoted in Sastri, *History of the Brahmo Samaj,* p. 230.

59. K. C. Sen, *The New Dispensation or Religion of Harmony* (Calcutta: Bidhan Press, 1903), pp. 258–259. This particular work is a compilation of his writings between May and December 1881.

60. See ibid., pp. 33–35.

61. Ibid., pp. 34–35.

62. Ibid., pp. 257, 86. On the demonstrability of Nava-Vidhan truths, see ibid., p. 250.

63. See Dhar, *Comprehensive Biography*, 1:66; and also Kopf, *The Brahmo Samaj*, pp. 204–206.

64. There are, of course, very important differences between the ideas of Sen and those of Vivekananda. The most important perhaps is Sen's uncompromising rejection of Advaita, which forms the bedrock of Vivekananda's philosophy. There are intriguing parallels, however, some of which will be made obvious in my discussion of Vivekananda.

65. There are many available biographies. See, e.g., Christopher Isherwood, *Ramakrishna and His Disciples,* 3d ed. (Calcutta: Advaita Ashrama, 1974); and also Romain Rolland, *The Life of Ramakrishna* (Calcutta: Advaita Ashrama, 1974). For a recent psychohistory, see N. R. Sil, *Ramakṛṣṇa Paramahaṁsa: A Psychological Profile* (Leiden: E. J. Brill, 1991).

66. Ramakrishna, quoted in Swami Saradananda, *Śrī Ramakrishna the Great Master,* trans. Swami Jagadananda, 5th rev. ed., 2 vols. (Madras: Sri Ramakrishna Math, 1978–1979), 1:162–163.

67. See Rolland, *The Life of Ramakrishna,* pp. 75–80.

68. For this selection, two main sources have been relied on. The major source is Mahendra Gupta, *The Gospel of Sri Ramakrishna,* trans. Swami Nikhilananda (New York: Ramakrishna-Vedanta Center, 1977). This is a detailed record, by the disciple Gupta, of the conversations of Ramakrishna from March 1882 to April 1886, only a few months before his death. It is an important source for any study of Ramakrishna's ideas. The second is Sri Ramakrishna Math, *Sayings of Śrī Ramakrishna* (Madras: Sri Ramakrishna Math, 1975). This is a considerably smaller work, based on Gupta's records, which attempts to arrange under subject headings some of his teachings.

69. *Sayings of Ramakrishna,* pp. 62–64, 68–69.

70. See ibid., pp. 64, 67; and *The Gospel of Sri Ramakrishna,* p. 625.

71. Ibid., pp. 543, 645–646, 476. On the multiplicity of religious texts, see ibid., p. 475.

72. *Sayings of Ramakrishna,* p. 263; see also pp. 278, 284. The concept of *samādhi* will be treated when I consider Vivekananda.

73. Isherwood, *Ramakrishna and His Disciples,* p. 115.

74. Walter G. Neevel, Jr., "The Transformation of Śrī Rāmakrishna," in *Hinduism: New Essays in the History of Religions,* ed. B. L. Smith (Leiden: E. J. Brill, 1976), pp. 55, 67.

75. Ibid., pp. 85–97. In another study, Freda Matchett ("The Teaching of Ramakrishna in Relation to the Hindu Tradition and as Interpreted by Vivekananda," *Religion* 11 [1981]: 171–184) argues along similar lines. Her work seems to draw heavily on Neevel's study, but she argues that no single strand of the Hindu tradition should be emphasized as determining the framework of Ramakrishna's thought.

76. See Heinrich Zimmer, *Philosophies of India* (New York: Pantheon Books, 1951), p. 569.

77. Kopf, *The Brahmo Samaj,* p. 4.

78. N. C. Ganguly, *Raja Ram Mohun Roy* (Calcutta: Y.M.C.A. Publishing House, 1934), p. 141.

79. Kopf, *The Brahmo Samaj,* pp. 15–26.

80. Sastri, *History of the Brahmo Samaj,* p. 336.

81. For a full discussion of the basic doctrines and arguments of Unitarian Christianity, see W. E. Channing, *The Complete Works* (London: Williams & Norgate, 1880), pp. 292–306.

82. Ibid., pp. xvii, 293.

83. Theodore Parker, *The Collected Works,* ed. Frances Power Cobbe, 12 vols. (London: Trubner, 1863–1865), 1:216.

84. Channing, *Complete Works,* pp. xvii, xii.

85. Parker, *Collected Works,* 1:140, 149–50; for full discussion of inspiration, see pp. 138–150.

86. Ibid., 1:7 (see generally 1:1–28).

87. Sen, "The Existence of God," p. 59.

88. For a discussion of Dayananda's life and the doctrines of the movement, see Lajpat Rai, *A History of the Arya Samaj* (Bombay: Orient Longmans, 1967). The development of the Arya Samaj is also well treated in K. W. Jones, *Arya Dharm* (Berkeley: University of California Press, 1976).

89. See Rai, *History of the Arya Samaj,* p. 82. For a full discussion of Dayananda's view of the Vedas, see Swami Dayananda Saraswati, *An Introduction to the Commentary on the Vedas,* trans. Pundit Ghasi Ram (Delhi: Jan Gyan Prakashan, 1973).

90. See Majumdar, *History of the Freedom Movement in India,* 1:264.

91. K. M. Panikkar, *The Foundations of New India* (London: Allen & Unwin, 1963), p. 29.

92. This by no means implies that there was agreement on all matters of doctrine between the Brahmo Samaj and Ramakrishna. They were divided on many issues, e.g., the doctrine of transmigration, the concept of the *avatāra,* the ultimate supremacy of Advaita, and the use of images in worship.

Chapter 2: Vivekananda's Concept of the Nature, Role, and Authority of the Vedas

1. See *The Complete Works of Swami Vivekananda (CW),* 8 vols. (Calcutta: Advaita Ashrama, 1964–1971), 1:204–206. (Documentation is hereafter given in the text.)

2. Śaṅkara clearly uses the word *āgama* as synonymous with the words of the *śruti* (see Ke.U = B 1.3, p. 49). Vivekananda translates *āpta* as "attained."

3. It is very interesting to note the similarity of this argument with the ones advanced by Śaṅkara for the necessity and justification of the Vedas as a *pramāṇa.* His general contention is that the Vedas are necessary to provide knowledge of those things that cannot be known through our normal pro-

cesses. They are not meant to inform us of subjects that can be known through perception and inference. For a discussion of Śaṅkara's view, see Anantanand Rambachan, *Accomplishing the Accomplished: The Vedas as a Source of Valid Knowledge in Śaṅkara,* Monographs of the Society for Asian and Comparative Philosophy, no. 10 (Honolulu: University of Hawaii Press, 1991), 39–46.

4. Again, there is a similarity between this criterion and Śaṅkara's argument that one *pramāṇa* does not contradict another but only provides information unknown through any other means (see Br.U = B 2.1.20, p. 209).

5. It is interesting to note that Vivekananda uses the concept of the *āpta* to argue for the acceptance of his translation of *The Imitation of Christ* among Hindu readers. He argues that the words of such persons have a probative force and are "technically" known as *śabda-pramāṇa.* This identification of *śabda-pramāṇa* with the words of the *āpta* is adopted by Vivekananda from the philosophy of Nyāya (see NYSG 1.7, p. 5). According to Nyāya, *śabda-pramāṇa* is twofold in its concern. It informs us of things that are the objects of perception and of those things that cannot be seen *(driṣṭa* and *adriṣṭa).*

6. This analogy is just one example of Vivekananda's continuous attempt to draw parallels between the spheres of science and religion and their respective methods and findings. It is an important feature of his thought, and we shall be examining this later. See also *CW,* 8:232.

7. The view that knowledge is within is a repeated assertion of Vivekananda's, and we shall be exploring this subsequently.

8. "The book is not the proof of your conduct, but you are the proof of the book. How do you know that a book teaches truth? Because you are truth and feel it. That is what the *Vedānta* says" (*CW,* 2:307; see also 1:369, 324).

9. The same idea is expressed in the view that belief is possible only when individuals become prophets (see *CW,* 6:13, 181).

10. With reference to Christianity, Vivekananda asserted that the ideal was not to follow the Bible but to become the Bible, to see it as a mere guidepost (see *CW,* 4:45). In connection with this, he presented Christ and the Buddha as states to be attained. The historical Christ and Gautama were persons who manifested it (see *CW,* 7:29, 8:105).

11. The concept of religion as realization is a central one in Vivekananda's philosophy of religion and will be explored later.

12. "Religion, which is the highest knowledge and the highest wisdom, cannot be bought, nor can it be acquired from books" (*CW,* 3:52; also 8:210).

13. For Vivekananda's references to *śravaṇa, manana,* and *nididhyāsana,* see *CW,* 1:177; 2:396; 3:402; 4:245; 5:302, 322; 7:37; 8:154–155.

14. Vivekananda also admires the Buddha for his discovery of truth by himself (see *CW,* 8:104).

15. This was in response to whether he believed that the Sermon on the Mount was preached by Christ.

16. "The Church tries to fit Christ into it, not the church into Christ; so only those writings were preserved that suited the purpose in hand. Thus the books are not to be depended upon and book-worship is the worst kind of

idolatry to bind our feet. All has to conform to the book—science, religion, philosophy; it is the most horrible tyranny, this tyranny of the Protestant Bible" (*CW*, 7:30).

17. Vivekananda also sees belief in books as being responsible for much of the fanaticism associated with religious persecutions.

18. One must admit, however, that Vivekananda simplifies and caricatures the Mīmāṁsā theory that creation proceeds out of the eternal words of the Vedas. It is not that one verifies the existence of anything by its mention in the Vedas. Vivekananda also attacks the view of the Vedas as a treasury of the sum total of all knowledge, past, present, and future, revealed to a particular group (see *CW*, 4:433). It is important to note that, in Śaṅkara's view, it is not the purpose of the Vedas to inform us of everything. They impart only beneficial knowledge that cannot be obtained through any other means.

19. For Śaṅkara's definition of these terms, and for his interpretation of their significance, see Rambachan, *Accomplishing the Accomplished*, pp. 85–92. For Vivekananda's discussion of these qualities, see *CW*, 1:405–416, 8:106–121.

20. In Vivekananda's treatment of these qualities, he presents them more as fully accomplished rather than as preparatory.

21. For a full discussion of Śaṅkara's orthodox views on this matter, see BS = B 1.3.34, pp. 229–234.

22. For Śaṅkara's views, see Br.U = B 3.5.1, pp. 334–341; Pr.U = B 1.16, pp. 424–425.

23. BS = B 1.1.4 is especially concerned with establishing this view. See also Rambachan, *Accomplishing the Accomplished*, pp. 61–67.

24. It must be added, however, that Vivekananda does not provide any detailed evidence to substantiate his accusations.

25. Ramakrishna's life, according to Vivekananda, was a working out of the underlying harmony of all religious groups in India.

26. Vivekananda sees the Bhagavadgītā as a good illustration of this principle of exegesis; it proposes, according to him, a gradual method of exegesis until the absolute is attained (see *CW*, 3:261–262).

27. Vivekananda often said that, by the term *śruti*, he meant primarily the Upaniṣads. He felt that, in the present times, most of the rituals of the *karmakāṇḍa* were impractical. For Śaṅkara's understanding of the relation between *śruti* and *smṛti*, see Rambachan, *Accomplishing the Accomplished*, pp. 50–54.

28. Vivekananda often spoke out against the problem of a plurality of authoritative sources and the prevalence of Tantra practices in Bengal. His tone was usually impassioned on these occasions. Without specifying the nature of the customs, he often vehemently denounced the *vāmācārā* (left-handed) practices of Tantra, describing these as "horrible debauchery." He felt that the texts authorizing these practices had replaced *śruti* in Bengal (see, e.g., *CW*, 3:332–333, 340–341).

29. In India, Vivekananda often said that he preferred the name *Vedāntist* rather than *Hindu*. He thought the latter term to be quite descriptively mean-

ingless, while *Vedāntist* signified the common acceptance of the authority of the Vedas.

30. It is obvious that, when Vivekananda spoke of religion as forming the rallying point of national unity, he was thinking primarily of Hinduism. Islam, e.g., was not mentioned in this context. National unity basically meant Hindu religious accord. Vivekananda did not seem to anticipate the fears and suspicions that this could have aroused among non-Hindus and the eventual division of his country over this very question.

31. The foundation of Vedānta on impersonal principles was one of the characteristics, Vivekananda claimed, that commended it as a universal religion. It is impossible, he argued, to unite all people around any particular human figure.

32. For the Indian expression of this interpretation, see *CW,* 5:206, 6:9, 103.

33. Vivekananda's attempt to reconcile Vedic statements on the principle of an evolution from dualism to nondualism also featured more prominently in his Indian addresses. Noted earlier was his ridicule of the Mīmāṁsā theory of the creation of the world from Vedic words. There is one occasion in India, however, when he showed considerable sympathy to this argument and offered an interpretation of it to a disciple (see *CW,* 6:495–499). The gist of Vivekananda's argument in this lengthy discussion is that, with reference to the origin of the universe from Vedic words, the term *śabda* (lit., "word") indicates subtle ideas. Even when the entire universe is withdrawn, the subtle idea or *śabda* state of every created object exists in *brahman,* and the gross objects are created out of these subtle ideas. In Śaṅkara's own discussion of this theory, he does not distinguish between *śabda* as word and *śabda* as idea.

34. It is possible to argue that, in the West, Vivekananda felt that Advaita could be made more acceptable if he gave little or no significance to the Vedas as its authoritative source. But Vivekananda's denunciation of the value of scripture was not confined to the Vedas, and the reasons for this censure are too broad to be explained away by this argument. Halbfass (*India and Europe,* p. 235) comments on Vivekananda's tendency to pay heed to the expectation of his listeners. Halbfass sees this as an indication of Vivekananda's ambivalent hermeneutical situation. For his wider discussion of Vivekananda, see ibid., pp. 228–242.

Chapter 3: Karma, Bhakti, *and* Jñāna *as Direct and Independent Ways to* Mokṣa

1. In this chapter, I confine myself to a discussion of *karma, bhakti,* and *jñāna. Rājayoga* is closely linked with the central spiritual experience about which Vivekananda continuously speaks, and I consider this method in chapter 4.

2. For elaborations of this argument, see *CW,* 2:385–388, 6:16–17, 137–138.

3. For Śaṅkara's understanding of *karmayoga,* see Rambachan, *Accomplishing the Accomplished,* pp. 92–96.

4. "Performing actions without attachment for the sake of *Iśvara,* man attains *mokṣa,* through attaining purity of mind *(sattva-śuddhi)*" (BG = B 3:19, p. 104).

5. Vivekananda often argues about the contradiction of the concept of a perfect life. Good and evil, he says, define each other, and the former is not possible without the presence of the latter. The sum total of pain in the world is always the same; the variation is only in expression (see *CW,* 1:83–84, 111–113).

6. Along with his attempt to enlarge the concept of *karmayoga,* one also finds in Vivekananda the search for new ways of justifying this means. The primary new rationale centers around the idea of *karmayoga* as the secret of activity or work. Sometimes this is emphasized in a manner that appears to take *karmayoga* out of the context of being a way to *mokṣa* and converts it into a pragmatic method of maximizing the success of any activity. The main argument in this context is that failure in accomplishing the ends of activity is often due to an obsession with these ends and insufficient attention to the means. *Karmayoga* remedies this by diverting attention from the result and stressing the perfection of the means (see *CW,* 2:1–9). Vivekananda also sees the self-restraint involved in being indifferent to rewards as leading to the cultivation of willpower. For a contemporary discussion of the *karmayoga* concept, see Ursula King, "Who Is the Ideal Karmayogin? The Meaning of a Hindu Religious Symbol," *Religion* 10 (1980): 41–59.

7. Among other reasons, the Buddha is described as an ideal *karmayogī* because of what Vivekananda considers to be his doctrinal indifference.

8. "So the only way is to give up all the fruits of work, to be unattached to them. Know that this world is not we, nor are we this world; that we are really not the body; that we really do not work. We are the Self, eternally at rest and at peace" (*CW,* 1:116).

9. These are very typical of the kinds of passages one encounters in trying to understand how *karmayoga* leads directly to knowledge. For other examples, see *CW,* 1:107, 110; 3:142; 4:436; 7:63, 69, 75, 110.

10. "Good works and all that (merely) make the mind a little quiet" (*CW,* 1:517; see also 5:240–241; 7:54, 159–160, 221–222).

11. Vivekananda defines *Īśvara* in accordance with BS 1.1.2: "From whom is the birth, continuation, and dissolution of the universe."

12. "The object of *bhakti* is God. Love cannot be without a subject and an object. The object of love again must be at first a being who can reciprocate our love. Therefore the God of love must be in some sense a human God. He must be a God of love" (*CW,* 8:153).

13. The disadvantage of this method, according to Vivekananda, is its tendency to degenerate into fanaticism. The reverse side of the singleness of attachment required in *bhaktiyoga* is often the deprecation of everything else, for we seem to be able to love our own ideals only by hating all others. This danger, however, says Vivekananda, is a possibility only in the lower and early stages of *bhaktiyoga.*

14. In commending the virtues of *bhaktiyoga,* Vivekananda mentions what he sees as some disadvantages and difficulties of *jñāna-* and *rājayoga. Jñānayoga,* he says, requires favorable circumstances and strenuous practice. There is also the danger of being caught "in the interminable net of vain argumentation" (*CW,* 7:198) and of knowledge being used to justify any kind of conduct. In *rājayoga,* the danger is the attraction for the acquisition of psychic powers.

15. In *karmayoga,* e.g., there is no emphasis on the necessity of a teacher. The main reason for the wealth of details that Vivekananda provides in his discussions of *bhaktiyoga* is the availability of a mass of traditional literature on the subject. In these discussions, he draws heavily on the commentaries of Rāmānuja.

16. For a full discussion of these qualifications, see *CW,* 4:1–12, 21–33; 3:45–56, 64–69. The Bhagavadgītā (17.7–10) relates the nature of the food preferred to the characteristics of the individual temperament. Preference is determined by the predominance of the qualities of *sattva, rajas,* or *tamas* (see also Ch.U 7.26.2).

17. Because of the secondary role that he ascribes to scripture and, therefore, exegesis, Vivekananda does not seem to consider the possibility that a knowledge of philology, etymology, and syntax may be of great value in arriving at the spirit of any scripture.

18. The question of Krishna's historicity was widely discussed at the turn of the nineteenth century in Bengal (see Ursula King, "True and Perfect Religion: Bankim Chandra Chatterjee's Reinterpretation of Hinduism," *Religion* 7 [1977]: 127–148).

19. Vivekananda explains that grace operates both within and outside the concept of law. While it naturally descends on the pure, it is not constrained by any conditions. The Lord has a playful nature, and grace can bring about even unsolicited release (see *CW,* 6:481–483).

20. For Śaṅkara's understanding of the role of reason, see Rambachan, *Accomplishing the Accomplished,* pp. 101–108; and also Wilhelm Halbfass, *Tradition and Reflection* (Albany: State University of New York Press, 1991), chap. 5.

21. See Rambachan, *Accomplishing the Accomplished,* pp. 106–108.

22. For arguments along the same lines, see also *CW,* 2:329–336, 3:423–424, 8:184.

23. Vivekananda also suggests that reason is the only guide able to decide among the conflicting claims of religion. Conflicting claims cannot be decided by each asserting the superiority of its authoritative text.

24. See Kopf, *The Brahmo Samaj,* pp. 42–86.

25. Vivekananda also sees as characteristic of scientific method the availability of a common experiential referent, against which the truth or fallacy of its conclusions can be readily evaluated. Because he can evaluate scientific claims by reference to his own experiences, the ordinary man, Vivekananda argues, has no difficulty in seeing their plausibility. It is important for him to identify this as describing the scientific approach, for in *rājayoga* he proposes

a method for arriving at such an experience in the religious sphere, against which its claims could be evaluated. It is clear here, however, that he is equating two different kinds of experiences, and in the next chapter we shall be looking at the difficulties that this equation presents. For a discussion of some of the problems of defining the nature of science, see A. F. Chalmers, *What Is This Thing Called Science,* 2d ed. (Milton Keynes: Open University Press, 1982).

26. For a good example of this, see "The Cosmos" (*CW,* 2:203–225). The Upaniṣads themselves, of course, frequently draw this analogy.

27. "Religion is the acceptance of all existing creeds, seeing in them the same striving toward the same destination. Creed is something antagonistic and combative" (*CW,* 7:286).

Chapter 4: The Meaning and Authoritativeness of Anubhava *in Vivekananda*

1. This, of course, challenges his own attempt to present the method of *jñānayoga* as a path to ultimate knowledge through independent reasoning.

2. In chapter 3, reference was made to his attempts to draw analogies with the methods and findings of science. The further significance of these attempts will become more obvious in his arguments for the imperative of a direct perception of religious truths.

3. Vivekananda distinguishes between internal and external experience. He classifies knowledge garnered from the former as psychology, metaphysics, and religion and that from the latter as the physical sciences (see *CW,* 2:432). Even when knowledge is gained from someone's words, says Vivekananda, one must presume the experience in a former existence because only through experience can one learn anything (see *CW,* 7:46).

4. For similar statements on the derivation of all knowledge from experience, see *CW,* 2:226; 6:81, 128, 132–133.

5. There are occasions in India, however, when Vivekananda asserted that the idea of religion as direct perception is unique to Hinduism (see *CW,* 3:345).

6. "The *Vedānta* says that Yoga is the one way that makes men realize this divinity" (*CW,* 5:282). Vivekananda is not very clear on the relation between the truths that, he claims, can be directly perceived through the practice of *rājayoga* and *mokṣa.* Is the direct perception of religious truth *mokṣa* or the way to attain *mokṣa?* (I am grateful to Professor Arthur Herman for drawing my attention to the significance of this distinction.) It appears, however, that Vivekananda does understand *mokṣa* to be more than the perception of religious truths. He speaks of it as a separation of the self from the body and all nature. For the problems associated with this argument, see chapter 5 below.

7. Vivekananda often enthusiastically describes the control of *prāṇa* in the body as leading to a control of all forces in the universe, to all knowledge, and eventually to freedom (see *CW,* 1:148–149).

8. The *kuṇḍalinī* is described by Vivekananda as a coiled-up, unmanifested energy lying at the base of the spinal canal. Its awakening through the practice

of *rājayoga* leads to its upward movement through a subtle, nonphysical hollow in the spinal column *(suṣumnā).* As it progresses, it passes through seven centers of consciousness *(cakras),* each step marked by distinct spiritual experiences. When it reaches the seventh, the thousand petaled *(sahasrāra cakra),* located in the brain, full spiritual illumination is gained (see *CW,* 1:160–170). For more information, see Agehananda Bharati, *The Tantric Tradition* (London: Rider, 1965).

9. See Georg Feuerstein, *The Philosophy of Classical Yoga* (Manchester: Manchester University Press, 1980). The word *Tantra* means a system or discipline. There is a great division of opinion among scholars over the origin of the beliefs and practices of Tantra. Although the earliest Tantric texts are not dated before the fifth century A.D., attempts have been made to find its roots in the Ṛg-Veda (see G. Feuerstein and J. Miller, *A Reappraisal of Yoga* [London: Rider, 1971]; and chapter 5 below). Other views suggest that it was the prevalent form of worship among the non-Aryans and that it was gradually encompassed by the Aryans. It has also been argued that the roots of Tantra are to be found in Mahāyāna Buddhism. According to T. W. Organ, the background of Tantra is largely Sāṅkhya. While Śiva is the passive *puruṣa,* Śakti is the dynamic *prakṛti.* The evolution and diversity of the world are traced to the interaction of the three *guṇas.* Tantricism classifies the Hindu scriptures into the *āgamas* and *nigamas,* equivalent to the traditional distinction between *śruti* and *smṛti.* Tantric texts, however, are accorded the status of *āgamas (śruti),* while the Vedas are grouped with the *nigamas (smṛti)* (see *The Hindu Quest for the Perfection of Man,* 1st paperbound ed. [Athens: Ohio University Press, 1980], chap. 5, pp. 319–329). For a good discussion of Ramakrishna in the context of Tantra, see Zimmer, *Philosophies of India,* pp. 560–595.

10. The nature of reason in Vivekananda is considered in detail in chapter 3 above.

11. It is significant that Vivekananda often substitutes the term *inspiration* for *samādhi* or superconsciousness (see, e.g., *CW,* 2:389–390). Keshub Chandra Sen also upholds inspiration as the highest instrument of spiritual knowledge. He presents it as direct communion with God made possible through God's mercy. I have suggested that Sen was deeply influenced in this matter by leading Unitarian writers of the time (see chapter 1 above).

12. Vivekananda often replaces the words *concentration* and *observation* with *meditation* and speaks of the latter as the great scientific method of knowledge, the process through which all scientific and other types of knowledge is gained (see, e.g., *CW,* 4:230, 249).

13. "In making money, or in worshipping God, or in doing anything, the stronger the power of concentration, the better will that thing be done. This is the one call, the one knock, which opens the gates of nature, and lets out floods of light. This, the power of concentration, is the only key to the treasure house of knowledge. The system of *Rāja-Yoga* deals almost exclusively with this" (*CW,* 2:391).

14. Vivekananda's arguments about the derivation of the fundamental doc-

trines of religion from the study of the mind are almost identical with Keshub Chandra Sen's views on this subject (see chapter 1 above).

15. *Ch.U.* 4.4.1–4.9.3 describes the method by which the student, Satyakāma, gains *brahmajñāna.* After convincing his teacher of his strict adherence to truth, he is initiated and given four hundred lean and weak cows to tender. He departs from his teacher, promising not to return until the herd has multiplied to a thousand cows. The text describes Satyakāma's instruction by a bull, fire, a flamingo, and an aquatic bird. According to Vivekananda, the student mistakenly interprets the knowledge that was coming from within himself as originating from the external world (see *CW,* 2:309–311).

16. Vivekananda uses Muhammad as an example of a prophet who accidentally encountered the state of *samādhi.*

17. "Then when the mind is free from activity or functioning, it vanishes, and the Self is revealed" (*CW,* 6:475; see also 1:203, 234).

18. "If you can get absolutely still for just one moment, you have reached the goal. The mind may go on working after that; but it will never be the same mind again. You will know yourself as you are—your true Self. Still the mind but for one moment, and the truth of your real nature will flash upon you, and freedom is at hand; no more bondage after that" (*CW,* 6:96–97; see also 1:453, 7:431, 434).

19. For the second account, see *CW,* 7:139. In this description, he says that he was able to return to the relative world only because of a persistence of the ego sense.

20. Some of the roots of this idea of religion as direct perception and realization, with its rejection of formal learning, organization, and worship, go back perhaps to the tradition of *bhakti* and, in Bengal, to its poet-saints. In a lecture on Ramakrishna, Vivekananda himself mentions the idea as being common among these poets (see *CW,* 4:164–165). This is an area that deserves further examination. In Vivekananda himself, the quest for some form of direct, authoritative, and immediate knowledge of God seems to have been well developed even before his meeting with Ramakrishna. Keshub Chandra Sen, with whom we have suggested certain significant parallels, could have been an important influence. The following questions put by Vivekananda to Ramakrishna are significant in understanding the kind of quest he was pursuing at that time. The words are Vivekananda's own: "I heard of this man, and I went to hear him. He looked just like an ordinary man, with nothing remarkable about him. He used the most simple language, and I thought 'Can this man be a great teacher?'—I crept near to him and asked him the question which I had been asking others all my life: 'Do you believe in God, Sir?' 'Yes.' 'How?' 'Because I see Him just as I see you here, only in a much intenser sense.' That impressed me at once. For the first time I found a man who dared to say that he saw God, that religion was a reality to be felt, to be sensed in an infinitely more intense way than we can sense the world" (*CW,* 4:179).

The search for an incontrovertible, self-validating experience must in part also be the result of the skepticism induced in his thought at college through his reading of the works of such writers as J. S. Mill, D. Hume, and H. Spencer. Reason seemed a meandering path with no visible end and failed to satisfy him. The kind of skepticism that seemed to have plagued him in his early days was evinced much later on, after the death of Ramakrishna. There were doubts in his mind about the authoritativeness of the Vedas and the reliability of its authors. He sought answers from Pramadadas Mitra of Benares, whose erudition he regarded highly (see the letter to Pramadadas Mitra in *Letters of Swami Vivekananda,* 4th ed. [Calcutta: Advaita Ashrama, 1976], pp. 7–11). It is quite possible that his search for a spiritual experience may also have been prompted, in part, by his study of English Romantic poetry, with its strong mystical bent and its preference for the faculties of intuition and feeling as opposed to reason. It is significant that one version of his life records as the motive for his first visit to Ramakrishna a discussion of a verse from Wordsworth's *Excursion,* describing a state of mystic rapture (see Dhar, *Comprehensive Biography,* 1:79–80).

21. "If God is true, we must feel Him as a fact, and if there is a soul, we ought to be able to see it and feel it" (*CW,* 8:39). These references are representative of his innumerable and almost identical statements on this issue. For similar affirmations, see *CW,* 1:232, 234; 2:129, 372, 410–411, 474; 4:30, 126.

22. Similar views, in almost identical language, are repeated in nearly every one of Vivekananda's major addresses.

23. In chapter 3, I have already considered some of the general difficulties raised in connection with Vivekananda's equation of Advaita and science.

24. For a brief, lucid discussion of many of the problems associated with evaluating religious experience, see P. Donavan, *Interpreting Religious Experience* (London: Sheldon Press, 1979).

25. For a discussion of Śaṅkara's position on this issue, see Rambachan, *Accomplishing the Accomplished,* chap. 2.

26. For a series of illuminating discussions of this issue, see S. T. Katz, ed., *Mysticism and Philosophical Analysis* (London: Sheldon Press, 1978); and also Ninian Smart, "Interpretation and Mystical Experience," *Religious Studies* 1 (1965): 75–87.

27. See chapter 2 above.

28. Among the differences mentioned by Vivekananda are the Śāṅkhya concept of a plurality of individual selves and the total separation of the self *(puruṣa)* from nature *(prakṛti).* He also argues against the concept of a plurality of infinites.

Chapter 5: Vivekananda and Śaṅkara

1. In *Accomplishing the Accomplished,* I attempt to clarify Śaṅkara's justification of the Vedas as a *pramāṇa* for the liberating knowledge of *brahman.* A short summary of his arguments may also be found in my "Śaṅkara's Rationale for the *Śruti* as the Definitive Source of *Brahmajñāna:* A Refutation of Some Contemporary Views," *Philosophy East and West* 36, no. 1 (January 1986): 25–40. The outline that follows draws from these two sources.

2. See BS = B 1.1.1, pp. 6–13; and also Rambachan, *Accomplishing the Accomplished,* pp. 65–67.

3. The desirable ends that can be attained by adopting the means prescribed in the *karmakāṇḍa* are sometimes classified as *dharma, artha* (prosperity), and *kāma* (pleasure). The *jñānakāṇḍa* is also referred to as Vedānta, literally meaning the end of the Vedas (i.e., the Upaniṣads). The end here is *mokṣa* (liberation).

4. See Rambachan, *Accomplishing the Accomplished,* pp. 37–39. The word *Mīmāṁsā* means "inquiry," and this system undertakes an analysis of the first *(Pūrva)* parts of the Vedas. The *sūtras* of Jaimini (ca. 200 B.C.) are the earliest work of this system and form its basis.

5. See Rambachan, *Accomplishing the Accomplished,* pp. 92–96.

6. See chapter 2 above.

7. The suggestion of *mokṣa* as obtaining only in the state of *samādhi* occurs throughout Vivekananda's presentation of *rājayoga*. For two specific discussions in which this view is very obvious, see *CW,* 1:197–199, 212–224.

8. In a recent article, Michael Comans points to Śaṅkara's cautious and infrequent use of the term *samādhi.* According to Comans, Śaṅkara does not uphold *nirvikalpasamādhi* as a goal. The aim of contemplation, in Śaṅkara, is the appreciation of a self that is already liberated. Comans also draws attention to the increase in *samādhi*-oriented practice after Śaṅkara (see "The Question of the Importance of *Samādhi* in Modern and Classical Advaita Vedānta," *Philosophy East and West* 43, no. 1 [January 1993]: 19–38).

9. As a system of dualistic realism, Sāṅkhya proposes two ultimate realities, *puruṣa* (self) and *prakṛti* (matter). These are absolutely separate and independent of each other, with respect to their existence. Unlike Advaita, there is an infinity of *puruṣas,* each distinct from the other. Through some unexplained process, *puruṣas* got mixed up with *prakṛti* and impose on themselves the qualities of *prakṛti.* In Śaṅkhya, *mokṣa* involves total isolation *(kaivalya)* of each *puruṣa* from *prakṛti* and from each other. Since *prakṛti* is as real as *puruṣa,* any association between the two would constitute bondage, and this seems to explain the emphasis on isolation or withdrawal. For a detailed account, see C. Sharma, *A Critical Survey of Indian Philosophy* (Delhi: Motilal Banarsidass, 1976), chap. 9; and also S. N. Dasgupta, *A History of Indian Philosophy,* 1st Indian ed., 5 vols. (Delhi: Motilal Banarsidass, 1975), vol. 1, chap. 7.

10. See Rambachan, *Accomplishing the Accomplished,* pp. 108–113.

11. See ibid., pp. 101–108.

12. In *CW,* 3:281–282, three such texts are mentioned by Vivekananda. These are Ke.U. 1.3 and 2.2 as well as Ta.U. 2.9.1. I am using Vivekananda's own translations.

13. For a discussion of Śaṅkara's approach to the problem of defining *brahman,* which lacks genus, quality, relation, and activity, see Rambachan, *Accomplishing the Accomplished,* pp. 67–78.

14. Vivekananda appears to be even more inconsistent when he describes the state of *samādhi* as being only temporary (see *CW,* 7:112).

15. See Rambachan, *Accomplishing the Accomplished,* pp. 83–85.

16. This is the last *sūtra,* and the repetition of the sentence in the Brahmasūtra indicates the end of the text.

17. See Rambachan, *Accomplishing the Accomplished,* pp. 112–113; and also Halbfass, *Tradition and Reflection,* chap. 6.

18. Rambachan, *Accomplishing the Accomplished,* pp. 67–68, 100–101.

19. Ch.U. 4.4.1–4.9.3, which Vivekananda interprets as affirming his theory of *brahmajñāna* as being within, is understood differently by Śaṅkara. When Satyakāma returns to his teacher's home, his teacher, noticing his radiant appearance, realizes that he had received instruction about *brahman.* He inquires about this and is told by Satyakāma that he received instruction from "people other than human beings." Unlike Vivekananda, Śaṅkara says that the student was instructed by deities. It is very interesting that, in the next verse (4.9.3), Satyakāma still requests instruction from his teacher. In his commentary, Śaṅkara paraphrases this request: "Further, it has been heard by me, in this connection, from sages like your reverence, that it is only knowledge learnt from a teacher that becomes best,—acquires its highest character; hence your reverence alone should teach me" (Ch.U = B 4.9.3, p. 198).

20. BG 4:32 advances the traditional method of the Upaniṣads for gaining knowledge. The student is advised to approach the teacher with reverence, service, and inquiry. Commenting on this verse, Śaṅkara says that the teacher should be asked about the cause of bondage, the means of deliverance, and the nature of ignorance and knowledge (see also Mu.U. 1.2.12–13, along with Śaṅkara's commentary). There is no suggestion in these texts discussing the role of the teacher that the knowledge imparted is already possessed by the student.

Chapter 6: The Legacy of Vivekananda

1. It is difficult to agree here with Wilhelm Halbfass, who argues that science is not a central issue in Vivekananda's rediscovery and reinterpretation of the Indian tradition (see *India and Europe,* p. 34). Vivekananda was clearly concerned to demonstrate the compatibility between Hindu methods and insights with what he understood to be the claims and methods of science.

2. For a detailed discussion of the impact of science in Bengal in the nineteenth century, see Kopf, *The Brahmo Samaj,* chap. 2, pp. 42–85.

Glossary

adhikārī	A qualified or eligible aspirant for liberation.
adhikārībheda	Differences in the eligibility of aspirants; this may require different teaching methods and techniques.
adhyāsa	Superimposition; used, in Advaita, to describe the erroneous identification of *brahman* with the qualities of the body and mind.
Advaita	Lit., "nonduality"; the view of reality systematized and expounded by Śaṅkara.
āgama	Traditional text or doctrine; sometimes used as a synonym for the *śruti.*
ajñāna	Ignorance, error, or invalid cognition.
anubhava	Experience, firm opinion; also used to designate knowledge gained from any valid source other than memory.
anubhūti	Experience; direct apprehension.
anumāna	Inference; one of the six sources of knowledge accepted by Advaita.
apauruṣeya	That which is not of human origin or nature; used as a description of the Vedas to distinguish them from texts having a human origin.
āpta	A credible, trustworthy, or authoritative person.
āptavākya	The words of a trustworthy person.
ātmajñāna	Knowledge of the *ātman.*
ātman	The self; posited, in Advaita, as identical with *brahman.*
avatāra	Incarnation or descent of God into the world.
avidyā	Ignorance or erroneous knowledge; in Advaita, it indicates incorrect knowledge of the self.
bhakta	Devotee or lover of God.
bhakti	Love or devotion for God.
bhaktiyoga	Path or way of loving devotion.
bhaktiyogī	One who follows the path of *bhaktiyoga.*

brahmajñāna	The knowledge of *brahman* that reveals the liberated state.
brahman	The limitless reality; identical, in Advaita, with the *ātman*.
brahmin	Member of the highest caste, whose primary duty is to study and teach the Vedas.
cit	Awareness; the nature of the self.
citta-śuddhi	Purity of the mind; a precondition for the knowledge of *brahman*.
guṇa	Quality or attribute; merit or excellence.
guru	Teacher, preceptor; one who instructs about *brahman*.
iṣṭadeva	One's chosen deity or form of God.
Īśvara	God; *brahman* conceived as creator and ruler of the universe and possessing the qualities of omniscience and omnipotence.
jīvanmukta	Lit., "living free"; one who retains the body after attaining liberation but who enjoys freedom and fullness in spite of the limitations of the body.
jñāna	Any kind of cognition, without regard to the question of truth or error; generally used, however, to designate valid knowledge.
jñānakāṇḍa	Last sections of the Vedas (namely, the Upaniṣads); seen, in Advaita, as having an independent purpose in revealing *brahman*.
jñānayoga	The way of knowledge; used, by Vivekananda, to indicate a spiritual path consisting primarily of the application of reason.
jñānayogī	One who follows the method of *jñānayoga*.
jñānī	One who possesses valid knowledge.
karma	Action or deed; also used to indicate the effects of deeds performed in past lives and the future effects of current actions.
karmakāṇḍa	First sections of the Vedas dealing with the performance of ritual actions; seen, in Advaita, as having a different aim and result from the *jñānakāṇḍa*.
karmayoga	The way of action; used, by Vivekananda, to indicate a spiritual path emphasizing unselfish action.
karmayogī	One who practices *karmayoga*.
manana	Thinking or reflection; the process of pondering the meaning of scripture with the aid of reason.
mantra	Sacred word or sentence from the scriptures.
mantra-draṣṭā	Seer or recipient of the sacred words and truths enshrined in the Vedas.
mokṣa	Lit., "freedom"; generally from the cycle of birth and death; in Advaita, this freedom is conceived as being coincident with the knowledge of *brahman* and attainable while one is living in the body.
mukti	Liberation; same as *mokṣa*.

nididhyāsana	Contemplation or attentive thinking.
nirguṇa	Free from all qualities; the nature of *brahman* in Advaita.
Nyāya	Logic; school of Indian philosophy systematized by Gautama.
parābhakti	The highest stage in the path of loving devotion *(bhaktiyoga)*.
pramāṇa	A source of valid knowledge.
pratyakṣa	Perception; one of the sources of valid knowledge.
Pūrva-Mīmāṁsā	School of Vedic exegesis systematized by Jaimini and concerned with the analysis of the first or ritualistic portions of the Vedas.
rājayoga	Lit., "the royal path"; used by Vivekananda to designate the eightfold Yoga system of Patañjali.
rājayogī	One who follows the path of *rājayoga*.
ṛṣi	Inspired poet or sage; used to describe the recipients of revelation.
śabda	Sound or word.
śabda-pramāṇa	A means of valid knowledge consisting of words; identified, in Advaita, with the Vedas and posited as one of the six sources of valid knowledge.
sādhana	Spiritual discipline or path.
sādhana-catuṣṭaya	The fourfold disciplines proposed as preparatory for the successful attainment of liberating knowledge.
saguṇa (brahman)	With qualities; *brahman* conceived of as creator and possessing all good qualities.
samādhi	Lit., "putting together"; concentration; absorption; the eigth and last stage in the Yoga system of Patañjali.
saṁsāra	Cycle of successive births and deaths, freedom from which constitutes liberation.
Sāṅkhya	Number; dualistic school of Indian philosophy founded by Kapila.
saṅnyāsin	Renunciant; one who has entered the fourth stage of Hindu life.
smṛti	Memory; name given to texts other than the Vedas.
śravaṇa	Listening or hearing; the acquisition of knowledge by listening to the words of the scripture or teacher.
śruti	Lit., "that which is heard"; synonym for the Vedas.
śūdra	Member of the fourth caste.
Vedānta	Lit., "the end of the Vedas"; applied to the last sections of the Vedas (the Upaniṣads) and to schools based on their exegesis.
Vedāntavākya	Words and sentences of the Upaniṣads.

Bibliography

Primary Sources in English Translation

Gambhīrānanda, Swāmī, trans. *Eight Upaniṣads: With the Commentary of Śaṅkarācārya.* 2 vols. (*Īśa, Kena, Kaṭha,* and *Taittirīya* in vol. 1; *Aitareya, Muṇḍaka, Māṇḍūkya, Kārikā,* and *Praśna* in vol. 2.) 2d ed. Calcutta: Advaita Ashrama, 1965–1966.

———, trans. *The Brahma-sūtra Bhāṣya of Śaṅkarācārya.* 3d ed. Calcutta: Advaita Ashrama, 1977.

Jha Ganganatha, trans. *The Chāndogyopanishad (A Treatise on the Vedānta Philosophy Translated into English with the Commentary of Śaṅkara).* Poona: Oriental Book Agency, 1942.

———, trans. *The Pūrva-Mīmāṁsā Sūtras of Jaimini: With an Original Commentary in English.* Varanasi: Bharatiya Publishing House, 1979.

Mādhavānanda, Swāmī, trans. *The Bṛhadāraṇyaka Upaniṣad: With the Commentary of Śaṅkārācarya.* 5th ed. Calcutta: Advaita Ashrama, 1975.

Sastry, A. Mahadeva, trans. *The Bhagavadgītā: With the Commentary of Śrī Śaṅkarāchārya.* Madras: Samata Books, 1977; reprint, 1979.

———, trans. *The Taittiriya Upanishad: With the Commentaries of Sri Sankaracharya, Sri Suresvaracharya and Sri Vidyaranya (Including Introduction to the Study of the Upanishads by Sri Vidyaranya and the Atharvana Upanishads: Amritabindu, Kaivalya).* Madras: Samata Books, 1980.

Vidyābhūṣaṇa, M. M. Satisa Chandra, trans. *The Nyāya Sūtras of Gotama.* Edited by Nandalal Sinha. Allahabad, 1930; reprint, Delhi: Motilal Banarsidass, 1981.

Works of Swami Vivekananda

The Complete Works of Swami Vivekananda (Mayavati Memorial Edition). 8 vols. Calcutta: Advaita Ashrama, 1964–1971.

Letters of Swami Vivekananda. 4th ed. Calcutta: Advaita Ashrama, 1976.

Secondary Sources

Arora, V. K. *The Social and Political Philosophy of Swami Vivekananda.* Calcutta: Punthi Pustak, 1968.

Ashby, P. H. *Modern Trends in Hinduism.* New York: Columbia University Press, 1974.

Baird, Robert, ed. *Religion in Modern India.* New Delhi: Manohar Publications, 1981.

Bali, Dev Raj. *Modern Indian Thought (Rammohun Roy to M. N. Roy).* Delhi: Stirling Publishers, 1980.

Banerji, G. C. *Keshab Chandra and Ramakrishna.* Calcutta: Navavidhan Publications, 1931.

Basu, Prem Chunder, ed. *Life and Teachings of Brahmananda Keshub Chunder Sen.* Calcutta: Navavidhan Publications, 1931.

Basu, S. B., and S. B. Ghosh, eds. *Vivekananda in Indian Newspapers, 1893–1902.* Calcutta: Dineshchandra Basu Bhattacharyya, 1969.

Bharati, A. *The Tantric Tradition.* London: Rider, 1965.

———. "The Hindu Renaissance and Its Apologetic Patterns." *Journal of Asian Studies* 29 (1970): 267–287.

———. *The Light at the Centre: Context and Pretext of Modern Mysticism.* Santa Barbara, Calif.: Ross Erickson Publishers, 1976.

Blichfeldt, Anders. "Tantra in the Ramakrishna Math and Mission." *Update* 6 (1982): 30–47.

Brown, L. K. "Mission, a Cultural Confrontation: Swami Vivekananda and the American Missionary Movement." *Journal of Dharma* 6 (1981): 167–189.

Burke, Marie Louise. *Swami Vivekananda in America: New Discoveries.* Calcutta: Advaita Ashrama, 1958.

Chalmers, A. F. *What Is This Thing Called Science.* Milton Keynes: Open University Press, 1982.

Channing, W. E. *The Complete Works.* London: Williams & Norgate, 1880.

Choudhary, K. P. S. *Modern Indian Mysticism.* Delhi: Motilal Banarsidass, 1981.

Collet, S. D., ed. *Lectures and Tracts by Keshub Chunder Sen.* London: Strahan, 1870.

Comans Michael. "The Question of the Importance of *Samādhi* in Modern and Classical Advaita Vedānta." *Philosophy East and West* 43, no. 1 (January 1993): 19–38.

Crawford, S. C. *Ram Mohan Roy: Social, Political and Religious Reform in Nineteenth Century India.* New York: Paragon House, 1987.

Das, Sisir Kumar. *The Shadow of the Cross: Christianity and Hinduism in a Colonial Situation.* Delhi: Munshiram Manoharlal Publishers, 1974.

Dasgupta, S. N. *A History of Indian Philosophy.* 1st Indian ed. 5 vols. Delhi: Motilal Banarsidass, 1975.

Datta, Bhupendranath. *Swami Vivekananda: Patriot-Prophet.* Calcutta: Nababharat, 1954.

Devaraja, N. K. *Hinduism and the Modern Age.* Delhi: Islam and Modern Age Society, 1975.

Devdas, Nalini. *Swami Vivekananda.* Bangalore: Christian Institute for the Study of Religion, 1968.

———. *Sri Ramakrishna.* Bangalore: Christian Institute for the Study of Religion and Society, 1969.

Dhar, S. N. *A Comprehensive Biography of Swami Vivekananda.* 2 vols. Madras: Vivekananda Prakashan Kendra, 1975–1976.

Donavan, P. *Interpreting Religious Experience.* London: Sheldon Press, 1979.

Eastern and Western Disciples. *The Life of Swami Vivekananda.* 8th ed. Calcutta: Advaita Ashrama, 1974.

Farquhar, J. N. *An Outline of the Religious Literature of India.* Oxford: Oxford University Press, 1920; reprint, Delhi: Munshiram Manoharlal, 1967.

———. *Modern Religious Movements in India.* Indian ed. Delhi: Munshiram Manoharlal, 1977.

Feuerstein, G. *The Philosophy of Classical Yoga.* Manchester: Manchester University Press, 1980.

Feuerstein, G., and J. Miller. *A Reappraisal of Yoga.* London: Rider, 1971.

French, Harold W. *The Swan's Wide Waters: Ramakrishna and Western Culture.* Port Washington, N.Y.: Kennikat Press, 1974.

Gambhīrānanda, Swāmī. *History of the Ramakrishna Math and Mission.* Calcutta: Advaita Ashrama, 1957.

———. *The Apostles of Ramakrishna.* Calcutta: Advaita Ashrama, 1972.

Ganguly, N. C. *Raja Ram Mohun Roy.* Calcutta: Y.M.C.A. Publishing House, 1934.

Ghanananda, Swami. *Shri Ramakrishna and His Unique Message.* 3d ed. London: Ramakrishna Vedanta Center, 1968.

Ghanananda, Swami, and Geoffrey Parrinder, eds. *Swami Vivekananda in the East and West.* London: Ramakrishna Vedanta Center, 1968.

Gupta, A. K., ed. *Studies in the Bengal Renaissance.* Calcutta: National Council of Education, 1958.

Gupta, K. P. "Religious Evolution and Social Change in India: A Study of the Ramakrishna Mission Movement." *Contributions to Indian Sociology,* n.s., 8 (1974): 25–50.

Gupta, Mahendranath. *The Gospel of Sri Ramakrishna.* Translated by Swami Nikhilananda. New York: Ramakrishna-Vivekananda Center, 1977.

Halbfass, Wilhelm. *India and Europe.* Albany: State University of New York Press, 1988.

———. *Tradition and Reflection.* Albany: State University of New York Press, 1991.

Heimsath, C. H. *Indian Nationalism and Hindu Social Reform.* Princeton, N.J.: Princeton University Press, 1964.

Isherwood, C. *Ramakrishna and His Disciples.* 3d ed. Calcutta: Advaita Ashrama, 1974.

Jones, K. W. *Arya Dharm: Hindu Consciousness in Nineteenth Century Punjab.* Berkeley: University of California Press, 1976.

Jordens, J. T. F. *Dayananda Saraswati.* Delhi: Oxford University Press, 1978.

Joshi, V. C., ed. *Rammohun Roy and the Process of Modernization in India.* New Delhi: Vikas Publishing House, 1975.

Katz, S. T., ed. *Mysticism and Philosophical Analysis.* London: Sheldon Press, 1978.

Killingley, D. "Rammohun Roy's Interpretation of the Vedānta." Ph.D. thesis, School of Oriental and African Studies, University of London, 1977.

———. "*Yoga-Sūtra* IV, 2-3 and Vivekananda's Interpretation of Evolution." *Journal of Indian Philosophy* 18 (1990): 151–179.

King, Ursula. "True and Perfect Religion: Bankim Chatterjee's Reinterpretation of Hinduism." *Religion* 7 (1977): 127–148.

———. "Who Is the Ideal Karmayogin? The Meaning of a Hindu Religious Symbol." *Religion* 10 (1980): 41–59.

Kinsley, D. R. *Hinduism.* Englewood Cliffs, N.J.: Prentice-Hall, 1982.

Kopf, D. *British Orientalism and the Bengal Renaissance.* Berkeley: University of California Press, 1969.

———. *The Brahmo Samaj and the Shaping of the Modern Indian Mind.* Princeton, N.J.: Princeton University Press, 1979.

Lavan, Spencer. *Unitarians and India: A Study in Encounter and Response.* Boston: Beacon Press, 1977.

Mahadevan, T. M. P. *Swami Vivekananda and the Indian Renaissance.* Coimbatore: Sri Ramakrishna Mission Vidyalaya Teachers College, 1965.

Majumdar, R. C. *History of the Freedom Movement in India.* 3 vols. Calcutta: Firma K. L. Mukhopadhyay, 1962–1963.

———, ed. *Swami Vivekananda Centenary Memorial Volume.* Calcutta: Swami Vivekananda Centenary Committee, 1963.

Matchet, Freda. "The Teaching of Ramakrishna in Relation to the Hindu Tradition as Interpreted by Vivekananda." *Religion* 11 (1981): 171–184.

Mazoomdar, P. C. *The Life and Teachings of Keshub Chunder Sen.* Calcutta: J. W. Thomas, Baptist Mission Press, 1887.

Mazumdar, A. K. *Understanding Vivekananda.* Calcutta: Sanskrit Pustak Bhandar, 1972.

Mital, S. S. *The Social and Political Ideas of Swami Vivekananda.* Delhi: Metropolitan Book Co., 1979.

Mitra, Sisirkumar. *Resurgent India.* Delhi: Allied Publishers, 1963.

Mukhopadhyay, A. K. *The Bengali Intellectual Tradition.* Calcutta: K. P. Bagchi, 1979.

Muller, F. Max. *Ramakrishna: His Life and Sayings.* Mayavati: Advaita Ashrama, 1951.

Narvane, V. S. *Modern Indian Thought.* New York: Asia Publishing House, 1964.

Neevel, Walter G., Jr. "The Transformation of Śrī Rāmakrishna." In *Hindu-*

ism: New Essays in the History of Religions, ed. Bardwell L. Smith. Leiden: E. J. Brill, 1976.

Nikhilananda, Swami. *Vivekananda.* 3d Indian ed. Calcutta: Advaita Ashrama, 1975.

Nivedita, Sister. *The Master as I Saw Him.* 12th ed. Calcutta: Udbodhan Office, 1977.

Olson, Carl. *The Mysterious Play of Kali: An Interpretative Study of Ramakrishna.* Atlanta: Scholars Press, 1990.

Organ, T. W. *The Hindu Quest for the Perfection of Man.* 1st paperbound ed. Athens: Ohio University Press, 1980.

Pangborn, Cyrus R. "The Ramakrishna Math and Mission: A Case Study of a Revitalization Movement." In *Hinduism: New Essays in the History of Religions,* ed. Bardwell L. Smith. Leiden: E. J. Brill, 1976; reprint, 1982.

Panikkar, K. M. *The Foundations of New India.* London: Allen & Unwin, 1963.

———. *Hinduism and the West.* Chandigarh: Panjab University Publications Bureau, 1964.

Parekh, M. C. *The Brahmo Samaj.* Calcutta: Brahmo Samaj, 1922.

———. *Brahmarsi Keshub Chander Sen.* Rajkot: Oriental Christ House, 1926.

Parker, Theodore. *The Collected Works.* Edited by Frances Power Cobbe. 12 vols. London: Trubner, 1863–1865.

Phillips, C. H., and M. D. Wainwright, eds. *Indian Society at the Beginnings of Modernization.* London: School of Oriental and African Studies, University of London, 1976.

Poddar, A. *Renaissance in Bengal.* 2 vols. Simla: Indian Institute of Advanced Study, 1970–1977.

Radhakrishnan, S. *Indian Philosophy.* 2 vols. London: Allen & Unwin, 1971.

Rai, Lajpat. *A History of the Arya Samaj.* Bombay: Orient Longmans, 1967.

Rambachan, Anantanand. "Is *Karmayoga* a Direct and Independent Means to *Mokṣa?*" *Religion* 15 (1985): 53–65.

———. "Śaṅkara's Rationale for the *Śruti* as the Definitive Source of *Brahmajñāna:* A Refutation of Some Contemporary Views." *Philosophy East and West* 36, no. 1 (January 1986): 25–40.

———. "The Place of Reason in the Quest for *Mokṣa:* Problems in Vivekananda's Conceptualization of *Jñānayoga.*" *Religious Studies* 23 (June 1987): 279–288.

———. "Where Words Fail: The Limits of Scriptural Authority in the Hermeneutics of a Contemporary Advaitin." *Philosophy East and West* 37 (October 1987): 361–371.

———. "Swami Vivekananda's Use of Science as an Analogy for the Attainment of *Mokṣa.*" *Philosophy East and West* 40 (July 1990): 331–342.

———. *Accomplishing the Accomplished: The Vedas as a Source of Valid Knowledge in Śaṅkara.* Monographs of the Society for Asian and Comparative Philosophy, no. 10. Honolulu: University of Hawaii Press, 1991.

———. "Where Words Can Set Free: The Liberating Potency of Vedic Words in the Hermeneutics of Śaṅkara." In *Texts in Context: Traditional Hermeneutics in South Asia,* ed. Jeffrey Timm. Albany: State University of New York Press, 1991.

Ray, Ajit Kumar. *The Religious Ideas of Rammohun Roy.* Delhi: Kanak Publications, 1976.

Ray, B. G. *Religious Movements in Modern Bengal.* Santiniketan: Visva-Bharati, 1965.

Ray, Niharranjan, ed. *Rammohun Roy: A Bi-Centenary Tribute.* New Delhi: National Book Trust, 1974.

Rolland, R. *The Life of Ramakrishna.* Calcutta: Advaita Ashrama, 1974.

———. *The Life of Vivekananda and the Universal Gospel.* Calcutta: Advaita Ashrama, 1975.

Rosselli, J. "Sri Ramakrishna and the Educated Elite of the Late Nineteenth Century Bengal." *Contributions to Indian Sociology,* n.s., 12 (1978): 195–212.

Saradananda, Swami. *Sri Ramakrishna the Great Master.* Translated by Swami Jagadananda. 5th rev. ed. 2 vols. Madras: Sri Ramakrishna Math, 1978–1979.

Saraswati, Swami Dayananda. *An Introduction to the Commentary on the Vedas.* Translated by Pundit Ghasi Ram. Delhi: Jan Gyan Prakashan, 1973.

Sarma, D. S. *Renascent Hinduism.* Bombay: Bharatiya Vidya Bhavan, 1966.

Sarma, N. S. *Hindu Renaissance.* Benares: Benares Hindu University, 1944.

Sastri Sivanath. *History of the Brahmo Samaj.* 2d ed. Calcutta: Sadharan Brahmo Samaj, 1974.

Satprakashananda, Swami. *Swami Vivekananda's Contribution to the Present Age.* St. Louis: Vedanta Society of St. Louis, 1978.

Schneiderman, Leo. "Ramakrishna: Personality and Social Factors in the Growth of a Religious Movement." *Journal for the Scientific Study of Religion* 8 (Spring 1969): 60–71.

Sen, Keshub Chunder. *Lectures and Tracts.* Edited by S. D. Collet. London: Strahan, 1870.

———. *The New Dispensation or Religion of Harmony.* Calcutta: Bidhan Press, 1903.

———. *Discourses and Writings.* Calcutta: Brahmo Tract Society, 1904.

Sharma, Arvind. *Ramakrishna and Vivekananda: New Perspectives.* New Delhi: Sterling Publishers, 1989.

Sharma, C. *A Critical Survey of Indian Philosophy.* Delhi: Motilal Banarsidass, 1976.

Sil, N. P. *Ramakṛṣṇa Paramahaṁsa: A Psychological Profile.* Leiden: E. J. Brill, 1991.

Sri Ramakrishna Math. *Sayings of Sri Ramakrishna.* Madras: Sri Ramakrishna Math, 1975.

Srivastava, R. S. *Contemporary Indian Philosophy.* Delhi: Munshiram Manoharlal, 1965.

Swami Vivekananda Centenary Committee. *Parliament of Religions (1963–64).* Calcutta, 1965.

Tagore, Debendranath. *Brahmo Dharma.* Translated by Hem Chandra Sarkar. Calcutta: H. C. Sarkar, 1928.

Vivekananda Prakashan Kendra. *The Indian Renaissance.* Madras: Vivekananda Prakashan Kendra, 1978.

Williams, George M. *The Quest for Meaning in Swami Vivekananda.* Chico, Calif.: New Horizons Press, 1978.

———."The Ramakrishna Movement: A Study in Religious Change." In *Religion in Modern India,* ed. Robert D. Baird. New Delhi: Manohar Publications, 1981.

———. "Swami Vivekananda: Archetypal Hero or Doubting Saint?" In *Religion in Modern India,* ed. Robert D. Baird. New Delhi: Manohar Publications, 1981.

Zaehner, R. C. *Hinduism.* London: Oxford University Press, 1966.

Index

About the Author

Anantanand Rambachan is associate professor of religion at Saint Olaf College in Minnesota. A native of Trinidad, Dr. Rambachan earned his Ph.D. at the University of Leeds. His publications include *Accomplishing the Accomplished: The Vedas as a Source of Valid Knowledge in Śaṅkara.*

Production Notes

Composition and paging were done on the Quadex Composing System and typesetting on the Compugraphic 8400 by the design and production staff of University of Hawaii Press.

The text typeface is Compugraphic Times Roman and the display typeface is Schneidler.

Offset presswork and binding were done by The Maple-Vail Book Manufacturing Group. Text paper is Glatfelter Offset Vellum, basis 50.